UNSUNG HEROES
of the
ROYAL NAVY
and
ROYAL MARINES

The Far East Prisoners of War
1941 - 1945

PAM STUBBS

*To Nick
with best wishes*

Pam

ISBN 978-1-907516-11-5

Published and Produced by TUCANN*design&print*,
19 High Street, Heighington, Lincoln LN4 1RG
Tel & Fax 0522 790009

Distributed by Pam Stubbs, 143 New Road,
Bromsgrove, Worcs B60 2LJ

DEDICATION
To my late husband Stanley Leslie (Les) Stubbs

ACKNOWLEDGEMENTS

—■—

Mention must be made first of Roderick Suddaby, Keeper of the Department of Documents at the Imperial War Museum, for the great help and encouragement he has given me since the death of my husband and for his kind words in the Foreword of this book.

Les and I began our research at the request of several RN FEPOWs after the publication of our book concerning the RAF FEPOWs in 2002. And it was soon after this that Ian McLeod turned up at one of the Reunions of the Java FEPOW Club (1942). His research related to RN and RM men who had served in the Pacific theatre in World War II. Ian was able to supply much information about the ships on which FEPOWs served and many of the Christian Names and Service Numbers which did not appear on the Documents we were using at the National Archives at Kew.

Great help, particularly with service numbers, was provided from Portsmouth by Andy Godfrey, Director of Naval Personnel, and Major V M Bentley of the Naval Historical Branch.

Eric Smith collected information about war fatalities in the twentieth century and was therefore able to supply much information including the dates of ships which had succumbed in the Atlantic and Indian Oceans.

Ron Bridge, whose research primarily concerned Civilians (including Merchant Seamen) held by the Japanese, provided valuable help, particularly relating to men who served in the Hong Kong Royal Naval Reserve and the Royal Malayan Naval Volunteer Reserve. He also solved many difficulties relating to the RN and RM men who had survived the sinking of the *Lisbon Maru*.

Mention must also be made of Eileen Small and Tony Hazzard for the help they gave at the National Archives at Kew.

Lists of FEPOWs held in various locations were received from many quarters, thanks to Larry Holder (Celebes), Alfred Hunt (Hong Kong), Henry Kavanagh (Pomelaa) and Fred Ryall (Haruku). Arthur Tindall too gave much information about Pomelaa.

Much of the background information in this book came from "Unsung Heroes of the RAF - the FEPOWs" for which Queenie Spink's poem "What is a FEPOW" was an inspiration and Alex Bourne's thoughts on "The FEPOW Spirit" was invaluable. David Nelson's book "The Changi Story" provided virtually all of the information about transports. Other details about transports were obtained from Sumio Adachi's report and the book by J H W Veenstra et al.

Finally, grateful thanks to Robert Hughes Mullock, Naval Historian at the Naval Historical Collectors & Research Association, for his constructive help with proof reading and also to my lifelong friend Rowena Drury.

CONTENTS

◼

FOREWORD - Roderick Suddaby 9

INTRODUCTION 11

PROLOGUE - THE RISING SUN...13

WHAT IS A FEPOW? by Queenie Spink 15

MAP 1 - Japanese Empire and Allies November 1941 16
MAP 2 - Japanese Empire and Allies June 1942 16
MAP 3 - Malaya and Sumatra...17
MAP 4 - Celebes 18
MAP 5 - Moluccas 18
MAP 6 - Java 19
MAP 7 - Borneo...19
MAP 8 - Burma and Thailand...20
MAP 9 - Japan..21
MAP 10 - Honshu Island 21

CHAPTER 1 - CAPTURED 22

CHAPTER 2 – STARVATION, TORTURE and DISEASE 24

CHAPTER 3 - WORKED THE DAY LONG.....................................26
The Burma/Thailand Railway...27
The Sumatra Railway..27
Mining, Smelting, Shipbuilding, Land Reclamation
and Dam Building...28
Airfield Construction and Road Building 28

CHAPTER 4 – HERDED LIKE CATTLE 29

CHAPTER 5 – THE SHANGHAI FEPOWs....................................30

CHAPTER 6 – THE HONG KONG FEPOWs 32

CHAPTER 7 – THE SINGAPORE FEPOWs.................................34

CHAPTER 8 – THE SUMATRA FEPOWs....................................38

CHAPTER 9 – THE CELEBES FEPOWs 42

CHAPTER 10 – THE JAVA FEPOWs 44

CHAPTER 11 – THE FEPOWs CAPTURED LATER 48

CHAPTER 12 – THE SPIRIT WAS STRONG by Alex Bourne 51

CHAPTER 13 – SOME COULDN'T MAKE IT 53

CHAPTER 14 - THE ROLL...56

EPILOGUE...115

TABLES OF RELEVANT TRANSPORTS
TABLE 1 – Into Singapore 116
TABLE 2 – Into Saigon, Burma and Thailand............................117
TABLE 3 – Into Taiwan, Korea and Japan 118
TABLE 4 – Into Borneo...120
TABLE 5 – Into New Britain, the Moluccas and Flores..............121
TABLE 6 – Into Java and Celebes...121
TABLE 7 – Into Sumatra 122

APPENDICES
APPENDIX 1 – RN and RM Personnel who survived the
sinking of the Lisbon Maru 123
APPENDIX 2 – FEPOWs Identified as working on the
Mergui Road 126
APPENDIX 3 – Vessels Sunk / Captured / Scuttled
North of Sumatra in February 1942..................... 127

APPENDIX 4 - FEPOWs in the Party from Makassar
to Pomelaa 128
APPENDIX 5 – Makassar FEPOWs Transported to Java
in October 1943..131
APPENDIX 6 – Ships Carrying FEPOWs Sunk by
Allied Action...132
APPENDIX 7 – War Cemeteries and Memorials relating to
RN and RM FEPOWs...134

BIBLIOGRAPHY..136

FOREWORD

─────────────────■─────────────────

When Les and Pam Stubbs published "Unsung Heroes of the Royal Air Force – the Far East Prisoners or War" in 2002, their book immediately became the first port of call for anyone with an interest in the fates of the officers and men of the RAF (Les unfortunately among them) who became prisoners of war in the Far East during the Second World War. Just one small but for me constant reminder of how useful this authoritative Roll of the names of over 6,000 personnel who were captured by the Japanese from December 1941 onwards has proved to be to researchers is the now very well-worn state of the copies of the book used for reference purposes in the Imperial War Museum.

I am therefore delighted to have been asked to write a foreword to "Unsung Heroes of the Royal Navy and Royal Marines – the Far East Prisoners of War" on which Les and Pam began their research in 2003 and that, since Les' death in 2006, Pam has completed and seen through to publication. This companion volume follows much the same formula that works so well in their first book. It explains with precision the circumstances in which some 2,700 officers and men were taken prisoner, not only from the Royal Navy and Royal Marines but also from Commonwealth and Dominion Navies, when and how they were moved between camps and the conditions that they endured during their period of captivity. At its heart, however, is the invaluable alphabetical Roll identifying the names and service numbers of all these men, the ships or shore establishments in which they were serving at the time of their capture, the different camps where they were held and, in all too many instances, the dates and places of their deaths and the details of where they are now buried or commemorated.

The growing number of people who, for genealogical, academic or other reasons are investigating the lives of individuals who became prisoners of war or civilian internees in Japanese hands are fortunate that far more information is now readily available to them, either in print or on the web, than was the case twenty-five years ago. This book is, I believe, another very significant contribution to that body of knowledge and, along with its companion volume, represents the crowning achievement of the wonderful service which Pam and her late husband have rendered in so many ways to the FEPOW community.

Roderick Suddaby

INTRODUCTION

■

After publication of "Unsung Heroes of the Royal Air Force – the Far East Prisoners of War" on the sixtieth anniversary of my late husband's capture, we were asked to do something similar for the Navy FEPOWs. We began collecting information, which in the case of the RAF had taken ten years to research, and had done a considerable amount towards its completion when Les died in June 2006. The original plan was not to publish but to hand the Roll to the Department of Documents at the Imperial War Museum and to COFEPOW, the Children and Relatives of the Far East Prisoners of War. However my Grandson Jack has persuaded me that I should write this book.

This book is a companion to "Unsung Heroes of the RAF – the FEPOWs" which as it happens was also intended to be simply a Roll lodged with the Imperial War Museum. However when, back in the mid 1990s, we advertised widely for information a great many of the letters we received from relatives said "captured in Singapore" and "worked on the Burma/Thai Railway" whereas in fact less than a hundred of the approximately six thousand RAF FEPOWs were captured in Singapore and only half of those went to Thailand. Consequently in order to put the record straight the first book came about.

How to put the information we had into some sort of logical order proved very difficult. It was only after Queenie Spink read her poem "What is a FEPOW?" at a Reunion of the Java FEPOW Club (1942) that the answer came to us - to use phrases from Queenie's poem as chapter headings.

Many of the chapter headings in this book also use Queenie's phrases. But more than a third of the RN and RM FEPOWs were held first in Celebes (now Sulawesi) whereas no RAF FEPOWs were. And more than a quarter of the RN and RM FEPOWs were held first in Hong

Kong compared with less than 1.5% of the RAF FEPOWS. It seemed more logical therefore not to detail separately the places of capture and the places into which there were transportations but to give each place of capture a Chapter heading and to follow the information about how the RN and RM men came to be there with details of their movements from it.

Pamela Stubbs

PROLOGUE
THE RISING SUN

■

The first Emperor of Japan ascended the throne in February 660BC.
When Hirohito ascended the throne on Christmas Day 1926 his
dominion included the Ryukyu Islands, Formosa (now Taiwan) and
the Pescadores Islands (now Penghu), Korea and part of Sakhalin.
Under the Treaty of Versailles three groups of islands in the Pacific
were also administered by Japan, namely the Marianas, the Carolines
and the Marshall Islands. Under various other treaties and agreements
extensive rights were also held in Manchuria in the administration of
the South Manchuria Railway.

Three years prior to Emperor Hirohito's succession a book had been
published in Japan in which a Dr Okaya argued that as Japan had been
the first state in existence it was her Divine Mission to rule the world.
In September 1931 the first move was made to achieve this objective.

By instigating what was to become known as the Manchurian Incident,
Japan acquired Manchuria renaming it Manchukuo. By instigating
what was to become known as the China Incident large areas of China
were acquired. In February 1939 the island of Hainan was captured.

Japan signed a Tripartite agreement with Germany and Italy in July
1940, ten months after the outbreak of war in Europe. Subsequently
pressure was put on the French Vichy Government enabling Japanese
troops to move into French Indo-China (now Vietnam) in February
1941, the purpose being to construct air and naval bases there. A naval
base was also constructed on the island of Saipan in the Marianas in
spite of this being forbidden under the terms of the Treaty of Versailles.
By September 1941, a decade after the Manchurian Incident, Hirohito's
domain had expanded considerably and Japan was poised to turn what
had been until then a European war into World War II.

On 7th December 1941 Japan attacked Pearl Harbour on Hawaii, and Midway Island. More or less simultaneously (but in fact on 8th December being on the other side of the International Date Line) three other attacks on the USA were made (the Philippines, Wake Island and the Mariana Island of Guam) and two on British Territories (Hong Kong and Malaya). On 9th and 11th December two more attacks on British Territories were made (the Solomon Islands and Burma).

Within six months America had lost the Philippines, Wake Island, the Mariana Islands and two of the Aleutian Islands. The Dutch East Indies had lost Dutch Borneo, Celebes, the Moluccan Islands, Sumatra, Java, Bali, Lombok, Sumbawa, Sumba, Flores, Timor and half of Dutch New Guinea. Britain had lost Burma, Hong Kong, British Borneo (Sarawak), Malaya, Singapore, the Gilbert Islands, the Solomon Islands, New Britain and New Ireland. And half of Papua New Guinea, administered by Australia, had been lost.

The sun was in its zenith.

WHAT IS A FEPOW?

By Queenie Spink

What is a FEPOW? A FEPOW is one
Who fought a great battle, without sword or gun,
Who suffered starvation, torture, disease,
When captured by the Japanese.

Stripped of his dignity, degraded and hit,
The FEPOW fought back with courage and grit.
No longer a fight for King and Country
But a fight for survival in captivity.

Herded like cattle, worked the day long,
His body grew weak but his spirit was strong,
Determined to win the fight to survive,
To outwit the Japs and to stay alive.

Some couldn't make it; laid to rest there,
No flowers, no parades, just a tear and a prayer.
Never forgotten, remembered still
By their comrades who buried them there on the hill.

So - what is a FEPOW? A FEPOW is one
Unique among men, a hero unsung.

October 1992

MAP 1 - Japanese Empire and Allies November 1941

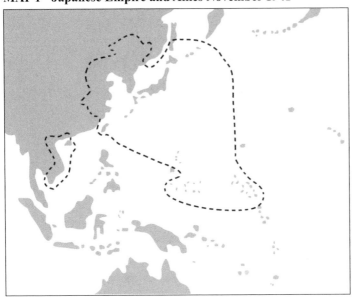

MAP 2 - Japanese Empire and Allies June 1942

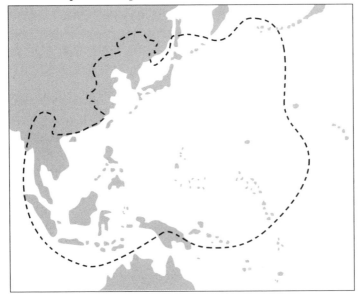

MAP 3 - Malaya and Sumatra (Scale 135 miles = 1 inch)

MAPS 4 - Celebes (Scale 150 miles = 1 inch)

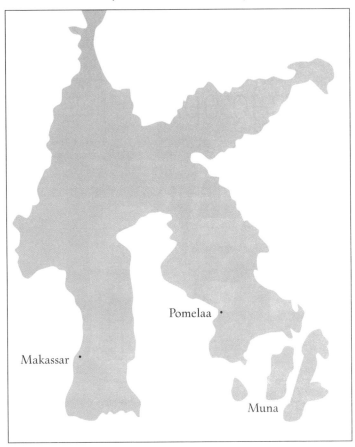

Map 5 - |Moluccas (Scale 150 miles = 1 inch)

MAP 6 – Java (Scale 240 miles = 1 inch)

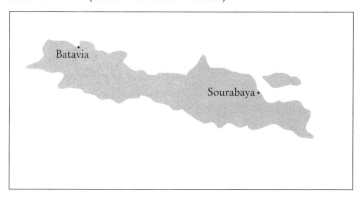

MAP 7 – Borneo (Scale 240 miles = 1 inch)

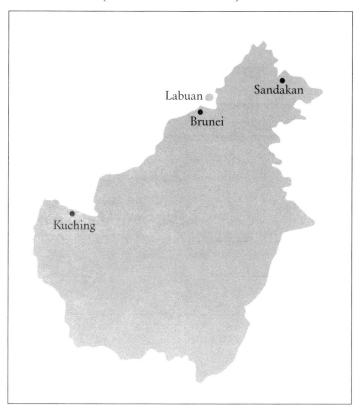

MAP 8 - Burma and Thailand (Scale 200 miles = 1 inch)

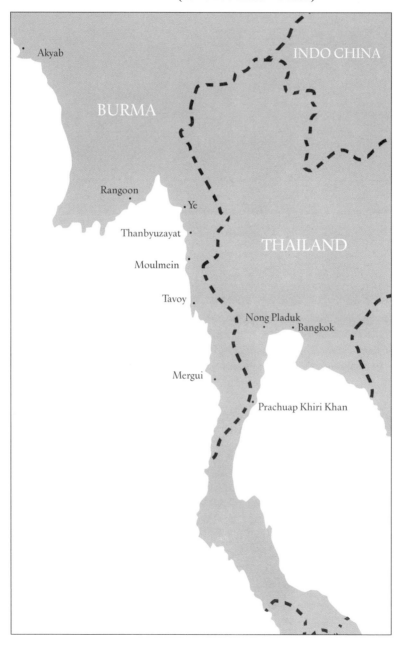

MAP 9 – Japan (Scale 300 miles = 1 inch)

MAP 10 - Honshu Island

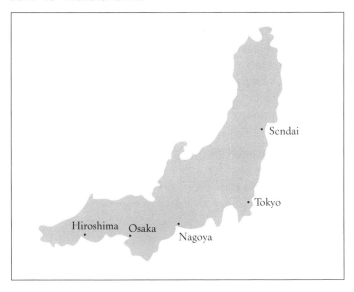

CHAPTER 1
CAPTURED

■

HMSO Cmnd 6832 dated June 1946 states that 2304 Navy Personnel were captured by the Japanese. However the Roll in this book lists 2698, the larger number being principally because Hong Kong Royal Naval Reserve, Malayan Royal Naval Reserve and some Commonwealth Navy personnel are included.

The largest group of RN and RM FEPOWs were held first in Celebes (now Sulawesi) being taken there from ships lost in the Battle of the Java Sea. Most were survivors from the heavy cruiser HMS *Exeter* and the destroyer HMS *Encounter.*

The second largest group of RN and RM FEPOWs were captured in or near Hong Kong and at Shanghai.

With the fall of Singapore imminent the Admiralty ordered the destruction of the naval base and the evacuation of the RN and RM personnel to Java, Australia and Ceylon. Many did not succeed in their bid for freedom, the loss of life north of Sumatra being tremendous, but those taken to or unable to get away from Sumatra make the third largest group.

Those RN and RM men who did not get away from Singapore were soon joined there by some of those captured north of Sumatra, mostly in or near Bangka Island, making those held first in Singapore the fourth largest group of RN and RM FEPOWs.

Of those reaching Java a few did get away but those who did not, either being captured in or returned to the island, make those RN and RM men held first in Java the fifth largest group.

By May 1942 most RN and RM who were FEPOWs had been captured. Those captured later were, in the first instance, principally in ships sunk in the South Atlantic or Indian Ocean. Later, towards the end of the war, they were mostly Navy airmen, not all of whom will have been identified because they fared very badly and details of who they were and what happened to them is not very prevalent.

CHAPTER 2
STARVATION, TORTURE
and DISEASE

---■---

Brutality, to a greater or lesser extent, was the order of the day for all FEPOWs. In the Japanese Army discipline was maintained by corporal punishment. Consequently severe beatings for prisoners of war were inevitable, not only for any misdemeanour but often because a guard needed to "save face" having himself been beaten by someone of senior rank.

A major difficulty was the unpredictability of the guards: an action which on one occasion would be applauded by them would on another be regarded as a misdemeanour as is illustrated by the case of RAF Cpl Owen Taylor. On board the *Tencho Maru*, one of the ships returning to Java from the Moluccan Islands, he took some dried fish. At the time of discovery he was in fact given more fish by one of the Japanese guards nicknamed "Yellow Boots" but after dark next day he was very badly treated before his execution.

Psychologically it was extremely difficult to cope with having to witness the ill-treatment and execution of comrades. It was also difficult not to react to violence against oneself and instances exist of prisoners of war striking or apparently about to strike a guard. On Ambon Island Trooper Henry Champion of the 3rd Kings Own Hussars, having raised his arm to protect his face from boiling water, was accused of attempting to strike a guard and murdered.

Brutality was not the only way in which the Japanese controlled their prisoners with a relatively small number of guards. Prisoners were made less physically able by being put on starvation rations.

Within a matter of months, if not weeks, signs of malnutrition and vitamin deficiency began to appear. "Happy feet" or "electric feet", the earliest sign of beri-beri, resulted from lack of vitamin B. Many developed pellegra, their finger nails turning black and their lips green. Nerve involvement was not only peripheral, frequently it affected the sight and in some cases blindness resulted.

Not only was there a lack of food, there was a lack of medicines and dressings, virtually all supplies from the Red Cross being withheld. Consequently there was no treatment for malaria or dysentery, diseases to which most prisoners of war succumbed. Neither were there dressings for the tropical ulcers which tended to develop from the smallest injury into dreadful holes exuding pus and growing both in circumference and depth.

Most prisoners of war had worms. Of the various species encountered one, strongyloides, is unique in that unlike all other worms affecting man, it does not at some time in its life cycle need to exist outside the human body. When it was realised that, if it was present, any treatment with steroids could result in death, its eradication became of major importance and the arrangement was set up whereby all ex-Far East Prisoners of War were entitled to a Tropical Diseases Investigation, courtesy of the Government's War Disability Pensions organisation.

Most dreaded of the diseases encountered by FEPOWs was cholera. But there were also other epidemic diseases, such as diphtheria. Tuberculosis existed and indeed many prisoners of war with this disease were, on their release, kept in hospital in South Africa and did not return to the United Kingdom for two or three years.

Shoes and clothing deteriorated rapidly. Whilst this was a hardship in tropical climes it was an extreme difficulty for those transported to colder regions. Many of those transported to Japan arrived at the start of winter with little clothing and consequently pneumonia was very prevalent.

CHAPTER 3
WORKED THE DAY LONG

■

The Japanese policy towards prisoners of war was to use them as slave labour to serve the needs of the Japanese war economy. This policy was directly contrary to the terms of the 1929 Geneva Convention but not having ratified the Convention, Japan regarded its terms as irrelevant.

For approximately six months, while Japan's Empire was expanding, work was not too arduous, consisting primarily of the repair of bomb damage to airfields and roads, followed by the dismantling of machinery such as aeroplanes, railway engines, engineering equipment, etc, for shipment overseas. Once the Japanese advance was stemmed the situation changed, prisoners of war then being transported great distances throughout the Japanese Empire in order to undertake much heavier work.

Food was issued on a per-capita basis for the number of men who worked. It was therefore important to the community at large for every man fit enough to work to do so. Nevertheless, the Japanese were never satisfied with the number of men considered fit to work. Constant arguments with Officers, including Medical Officers, took place because men who could stand, however weakly, were automatically considered by the Japanese to be fit to work. Much brutality resulted.

The work was heavy. Tools were primitive. Often a long march to and from work was necessary. Usually the environment was inhospitable. Always the day was very long. The work would have been arduous for fit, well-fed men, but for unfit starving men it was unbearable and indeed in his book "Samurais and Circumcisions" Dr Leslie Poidevin reports on men being "literally worked to death".

Railway Construction was the work undertaken by the largest number of prisoners of war on two projects, the Burma/Thailand Railway and the Sumatra Railway. Mining, Shipbuilding and other Heavy Industry occupied the next largest number of prisoners of war, mostly in Japan. Many FEPOWs were also employed on Airfield and Road Construction.

The Burma/Thailand Railway

In "The Story of Changi" David Nelson records almost 61,000 UK, Australian, Dutch and USA prisoners of war being transported to Burma and Thailand. In addition it is believed that some 20,000 Asians worked on the project.

Because of heavy losses at sea in supplying her forces in Burma, Japan decided to create an overland route and avoid the 2250 mile voyage from Bangkok to Rangoon, the final 900 of which were especially vulnerable to Allied attack. A railway line was already in existence in Burma from Ye to Moulmein, Thanbyuzayat lying equidistant between the two towns. In Thailand there was a rail link from Bangkok to Nong Pladuk, from where the line continued to Singapore. Between Thanbyuzayat and Nong Pladuk lay 415 km (257.7 miles) of jungle covered mountains through which a metre wide railway track with passing places would be constructed. The route determined lay along the north-eastern bank of the Mae Khlaung River from Nong Pladuk to Kanchanaburi where a bridge would be constructed so that the railway could follow the Kwai Noi River to Nikki and continue to the Burma border at Three Pagodas Pass. Work commenced in June 1942 at both ends of the railway and the two sections were joined on 25th October 1943 near Kon Kuta.

The Sumatra Railway

In May 1944 work began on the construction of a railway through central Sumatra. Japan expected an Allied landing on the south-west coast which she would need to supply from Singapore. The Siak River on the north-east coast was navigable inland to Pekanbaru, 48 hours sailing distance from Singapore. From Padang on the south-west coast there was an existing railway inland to Muaro. The railway was built between Pekanbaru and Muaro over some 220 km (136.6 miles) of swamps and mountains covered with equatorial forest. The single track railway was completed on 15th August 1945, the very day that Japan capitulated.

Neumann & Van Witsen in their book "The Sumatra Railway" report that some 4967 prisoners of war and 30,000 Romushas (Indonesians) worked constructing the railway. The majority of the prisoners of war were Dutch. A few were Australian Infantry and it is estimated that approximately 800 were UK men.

Mining, Smelting, Shipbuilding, Land Reclamation and Dam Building
With virtually all of its young men in the forces, Japan was extremely short of man power for its mines and heavy industries and a large number of prisoners of war were therefore transported to Japan, Taiwan and Korea.

Approximately 29,000 prisoners of war are known to have left Celebes, Hong Kong, Java and Singapore for Japan, Taiwan and Korea. In addition Sumio Adachi's papers indicate that approximately 11,000 were transported from the Philippines for Japan and Taiwan.

In Japan camps were scattered throughout the four main islands of Honshu, Hokkaido, Kyushu and Shikoku and two were on small islands to the south of Honshu in the Inland Sea. Most camps were comparatively small and often men in one camp did not work at the same location.

Airfield Construction and Road Building
Throughout the Japanese Empire military airfields were built using prisoner of war labour. Some 14,000 men are estimated to have been involved. Airfields were built in eastern Sumatra at Palembang and Pangkalan Bali, in the Moluccan Islands of Ambon, Haruku and Ceram, in Borneo at Sandakan and Kuching, and, after completion of the Burma/Thai Railway, in the north of Thailand.

Two major roads were built using prisoner of war labour. One was in western Sumatra at Atjeh (now Aceh) between Blangkedjeren and Takengon and the other in Thailand from Prachuap Khiri Khan to Mergui in Burma.

CHAPTER 4
HERDED LIKE CATTLE

Although the Japanese almost immediately began to move their prisoners of war between camps in the country of capture, there was little movement from country to country for about six months. Thereafter very few did not undertake a long journey either by train or sea or both. Overcrowding was extreme. Conditions were unventilated, hot and dirty.

The holds of cargo ships were fitted with staging so that the floor space was doubled or even trebled. On some ships there was no staging and the prisoners of war had to lie on top of the cargo; many mention having to lie on top of petrol drums. Often, crowding was such that it was not possible to lie down and there was usually insufficient height to sit comfortably. In these cramped conditions prisoners remained for weeks.

Exercise was sometimes impossible, sometimes restricted to half an hour on deck daily. Food and water were in very short supply. Washing was impossible. Toilet facilities were negligible, consisting of wooden crates hung over the sea at the stern of the ship and in their weakened condition FEPOWs found climbing into these most difficult.

On disembarkation, unloading of the ship was usually required. Frequently this was followed by a lengthy march.

CHAPTER 5
THE SHANGHAI FEPOWs

O n the very day that Japan launched her attacks on the USA and Great Britain the first Naval personnel were captured, all being held in Shanghai.

Of the 15 men, 14 were from the crew of HMS *Peterel*, which had been berthed for almost nine months in Shanghai docks as a floating wireless station for the British Consulate where the Senior Naval Officer in the port, Commander John Wooley, was stationed. On 8th December 1941 *Peterel* was attacked and despite a valiant fight the ship was sunk and the surviving crew taken into captivity. However on shore at the time of the attack were James Cuming, Kenneth Wainscott and Caradoc Williams. Later in December and on separate occasions Kenneth Wainscott and Caradoc Williams went to the Swiss Consulate only to be told that there was no alternative but to hand them over to the Japanese. However James Cuming evaded capture, eventually being heavily involved in espionage. His story is told in Desmond Wettern's "The Lonely Battle".

Also on 8th December 1942 the SS *Ben Nevis* was captured, the crew being taken later to Shanghai. Mostly they were Merchant Navy personnel but one RN man (Edward White) has been identified.

• • • • • •

Kenneth Wainscott and Caradoc Williams were held first in the notorious Bridgehouse Prison and very badly treated before joining the other crew members of *Peterel* in the POW camp at Woosung. Details of their time in Shanghai before capture is given in "The Lonely Battle".

After an early unsuccessful attempt to escape Commander Wooley, with three Americans, was transferred from Woosung to the Shanghai Prison. From there, in October 1944, Commander Wooley and Lt Commander Smith of the USS *Wake* did escape successfully.

During 1943 from Woosung 8 RN personnel were transported to the Osaka Area of Japan's Mainland Island of Honshu where William Lidington and Edward White died. The others were moved to the Tokyo Area in May 1945. The remaining 7 RN men stayed at Woosung until May 1945 when they were moved to Peking (now Beijing) for two months, then going on to Japan's northern island of Hokkaido.

CHAPTER 6
THE HONG KONG FEPOWs

O n 8th December 1941 Hong Kong was invaded, the Japanese crossing the border from China into the Mainland Territory.

By 13th December the Mainland Territory had been evacuated and during the evening of 18th December the Japanese landed in the north-east of Hong Kong Island. By dawn on 19th December the situation on the island was serious and 3 crew members of one of the Royal Navy's Motor Torpedo Boats (MTBs) namely Albert Gibson, James Hooker and Alfred Hunt had been captured.

Repeated demands for capitulation were made by the Japanese but were resisted until the afternoon of Christmas Day 1941. The RN and RM personnel captured numbered 711, many being stationed at HMS *Tamar*, the shore base.

$$\cdots \cdots$$

Several FEPOWs escaped from Hong Kong but only one RN man (Ralph Goodwin) has been identified. He did so in July 1944.

Almost a quarter of all of the RN and RM FEPOWs who did not survive captivity died on 2nd October 1942 when the *Lisbon Maru* was torpedoed and sunk en route from Hong Kong to Japan. Some 159 RN and RM personnel were among 839 losing their lives that day. The 196 RN and RM survivors are listed in Appendix 1 and of these Arthur Evans, James Fallace and William Johnstone avoided recapture. Some survivors who reached Shanghai after the sinking were in such a serious condition that they died very soon afterwards and among these were 7 RN men. Of the others who reached Shanghai 3 remained in Woosing until May 1945, when they were taken via Peking (now Beijing) to the northern Japanese Island of Hokkaido. The other

Lisbon Maru survivors had been taken to the Osaka Area of Japan's Mainland Island of Honshu, where within a month of the sinking 28 had died. From the Osaka Area Harry Bevis and John Cowling were moved in August 1943 to the officers camp at Zentsuji on Shikoku Island where they remained until June 1945. They were then moved to Miyata on Kyushu Island. In June 1945 Dudley Gore was moved from the Osaka Area to the Nagoya Area probably because the camp he was in was heavily bombed. There is a book about the ship – Tony Banham's "The *Lisbon Maru*".

The *Lisbon Maru* was the second of six transports from Hong Kong to Japan, the first leaving in August 1942 and the others in January 1943, August 1943, December 1943 and April 1944.

Most of the transports to Japan berthed on Japan's southern island of Kyushu the FEPOWs then crossing by ferry from Moji to Shimonoseki on Mainland Honshu and travelling on by train. A few, including Surgeon Lt John Page, remained in Kyushu for about three months.

The 55 RN and RM men on the January 1943 transport will have gone to the Osaka Area. Not all remained there, 7 being moved on to the Hiroshima Area and 18 to the Nagoya Area, presumably because of their camps having been bombed.

No RN or RM men from Hong Kong have been identified as being on the December 1943 transport. The 58 leaving in January 1944 were taken to the Nagoya Area. And the 58 released in the Tokyo or Sendai Areas left the colony either in August 1942 or April 1944, those in Sendai probably moving there from Tokyo as a result of the heavy bombing of that city.

The only other RN and RM FEPOWs to leave the colony did so in August 1943. Consisting primarily of Senior Officers and Diplomats they were taken to Taiwan and in October 1944, after the United States had landed on one of the Philippine Islands, most were moved to Mukden in Manchuria. Amongst those involved were 4 of the 5 RN FEPOWs from Hong Kong.

CHAPTER 7
THE SINGAPORE Fepows

■

On 8th December 1941 at 0100 hours standardised time, one and a half hours before the attack on Pearl Harbour, Japanese troops landed on Kota Bharu beach on the north-east coast of Malaya. Despite fierce resistance and a series of air attacks from Allied bombers, a bridgehead was secured.

Singapore that day experienced its first air raid and Force Z - the aging battlecruiser HMS *Repulse* and the modern battleship HMS *Prince of Wales* together with a screen of destroyers - was despatched in a bid to engage the enemy off the eastern coast of Malaya.

The history of what followed is given in Chapters 8 and 9 of Richard Hough's "The Hunting of Force Z". Both ships were sunk on 10th December 1941 and of the total complement of 2,921 officers and men, 840 did not survive. After picking up the survivors the destroyers returned to Singapore.

From Singapore a number of Royal Marine personnel from *Repulse* and *Prince of Wales* joined the Argyle and Sutherland Highlanders Regiment fighting in Malaya, becoming known as the Plymouth Argyles, Plymouth being the home port of many of them. But despite noble efforts on the part of those fighting in Malaya the Japanese advanced down the peninsular at an average rate of 8 miles per day and on 8th February 1942 the retreating troops were piped by the Argyles across the causeway linking Malaya to Singapore.

By this time the Asian crews of most of the merchant vessels had been replaced by Navy personnel, some being survivors of *Repulse* and *Prince of Wales* and others being stationed at the outbreak of war in Singapore itself in the shore base on the Johore Strait HMS *Sultan*, (previously HMS *Terror*). The immovable sloop HMS *Laburnum*, the

RNVR Headquarters ship, was moored in the Telok Ayer Basin.

Singapore fell on 15th February 1942 by which time most Naval personnel had been evacuated. Some 130 RN and RM men were left to be captured being joined shortly afterwards by 71 from the Bangka Area, north of Sumatra. They had either been kept in or returned to vessels which had been captured.

In April 1942 the 10 men in Col Francis Dillon's party arrived in Singapore. Having crossed Sumatra to Padang on the south-west coast in their bid to escape capture they left in a native prau but were spotted by Japanese tankers to the west of Sumatra and forced to heave to. In the party were 3 Navy men (Reginald Holloway, Cecil Hooper and Patrick Shellard).

Arriving in Singapore in early June 1942 was a party of 24 in which were 11 RN and RM men (Charles Day, Charles Firbank, Thomas Johncock, Ronald Johnson, William Padden, Richard Pool, Victor Richardson, William Smith, James Sneddon, Hubert Tucker and Allan Tweedale). They were the survivors of the motor launch *ML310*. The launch had been chased by an enemy destroyer and in an attempt to escape had run aground on 15th February 1942 on Jibbia Island, one in the Seven Brothers Group about forty miles north-west of Bangka Island. Disease was rife and many died, including Rear Admiral E J Spooner DSO RN and Air Vice Marshal C H Pulford RAF. Eventually the survivors found a small abandoned native boat which they repaired and some were able to make an attempt to reach Sumatra. In the vicinity of Sinkep Island, on learning that all of the southern region had been captured by the Japanese, they surrendered and were taken to Singapore. The Japanese were informed of those left behind on Jibbia and these too were taken on to Singapore. Squadron Leader George Atkins, Lt Ian Stonor (Argyle and Sutherland Highlanders) and Lt Richard Pool RN were taken to the Kempei Tei Headquarters and brutally interrogated for fifteen days before joining the others in Changi.

Also taken later to Singapore was Richard Danger, a Lt from HMS *Thanet* which had evaded capture in Hong Kong but been sunk on 17th January off Malaya. He had been picked up by a Japanese destroyer near the mouth of the Endau River, and like the crew of a Blenheim bomber from RAF No. 60 Squadron shot down in Thailand, taken first to Saigon.

• • • • • •

Excluding those captured later and detailed in Chapter 11, of the 216 RN and RM men held first in Singapore or taken there soon after its fall at least 130 were transported.

Although the first movement of FEPOWs was in April 1942 to Saigon, no RN or RM men were involved. It was in June 1942 that the first of the Singapore RN and RM men were moved. This draft was to Thailand for the construction of the Burma/Thai Railway and Table 2 includes details of the transports to Thailand. Of the Singapore FEPOWs 113 RN and RM men have been identified. Those in F and H Forces returned to Singapore and those identified number 5 (Bernard Campion, Charles Day, Kenneth Glover, Cecil James and George Jones).

After the completion of the railway in October 1943 approximately 8700 men who had worked on it were transported to Japan (see Table 3). There were 7 RN and RM men first held in Singapore who died on the voyage, 4 when the *Rakuyo Maru* was sunk on 12th September 1944 and 3 when the *Toyofuku Maru* was sunk on 21st September 1944. Among those reaching Japan safely were 11 RN and RM men, all being released on Kyushu Island with the exception of Charles Miller who was released in the Hiroshima Area of Honshu. One other RM man (Nicholas Jones) was aboard the *Asaka Maru*, sunk by a typhoon off Taiwan on 13th August 1944. He remained in Taiwan until his release.

In the direct transport to Taiwan from Singapore in August 1942 were 6 RN and RM men held first in Singapore. In June 1944 John Dunn died there, the others being transported in October 1944 to the Tokyo Area of Japan. Subsequently 2 (Ivor Butler and Kenneth Sheargold) were moved on to the Sendai Area where Kenneth Sheargold died.

The first transportation of Singapore men to Borneo was in July 1942, but all were Australians. It was in March 1943 that 8 RN and RM men were amongst those Singapore men transported and one of them (Albert Summers) was later in the Labuan Party (see Chapter 13).

In May 1943, 3 RN and RM men were among those transported to the northern Japanese island of Hokkaido.

By the beginning of 1945 the Japanese were in retreat in Burma and consequently, to enable their troops to escape, work began on a road from Prachap Khiri Khan in Thailand to Mergui in Burma. Approximately 1000 FEPOWs who had been involved with the construction of the Burma/Thailand Railway were therefore moved south. Those RN and RM men who had been held first in Singapore and identified as being in this party are listed in Appendix 2 Much information about the Mergui Road is contained in Don Few's "A Helping Hand".

CHAPTER 8
THE SUMATRA FEPOWs

The great evacuation from Singapore began shortly before British forces withdrew to the Island on 8th February 1942. Richard Gough in "The Escape from Singapore" lists 150 vessels. From information gathered from FEPOWs passing through Singapore David Nelson, in "The Story of Changi", lists 143. And in Geoffrey Brooke's aptly named "Singapore's Dunkirk" many of the vessels are named in the text and he points out that whilst the evacuees from Dunkirk were all fighting men and the distance to safety only forty miles, from Singapore the distance was more like five hundred miles, soon to double, and about a third of the evacuees were civilians many of whom were women and children.

Those vessels leaving late in the evacuation fared badly. The fate of many is unknown but north of Sumatra 57 are known to have been sunk, scuttled because of damage sustained, or captured (see Appendix 3). The loss of life was tremendous and shipwrecked survivors were scattered on many of the numerous islands off the north-east coast of Sumatra and also on that coast.

Many vessels were sunk or captured near Bangka Island and as mentioned in Chapter 7 some of the Navy men were taken back to Singapore. But the majority of men captured were held first in Bangka and moved later to Palembang which had fallen on 15th February 1942.

Also taken to Palembang were a few who were captured, or recaptured, later, James Brander and Maurice Leehan being two. Aboard HMS *Sin-Aik-Lee* they were leaving Java and sunk in the Sunda Strait on 1st March 1942 managing to reach Sumatra where they were captured.

Wilfred Blake and Noel Jackson whose actual names were Wilfred Barber and Noel Britt were also taken later to Palembang. They had assumed false names so as not to be identified as the two prisoners who had escaped earlier whilst on a working party. Noel Britt had been in *Thanet*, sunk in January 1942 near the mouth of the Endau River in eastern Malaya but had reached Singapore and taken part in Singapore's Dunkirk. Two others from *Thanet* had done likewise, William Press and Albert Young.

The survivors of vessels lost to the west of Bangka Island were mostly able to make their way through Sumatra via two escape routes. One was established by the Dutch and was via Djambi to Padang on the south-west coast. The other was established by Lt Col Alan Warren RM and was along the Indragiri River to Rengat and on to Padang. Most UK servicemen reaching Padang did so via Col Warren's route and some were able to get away to Ceylon (now Sri Lanka) or Australia. There were, however, insufficient boats and those remaining were captured when Padang fell on 17th March 1942.

Amongst those to leave Padang were John Cunyngham-Brown and Owen Henman. They sailed westwards in a prau but were captured to the north-west of Sumatra, eventually being taken to Medan on the north-east coast.

An attempt was made to rescue those stranded at Padang by SS *Chilka* which left Ceylon but was attacked about a hundred miles from the west coast of Sumatra on 11th March. Only one RN survivor has been identified, Robert Pope, who was taken later to Medan.

Also taken to Medan were 6 RN men who did not reach Padang (Philip Conway, Wilfred Farley, Rex Gillman, Francis McNelley, William Portch and Alexander Sim), most after a spell in Rengat Hospital.

And eventually all of the FEPOWs captured at Padang were taken to Medan.

• • • • • •

Excluding those captured towards the end of the war and mentioned in Chapter 11, the number of RN and RM men held first in Sumatra was 570. In the west, at Medan, were 206. In the east, at Palembang, were 364 from where Thomas Parsons escaped only to be recaptured in Java.

The first of only two departures from Palembang was in July 1942 when 26 RN and RM men were in the Technical Party, which left for Singapore. They then departed for Taiwan leaving Ronald Banks and Ernest Langdon at Singapore eventually to be transported to Thailand. After two months 18 of the group in Taiwan were taken to the Tokyo Area of Japan. It was from here in August 1943 that 3 were moved to the Officers' Camp at Zentsuji on Shikoku Island until June 1945 when 2 returned to the Tokyo Area, the other being taken to Miyata on Kyushu Island. Towards the end of the war 10 of those in the Tokyo Area were moved to the Sendai Area. Of the 6 who had remained in Taiwan in 1942 only one was released there, another dying there. In October 1944, after American Forces had landed on one of the Philippine Islands, 2 were taken to Mukden in Manchuria. Later the other 2 were taken from Taiwan to Japan, one to the Hiroshima Area and the other to Hokkaido Island.

It was not until May 1945 aboard two ships that there was another transport from Palembang. It was to Singapore and Commander Philip Reid RN the Senior British Officer, was among the 74 RN and RM on the transport.

Two books by Palembang FEPOWs have been published - "Prisoner of Nippon" is by Ray Stubbs (no relation to author) and "No Bamboo for Coffins" is by David Elio Roberts.

From Medan there were four departures. The first was in March 1942 and was of RN or RAF officers who had been captured in Padang. They were taken to Singapore from where all but one of the 14 RN and RM were subsequently transported to Thailand.

The next transport from Medan was in May 1942 when 501 UK FEPOWs who had been captured in Padang were transported to Burma. The RN and RM numbered 82. Known as the British

Sumatra Battalion under the command of Captain Dudley Apthorp of the Norfolk Regiment, they were the only United Kingdom FEPOWs to work from the Burma end of the Burma/Thai Railway. In Burma the Battalion was at Mergui for three months before being taken on to Tavoy for a further two months, then being moved to Moulmein from where a train journey took them to Thanbyuzayat, the western terminus of the proposed railway. When the war ended many of the British Sumatra Battalion were in Saigon awaiting transportation to Japan but one (Percy Watson) had died on the Mergui Road (see Chapters 3 and 7). In 1988 Dudley Apthorp's widow, A.A. Apthorp, published "The British Sumatra Battalion" much being quoted from her husband's papers.

In March 1944 approximately half of the FEPOWs remaining at Medan were moved north to Atjeh (now Aceh) for road building and 22 RN and RM men have been identified as being in this group. In October or November 1944 they went to central Sumatra for work on the Sumatra Railway.

The others remained at Medan until June when they were put aboard the *Harikiku Maru (Van Waerwijck)*. This transport was sunk on 26th June 1944 quite soon after departure with the loss of 25 RN and RM men. Those picked up were taken to Singapore from where all are believed to have stayed for about a month before departing for Pekanbaru, the northern terminus of the Sumatra Railway. Those known to have done this number 16 and those known to have stayed in Singapore until their liberation number 7.

CHAPTER 9
THE CELEBES FEPOWs

■

The Battle of the Java Sea commenced on 27th February 1942 and continued intermittently until 1st March. The Dutch cruiser HNLMS *De Ruyter* was the flagship of the Allied force comprising four cruisers (the Dutch HNLMS *Java,* HMS *Exeter,* USS *Houston* and HMAS *Perth)* and nine destroyers (HM Ships *Electra, Encounter* and *Jupiter,* US Ships *Edwards, Alden, Ford* and *Paul Jones* and the Dutch HNLM Ships *Kortenaer* and *Witte de Witt*s).

The heavy cruiser *Exeter* was damaged by a shell in her boiler room and was ordered to Sourabaya with *Encounter* escorting. Engineers worked furiously to repair the damage and on 28th February the two ships together with the USS *Pope,* received sailing orders. Disaster struck on 1st March and all three were sunk, survivors being picked up by the Japanese and eventually taken to Makassar in the Celebes.

On arrival they discovered RN and RM men already there. They were survivors from the destroyer HMS *Stronghold,* sunk off south Java, and SS *Francol.* There were also RN Liaison Officers from the Dutch vessels *Java and De Ruyter* and two survivors from the sinking of HMS *Anking* (Alfred Dawson and Charles Morgan) who had, it is believed, been picked up by *Francol.*

There were then at Makassar a total of 939 RN and RM men.

· · · · · ·

A month after capture Captain Oliver Gordon RN, *Exeter's* commander, and 16 others left Makassar for Japan. They were taken to Ofuna in the Tokyo area of Honshu Island, from where in September 1942 most were moved to the officers camp at Zentsuji on Shikoku Island until June 1945, then being moved back to the Tokyo Area, to Mitsushima.

There was a second draft to Japan, known as the Technical Party, on 14th October 1942. They were transported on the *Asama Maru* and of the 1000 prisoners on board 213 were RN or RM personnel. They were taken to Japan's Kyushu Island. Ted Anderson was in this Party and his story is told in the book "Nippon's Guest – a Sailor Prisoner of War in Japan". April 1945 saw 5 from the Technical Party being moved to Mukden in Manchuria.

In 1943 on 17th January 200 UK prisoners of war were transported from Makassar on the western leg of the Celebes to Pomelaa on the eastern leg and one of the Chapters in George T Cooper's book "Never Forget, Nor Forgive" is devoted to this party. They remained at Pomelaa for eight months, the 184 survivors returning in the middle of September in such a state that "it was difficult to recognise them individually". A list of those in this Party is given in Appendix 4.

After Captain Gordon's departure the Senior British Officer at Makassar was George Cooper. In October 1943 he was one of the 27 RN Officers listed in Appendix 5 to be taken to Java. Most remained there but some were moved on, 5 to Singapore and 2 to Sumatra. Of those reaching Singapore, 2 remained, the others going on to Japan aboard the *Tamahoko Maru,* one not surviving its sinking in Nagasaki Bay in June 1944. The 2 who reached Japan (Philip Cranefield and John Hickley) were first in Fukuoka 14 Camp at Nagasaki, only 1750 metres from the epicentre of the atom bomb, but had been transferred to Mukden in Manchuria in April 1945. Of those transported to Sumatra one (John Wyatt) was taken to Padang in May 1944 for work on the Sumatra Railway, the other (David Hazelton) left Java in September 1944 on the *Junyo Maru,* not surviving its sinking.

The other 41 Makassar FEPOWs to be transported to Java were moved in July 1945.

CHAPTER 10
THE JAVA FEPOWs

———————————————■———————————————

Among the casualties of the Battle of the Java Sea were HM Ships *Electra* and *Jupiter,* both being sunk on 27th February 1942. Survivors from both ships were able to reach the north coast of Java.

The Battle had been conducted from Sourabaya in the east of Java by the Combined Striking Force. In the west at Batavia (now Jakarta) was the Western Striking Force, formed from those few ships available including HM Ships *Danae, Dragon, Scout* and *Tenedos.* *Scout* had left Hong Kong as the Japanese crossed the border of the mainland territory afterwards being with HMS *Kudat* which was bombed and sunk at Port Swettenham on 30th December 1941. Patrolling the Sunda Strait were the naval auxiliaries *Rahman, Gemas*, *Jeram*, *Sin-Aik-Lee, Wo Kwang* and *Hong Kwong* together with six Dutch vessels. HMS *Anking* was the Depot Ship providing accommodation for the RN drafts from Singapore.

The first air attacks on Java had taken place on 3rd February and had been on Sourabaya plus two airfields in the vicinity. More air attacks followed and invasion seemed imminent.

After refuelling the Western Striking Force sailed from Batavia on 27th February 1942 with orders to sweep north and make a night attack on an enemy force reported 110 miles north of Java. The orders were that if the enemy was not met by 0430 hours the following day to reverse course, pass through the Sunda Strait and proceed to Padang on the south west coast of Sumatra. Merchant shipping had been ordered to leave Java on 19th February 1942 and by 26th February 1942, when *Anking* departed, 36 had left.

On 21st February 1942 General Wavell, Supreme Commander, signalled the Prime Minister to the effect that the defence of Java could not last long, consequently being ordered to India. He was replaced by Air Vice-Marshal Paul C Maltby who on 26th February 1942 received a personal telegram from the Prime Minister, Serial No T 302/2, which read *"I send you and all ranks of the British Forces who have stayed behind in Java my best wishes for success and honour in the great fight that confronts you. Every day gained is precious and I know that you will do everything humanly possible to prolong the battle".* Amongst those who had stayed behind were several RN and RM men, many of whom had reached Java from Singapore but been unable to leave on the departing vessels.

The Japanese landed on Java at three places soon after midnight on 28th February and on 8th March a Dutch proclamation was made declaring that all organised resistance had now ceased.

Hong Kwong was abandoned at Batavia and losses were considerable among the ships which left Java. *Rahman,* at the time towing the yacht *White Swan,* was one. Others were *Anking, Gemas, Jeram and Sin-Aik-Lee.*

Survivors from these ships joined those who had been "left behind" and captured in Java, as did some men who reached Java from Sumatra.

Amongst the latter 13 RN and RM men have been identified. Duncan Kinnear, Thomas Marr, John Sharples, Vernon Wade and Stanley Willimot were in a group of 7 from HMS *Siang Wo* who reached Java in a sampan. Percy Dunn and Henry Swift had been aboard *ML311,* sunk in the Bangka Strait on 15th February. David Kerr, an HMS *Repulse* survivor, was aboard HMS *Fan Lin,* also sunk in the Bangka Strait; he reached Java in a fishing boat. Hugh Morton, captain of HMS *Giang Bee*, plus George Hayes, Frank Rowe and Arthur Williamson reached Java in a small boat. And Thomas Parsons, a *Prince of Wales* survivor, had been captured on Bangka Island after the sinking of HMS *Li Wo* but had escaped with 3 others and reached Java, only to be betrayed and captured again.

Excluding those detailed in Chapter 11 as being captured later and, 153 RN and RM men were captured in Java.

Most of the RN and RM men held first in Java were transported. They went to Borneo, Japan, Thailand, the Moluccan Islands and Sumatra.

The first to leave did so in September 1942 and were transported via Singapore to Borneo, all 20 RN men involved going to Kuching. From Kuching 3 (Ernest Burnett, Reginald Redfern and William Simpson) were later in the Labuan Party (see Chapter 13).

Amongst those held first in Java and transported to Japan were 24 RN and RM men. All went via Singapore, though not all went into camp there. Those leaving in October and November 1942 included 8 naval men who were taken either to Kyushu Island or to the Hiroshima Area of Honshu. Leonard Cooper, Duncan Kinnear and Stanley Willimot were amongst those in the Hiroshima Area but were moved in February 1943 to the officers camp at Zentsuji on Shikoku Island until its closure in June 1945 when Leonard Cooper was moved to the Tokyo Area and Duncan Kinnear and Stanley Willimot to Kyushu. To the Osaka Area of Honshu in November 1943 went 12 RN and RM men. And the last draft of Java FEPOWs to Japan left in June 1944 and were aboard the *Tamahoko Maru* which was sunk on 24th June 1944 in Nagasaki Bay with the loss of all 4 of the Java RN men being transported.

Only 4 Java RN men were transported to Thailand. They were among 547 UK FEPOWs from Java to be in the 3,270 strong H Force which left Singapore in May 1943 for Hintok. George Giffin died in Thailand, The other 3 were returned to Singapore, as were all the survivors of F and H Forces.

The transports from Java to the Moluccan Islands were not routed through Singapore. They travelled direct on four ships leaving in April 1943. Of the approximately 4000 FEPOWs involved 59 RN/RM men have been identified, 2 of whom (Derek Freeman and Norman Slade) went to Ambon Island. The others went to Haruku Island. The purpose was to build airfields but within eighteen months, the airfields having been completed/abandoned, all surviving FEPOWs had left the islands on six drafts some of which involved two vessels. One of the ships on the first draft, the *Suez Maru* (see Chapter 13), was sunk with no survivors, one casualty being an RN man. Thereafter at one time or another the Haruku FEPOWs were moved to Ambon from where the other departures took place. There were 3 RN men not surviving the voyages of the second, third and fourth drafts, but 11 died on the fifth draft aboard the *Maros Maru (Haruyoshi Maru)* which, after picking up survivors from the other ship on the draft, was marooned off Makassar for forty days because of engine trouble until Frank Platt, an Engine Room Artificer from *Jupiter*, undertook the repair. The last draft of 435 FEPOWs left in October 1944 being marooned for at least six months on Muna Island to the south of the eastern leg of Celebes (now Sulawesi). An attempt to leave after one month, one boat towing another, failed because both were set alight following an air attack. Amongst those to lose their life on this transport (*Transport 125*) was one RN man. Successful were three later attempts in April, July and August 1945, the last not leaving until 16th August unaware that the war was officially over. Details of the transports to and from the Moluccan Islands are given in Tables 5 and 6 and were obtained from the book by Veestra et al "Als Krijgsgevangene naar de Moluccen en Flores". There are several books by Haruku FEPOWs one being "The Forgotten Men" by RN Boy Harold Lock, but that giving the overall story is "Spice Island Slaves" by RAF Fl Lt Leslie Audus.

The first draft to Sumatra from Java left in November 1943 and was to the east of the island, the purpose being to build an airfield at Pangkalan Bali near Palembang. The RN men involved numbered 11, most being moved in May 1945 to Singapore. The other three drafts to Sumatra were for the building of the Sumatra Railway and from the RN and RM men held first in Java there were 15, at least one of whom had returned to Java from the Moluccan Islands. Most left on the first transport in May 1944 being taken directly to Padang on the south-west coast. The second transport in July 1944 went via Singapore to Pekanbaru on the north-east coast with 2 RN men on board. The third was direct but off Padang the *Junyo Maru* was torpedoed and sunk in September 1944. Among the survivors were 2 RN men, John Halls and Herbert Upton.

CHAPTER 11
THE FEPOWs CAPTURED LATER

■

The Japanese launched their attack on the Philippine Archipelago on 8th December 1941, the battle continuing for months. It has not been possible to establish just when and how 6 crew members of the MV *Tantalus* were captured. But it is known that they were first held as civilians and that in January 1943 they officially became prisoners of war. All but one were transported to Japan, 3 to Kyushu Island, one to Osaka Area of Mainland Honshu and one to the Tokyo Area of Honshu.

Several ships were sunk in the South Atlantic by German raiders, the survivors becoming FEPOWs. Most, including R David Wilson who for many years was Secretary of the National Federation of FEPOW Clubs and Associations, were merchant seamen, but 30 were RN or RM men, 23 of whom were taken to Japan. Arriving there in May 1942 were survivors from SS *Kirkpool* sunk on 10th April, MV *Patella* sunk on 19th April, SS *Wellpark* sunk on 28th March and SS *Willesden* sunk on 1st April. Arriving in Japan later were survivors from SS *Gemstone* sunk on 4th June 1942, SS *Lyle Park* sunk on 11th June 1942 and SS *Dalhousie* on 9th August 1942. Survivors from two other ships sunk in the South Atlantic were taken to either Singapore or Java, 7 being RN men. In July 1942 SS *Gloucester Castle* was sunk the 2 RN survivors being taken to Singapore and on 4th September 1942 MV *Empire Dawn* succumbed, the 5 survivors being taken to Java and being transported in November 1943 to Pangkalan Bali in Sumatra, then moving to Singapore in May 1945.

Several ships were captured or sunk in the Indian Ocean. In May 1942 SS *Nankin* was captured and in July 1942 SS *Harauki* was sunk. In February 1943 SS *Empire March* and SS *Eugene Livano* succumbed. And in March 1944 SS *Nancy Moeller* was sunk by a Japanese submarine. There were 22 RN and RM survivors from these ships.

The one from *Nancy Moeller* was taken to and remained in Singapore and the one from *Harauki* after a spell in Singapore was transported to Japan. The others were all taken directly to Japan where Joseph Blackburn of SS *Nankin* was moved in August 1943 to the officers camp at Zentsuji on Shikoku Island until June 1945.

In March 1944 the MV *Behar* was crippled by the Japanese cruiser *Tone* in the Indian Ocean and sank within minutes. Survivors were picked up by *Tone* most being massacred but the 3 RN men on board were taken to Java for interrogation. The history is documented in David Sibley's "The Behar Massacre".

In Burma only one Navy FEPOW has been identified. He was Aubrey Chappell who was in the Royal Marines Special Branch. His story is told in Peter Haining's "The Banzai Hunters - the forgotten Armada of little ships that defeated the Japanese 1944-1945". In November 1944 30 Marines sailed in a motor launch towing a landing craft down the Arakan coast to Elizabeth Island which lies in Hunter's Bay just south of Akyab. The object of the mission was to collect information and if possible capture a Japanese prisoner. After marching two and a half miles the party fell upon a Japanese section post. Aubrey Chappell was surrounded by Japanese soldiers and after shooting several of them was forced to surrender, being taken away bound hand and foot.

In November 1944 the HM Submarine *Stratagem* was depth charged in the Malacca Strait, the 8 crew members being taken to Singapore. A month later 3 were taken on to Japan and were the only survivors. The Commonwealth War Graves Commission gives 31st December 1944 as the date of death for Reginald Howlett, Francis Phillips, Stanley Ritchen, Peter Webb and Arthur Westwood but it has not been possibly to determine what happened to them.

The other Navy men captured later in the war were all Fleet Air Arm personnel, having flown off HM Carriers *Illustrious, Indefatigable, Indomitable* and *Victorious.* From the Andaman Islands off the west coast of Malaya 3 men from *Illustrious* were captured in June 1944 and taken to Japan. In 1945 from *Illustrious, Indomitable* and *Victorious* 9 aircrew in four aircraft were shot down in or near Sumatra, taken to

Palembang and then to Singapore. The Commonwealth War Graves Commission give the dates of death of Ivor Barker and John Burns as 29th January 1945, of Donald Roebuck as 30th April 1945 and of Evan Baxter, Kenneth Burrenston, John Haberfield, William Lintern, William McRae and Reginald Shaw as 31st July 1945 but it is known that they were executed on or after 15th August 1945. *Indefatigable* was in the Pacific Ocean in 1945 and launched many planes over Japan. From those shot down 5 men are known to have been captured, the last being Fred Hockley whose plane was shot down in the Tokyo Bay area on the very day Japan surrendered and who was subsequently executed.

CHAPTER 12
THE SPIRIT WAS STRONG
By Alex Bourne

The Spirit found life amidst despair, degradation, disease and death. It was a spark of HOPE, struggling to live amongst sickness, starvation and brutality. The spark needed fuel to survive; this came from several sources:

FAITH in ourselves, our comrades and families, in our armed forces to overcome the enemy and for most of us a faith in God.

DETERMINATION to survive. This was not easy when the pains of dysentery, beri-beri, and tropical ulcers were doing their worst, or the body burning with fever, the mind hovering between fantasy and hallucination.

FRIENDSHIP, A friendly encouraging voice, a tin of cold water pressed to burning lips, knowing you were not alone and that someone was sharing your misery and giving help.

SHARING was very important - to share with your "oppo" an item of food or a cigarette and at the end of the day when a quiet moment was possible, to sit with your mates and share thoughts, hopes for the future and memories of happier days and of home. We shared troubles. We shared jokes, often at the stupidity of our captors and there was always some character who would try to raise a smile, act a part or play the fool. Sing-songs were shared. Where they were possible, church services were shared: where they were not, all shared in the prayer "Please God Help Us". Sharing was charity.

For some of our comrades the overwhelming burden of disease and lack of medication and food was too great and they lost the fight despite the skill and dedication of doctors and medical orderlies, both official and unofficial, often at the sacrifice of their own health. When our comrades died, we all shared the loss and shared our respect as they were laid to rest.

These are some of the facets that fuelled the FEPOW Spirit that kept us going. The spirit that was forged in the face of a man-made hell and led us through the dark tunnel that was captivity. The Spirit, even after fifty years, links FEPOWs together as when we were brothers in adversity.

February 1993

CHAPTER 13
SOME COULDN'T MAKE IT

∎

The number of RN and RM men listed in this book's Roll as dying in captivity is 669, being 456 on land and 213 at sea.

Many deaths were due to the dreadful conditions in the camps: malnutrition, disease, brutality and hard labour. Had FEPOWs not had to work so hard, the meagre food supplied would have been a little more adequate and fewer men would have died. And had brutality not been used to make FEPOWs work harder, fewer men would have died. Of the 456 who died on land, 198 (30% of all RN and RM fatalities) lie in Ambon War Cemetery and of these 193 were originally buried in the Commonwealth War Graves Commission's Cemetery at Makassar, moved to Ambon in 1961 at the request of the Indonesian Government.

Had FEPOWs not been transported in order to work, the great loss of life at sea would not have occurred. Most of those who died at sea died as a result of Allied action (See Appendix 6). Of the 213 Navy FEPOWs who died at sea some 199 (75%) lost their lives for this reason, and of those aboard transports which were sunk, 159 (80%) died on 2nd October 1942 when the *Lisbon Maru* was torpedoed.

The ships in which they were being transported gave no indication that there were prisoners of war aboard. The one exception was the *Suez Maru* with sick prisoners of war on board which, although marked with a red cross, carried damaged aircraft on deck. Being battened in the holds prevented many prisoners of war from abandoning ship. Often any prisoners of war who did manage to abandon ship were machine gunned in the water as Allan Jones's "The *Suez Maru* Atrocity" records.

Conditions on board ship were grim and, bad though conditions were when working, most prisoners of war will say that their worst experience was being transported. Sickness prevailed and on the *Maros Maru (Haruyoshi Maru)* cerebral malaria caused many deaths. Lord Russell of Liverpool in "The Knight's of Bushido" devotes much of Chapter VII "The Prison Hulks" to this transport.

Sickness also prevailed on land, of course. On the Moluccan Island of Haruku dysentery was difficult to combat in the dreadful living conditions and, although very few Navy men were involved, within the first six months 256 of the 2000 transported there died.

The greatest tragedy of all, however, unfolded in Borneo, primarily as a result of four death marches, three of which were from Sandakan, the other being from Labuan, all occurring after Leyte Island in the Philippines had been secured by the Allied on 25th December 1944. No RN or RM men were at Sandakan, where of an estimated 2750 prisoners of war the only survivors were some of the officers who had been transferred to Kuching after the discovery of a secret radio and six Australians who were successful in bids to escape. There were no survivors among the 300 Labuan Party, 200 being from Kuching from where they departed on 15th August 1944 to join the 100 from Sandakan already there since 16th June 1944. Many died at Labuan before the survivors were moved to Brunei on 8th March 1945. On 3rd May 1945 those still alive were marched inland and on or about 10th June 1945 there was a massacre. The information about the 4 Navy men in the Labuan Party was obtained from the Rolls in Lynette Ramsay Silver's "Sandakan - A Conspiracy of Silence" and Don Wall's "Kill the Prisoners".

Had the war not ended dramatically following the dropping of the atom bombs at Hiroshima and Nagasaki, it is undoubtedly true that all prisoners of war would have been massacred by the Japanese. With the end of the war in Europe in May 1945, the Japanese began to move many of their prisoners of war to sites where they could easily be massacred. In Japan, many were moved from shipbuilding, land reclamation, etc, to mining. In Singapore, work began on extensive tunnelling. In Java, nearly all prisoners of war were moved into the hills at Bandung where straw was stacked around the perimeter of their camp ready to be set alight.

A secret telegram sent on 17 March 1945 by the Japanese War Ministry to prison camp commanders stated "*Prisoners of war must be prevented by all means available from falling into enemy hands. They should be either relocated away from the front or collected at suitable points and time with an eye to enemy air raids, shore bombardments, etc. They should be kept alive to the last whenever their labour is needed.*" And indeed 10 FEPOW Naval aircrew have been identified as not being allowed to "fall into enemy hands" being executed on or after the day Japan surrendered.

CHAPTER 14
THE ROLL

∎

The most difficult problem in compiling the Roll in this book related to the man's ship. Whereas in many cases the ship in which he served at the outbreak of war is known what happened thereafter is difficult to ascertain. Some men were allocated to Straits Settlement ships after the native crews were dismissed. And most who took part in the evacuation from Singapore were passengers on ships that sank, subsequently being picked up by another ship, sometimes more than once. As far as possible therefore the ship given in the Roll is that at the outbreak of war. Once COFEPOW's database is complete on their website (www.cofepowdb.org.uk) and the information contained in the Liberation Questionnaires included, much more information will be available, although not all FEPOWs who survived completed a Liberation Questionnaire possibly because they were too ill or possibly because, being designed for prisoners of war who had been held in Europe, many of the questions on them were irrelevant. Inspection of some of those who did complete a questionnaire revealed a few problems. Some mention ships known not to have been sunk, scuttled or captured which reached Ceylon (now Sri Lanka) or Australia. Presumably these men were left in port as the ship passed through. For example Edward Breakspear and John Staples who were captured in Singapore give their ship as HMS *Kedah,* known to have left Singapore on 13th February and to have reached Java from where she departed with General Wavell on board and also known to have been the ship leading the Royal Navy into Singapore after Japan's surrender.

Another problem related to the country in which the FEPOW was held. The National Archives documents WO392/23 – WO392/26 list 56,813 UK men held by the Japanese giving Rank and Service Number, Branch of Service, Date of Capture, Date of Liberation (or Death) and Where Released (or Died). Where Released is the Japanese Command Area, of which there are 20.

Within Japan there are 7 Commands, 5 of which are on the main island of Honshu. On the Roll these are given as Tokyo Area, Sendai Area, Osaka Area, Nagoya Area and Hiroshima Area. The other Commands are Fukuoka, which was Kyushu Island, and Hakadate, which was Hokkaido Island; on the Roll these are given as Kyushu and Hokkaido. Also appearing on the Roll is Shikoku although this island was in fact in Hiroshima Command.

The Japanese Commands outside Japan cover much greater areas. Java Command covered not only Java but also the Celebes and the Moluccas and these three are named in the Roll. Thailand Command covered not only Thailand but also Saigon, and since all of the RN and RM men released in Saigon had previously been in Thailand no serious effort has been put into discovering those who moved on to Saigon. Malaya Command covered not only Singapore (then part of Malaya) but also Sumatra and Burma and these three are named in the Roll. Within Sumatra the UK FEPOWs fell into two categories between which there was no movement. Therefore Palembang is listed for those captured to the east of the island and Medan for those captured to the west.

Fortunately at the end of 1995, some twenty-five years earlier than the allotted date of 2021, the National Archives at Kew released Documents WO345/1 to WO345/58, each document being a box of approximately a thousand Japanese cards of their UK prisoners of war. These are mostly in Japanese. But from research into the Roll in "Unsung Heroes of the RAF – the FEPOWs" it was possible to use the dates on the cards to decode a great deal of information.

Place names in the Roll are those of the time. The exceptions are Taiwan (was Formosa), Thailand (was Siam) and names where the Dutch "oe" has been replaced with the Indonesian "u" - e.g. Haruku (was Haroekoe) and Muna (was Moena).

Dates of death are as given in the Registers of the Commonwealth War Graves Commission on the Commission's website (www.cwgc.org.uk) with a few exceptions. For the 10 airmen executed after Japan's surrender, >15.8.45 appears on the Roll.

Details of the War Cemeteries and Memorials relating to RN and RM FEPOWs appears in Appendix 7.

ABBISS Frederick - P/JX212426 - HMS Anking - Held Java, Singapore, Japan (Osaka Area)

ABEL Clifford Alan - D/SR8625 - HMS Tamar - Held Hong Kong - Died Lisbon Maru 2.10.42 - Named Plymouth Memorial

ACOCK George Richardson - C/K66405 - HMS Scorpion - Held Singapore (from Bangka)

ACOTT Louis Frederick Henry - D/J19255 - HMS Exeter - Held Celebes

ADAMS Alfred James - RM - PLY/21777 - SS Wellpark - Held Japan (Tokyo Area) - captured in S Atlantic

ADAMS Hedley - RM - RMB/X1535 - HMS Exeter - Held Celebes

ADAMS Leonard George - D/JX130985 - HMS Thracian - Held Hong Kong, Japan (Osaka Area) - Died Japan 30.10.42 - Buried Yokohama

ADAMS Thomas John George - D/J111409 - HMS Exeter - Held Celebes

ADDIS William Thomas - D/JX188455 - HMS Exeter - Held Celebes - Died Makassar 3.5.45 - Buried Ambon

AFFLECK John - D/SSX15176 - HMS Jupiter - Held Java, Moluccas - Died Suez Maru 29.11.43 - Named Plymouth Memorial

AINDOW Frederick - D/JX145433 - HMS Exeter - Held Celebes

AINSWORTH William George - D/JX133537 - HMS Prince of Wales - Held Sumatra (Palembang)

AIRTON Jack - RM - PLY/X101360 - HMS Repulse - Held Singapore, Thailand

AITKEN James Shaw - D/JX190455 - HMS Sultan - Held Sumatra (Medan, Railway) - Died Sumatra Railway 26.6.45 - Buried Jakarta

ALBISTON Joseph - P/J13252 - HMS Prince of Wales - Held Singapore (from Bangka Strait)

ALDWELL Basil Willington - .Lt - HMS Illustrious - Held Andaman Is., Japan (Tokyo Area)

ALEXANDER Caledon Charles - Com - HMS Sultan - Held Sumatra (Medan), Singapore, Thailand

ALEXANDER John - P/J58722 - HMS Redstart - Held Hong Kong, Japan (Osaka Area)

ALEXANDER Ronald - D/J107962 - HMS Repulse - Held Sumatra (Palembang)

ALLAN George - Lt - HMS Sultan - Held Singapore, Thailand

ALLAN John - P/JX212208 - HMS Giang Bee - Held Sumatra (Palembang)

ALLAN John C - P/JX262538 - MV Tantalus - Held Philippines

ALLANSON Walter - D/JX151706 - HMS Jupiter - Held Java, Moluccas, Celebes - Died Muna 7.3.45 - Buried Ambon

ALLARDYCE Maurice - P/JX273292 - HMS Hung Jao - Held Sumatra (Medan), Singapore, Sumatra (Railway)

ALLEN Fred - D/KX134324 - HMS Sultan - Held Sumatra (Medan) - Died Harikiku Maru 26.6.44 - Named Plymouth Memorial

ALLEN Graeme Phillip - Sub Lt - HMS Exeter - Held Celebes, Java

ALLEN Henry Vernon - D/JX184691 - HMS Exeter - Held Celebes - Died Makassar 7.5.45 - Buried Ambon

ALLEN Jesse Arthur - C/JX37199 - Ship not known - Held Sumatra (Palembang), Singapore

ALLEN Reginald Walter - D/JX170288 - HMS Exeter - Held Celebes - Died Makassar 19.4.45 - Buried Ambon

ALLEN Ronald James - D/JX171792 - HMS Exeter - Held Celebes

ALLEN William Richard - RM - PLY/X2196 - HMS Tamar - Held Hong Kong - Died Lisbon Maru 2.10.42 - Named Plymouth Memorial

ALLISON Desmond Heslop - C/JX262276 - Ship not known - Held Sumatra (Medan), Burma, Thailand

ALLISON George Dennis - C/MX69368 - HMS Encounter - Held Celebes

ALLISON John - D/MX45771 - HMS Tamar - Held Hong Kong, Japan (Osaka Area) - Died Japan 23.10.42 - Buried Yokohama

ALLISTONE Albert Percy - P/J97838 - HMS Redstart - Held Hong Kong, Japan (Osaka Area)

ALMOND Harold - P/SSX32264 - HMS Sultan - Held Sumatra (Medan, Railway) - Died Sumatra Railway 28.8.45 - Buried Jakarta

AMBROSE Fred - RM - PLY/22402 - HMS Tamar - Held Hong Kong - Died Lisbon Maru 2.10.42 - Named Plymouth Memorial

AMBROSE Frederick George - C/J97958 - Ship not known - Held Sumatra (Medan), Burma, Thailand

AMBROSE Frederick William - HKRNVR - Sub Lt - Ship not known - Held Hong Kong

AMBURY Edward Thomas John - D/JX179581 - HMS Sultan - Held Sumatra (Medan)   Died   Harikiku Maru 26.6.44 - Named Plymouth Memorial

ANDERSON Alexander - D/MD/X2403 - HMS Exeter - Held Celebes - Died Makassar 5.3.45   B u r-
ied Ambon

ANDERSON Arthur - D/MX50913 - HMS Encounter - Held Celebes, Japan (Kyushu)

ANDERSON Edward John - D/KX82481 - HMS Exeter - Held Celebes, Japan (Kyushu)

ANDERSON John - P/CDX2459 - HMS Tamar - Held Hong Kong - Died Hong Kong 16.8.42 - Buried Stanley

ANDERSON Thomas Albert - C/JX144913 - HMS Tamar - Held Hong Kong, Japan (Osaka Area) - Died Japan 29.10.42 - Buried Yokohama

ANDERSON William Holm - C/JX201212 - HMS Ying Pin - Held Sumatra (Palembang), Singapore

ANDREW Stanley - D/SSX25316 - HMS Prince of Wales - Held Sumatra (Palembang)

ANDREWS Thomas Amwel - D/KX81558 - HMS Exeter - Held Celebes, Japan (Kyushu)

ANDREWS William Henry Austin - D/JX163086 - HMS Tamar - Held Hong Kong, Japan (Osaka Area) - Died Japan 22.3.43 - Buried Yokohama

ANDREWS William Lewis - D/M34376 - HMS Exeter - Held Celebes, Japan (Kyushu) - Died Japan 5.2.43 - Buried Yokohama

ANGUS John - D/KX88406 - HMS Exeter - Held Celebes, Japan (Kyushu)

ANSELL Edward Ernest - C/JX313895 - MV Dalhousie - Held Japan (Osaka Area) - captured in S Atlantic

ANSON Peter - Sub Lt - HMS Exeter - Held Celebes, Java

ANTHONY Kenneth   RM - PLY/X3773 - HMS Repulse - Held Singapore, Thailand - Died Thailand 1.6.43 - Buried Kanchanaburi

ARBUCKLE Robert - C/JX129223 - HMS Encounter - Held Celebes - Died Makassar 28.3.45 - Buried Ambon

ARCHER Albert William John - C/KX105774 - HMS Tamar - Held Hong Kong - Died Lisbon Maru 2.10.42 - Named Chatham Memorial

ARCHER Robert Walter - P/JX125703 - HMS Sultan - Held Sumatra (Palembang) - Died Palembang 17.8.45 - Buried Jakarta

ARKLEY Robert Thirlway - RNZN - Sub Lt - ML 433 - Held Sumatra (Palembang)

ARMSTRONG John McPhail - D/JX237727 - SS Kirkpool - Held Japan (Tokyo Area) - captured in S Atlantic

ARMSTRONG Joseph - D/JX136887 - Ship not known - Held Sumatra (Palembang), Singapore, Taiwan, Japan (Tokyo Area, Sendai Area)

ARMSTRONG Robert Nelson - C/MX76758 - HMS Sultan - Held Sumatra (Palembang)

ARNOLD Jack Lawrence - MRNVR - Sub Lt - HMS Scorpion - Held Sumatra (Palembang), Singapore

ASHCROFT Walter - D/K66889 - ML 433 - Held Sumatra (Palembang), Singapore, Taiwan, Japan (Tokyo Area, Sendai Area)

ASHER Cecil Anthony - D/JX188588 - HMS Exeter - Held Celebes

ASHFORD Ronald Edward - P/JX201901 - HMS Tamar - Held Hong Kong - Died Lisbon Maru 2.10.42 - Named Plymouth Memorial

ASHMORE Raymond George - C/MX76835 - HMS Dymas - Held Singapore (from Bangka)

ASHTON Cyril Richard - C/SSX20134 - HMS Tamar - Held Hong Kong, Japan (Osaka Area) Died Japan 1.11.43 - Buried Yokohama

ASHWORTH Cecil Walter - D/MX51328 - HMS Prince of Wales - Held Sumatra (Palembang), Singapore

ASTON Joseph Thomas Charles - D/JX171806 - HMS Repulse - Held Sumatra (Palembang)

ATKINS Charles Frederick - P/JX27344 - HMS Tapah - Held Singapore (from Bangka Strait)

ATKINS James Ernest Tyndale - D/MX68126 - HMS Prince of Wales - Held Singapore

ATKINSON Robert - D/J108082 - HMS Tamar - Held Hong Kong - Died Lisbon Maru 2.10.42 - Named Plymouth Memorial

ATTERSOLL John Walter - P/JX251209 - HMS Sultan - Held Sumatra (Medan), Burma Died Burma (Railway) 30.10.43 - Buried Thanbyuzayat

ATTEWELL Danton - D/MX71926 - HMS Exeter - Held Celebes, Japan (Kyushu)

ATTWELL Gerald - D/SSX20157 - HMS Tamar - Held Hong Kong - Died Lisbon Maru 2.10.42 - Named Plymouth Memorial
AUSTIN John Edward - P/SSX21588 - HMS Prince of Wales - Held Sumatra (Medan), Burma, Thailand
AYLWIN Claude Derek Lawrence - RM - Capt - HMS Prince of Wales - Held Singapore, Thailand
BACK Percy George Edward - RM - PLY/X21505 - HMS Prince of Wales - Held Singapore, Thailand - Died Thailand 25.12.43 - Buried Chungkai
BACON Richard Stanley - D/KX95098 - HMS Exeter - Held Celebes
BADGER Wilfred Harold - D/KX90250 - HMS Exeter - Held Celebes
BAGGS Kenneth George - D/MX54450 - Ship not known - Held Hong Kong, Japan (Osaka Area)
BAILEY George Albert - D/SSX22354 - HMS Jupiter - Held Java, Moluccas, Java
BAILEY Godfrey Henry - C/SSX33182 - HMS Encounter - Held Celebes
BAILEY Henry Preston - HKRNVR - Lt - Ship not known - Held Hong Kong
BAILEY Reginald Kenneth - C/MX52582 - HMS Tamar - Held Hong Kong - Died Lisbon Maru 2.10.42 - Named Chatham Memorial
BAILEY Stanford Arthur - Boom Skipper - HMS Tamar - Held Hong Kong - Died Shanghai after sinking of Lisbon Maru 7.10.42 - Buried Yokohama
BAILEY Thomas Henry A - D/MX65178 - HMS Repulse - Held Sumatra (Palembang)
BAILEY William Edward - D/JX164181 - HMS Exeter - Held Celebes
BAILLIE William Arnold - D/SSX32756 - HMS Encounter - Held Celebes
BAINBOROUGH George Harry - D/MX58724 - HMS Tamar - Held Hong Kong, Japan (Osaka Area)
BAINES Arthur - D/JX140270 - Ship not known - Held Singapore (from Bangka)
BAIRD James - P/JX274435 - HMS Tanjong Pinang - Held Sumatra (Palembang), Singapore
BAIRSTOW Terence Benjamin - D/KX108124 - HMS St Breock - Held Singapore (from Bangka)
BAKER Arthur - C/SSX33461 - HMS Encounter - Held Celebes, Japan (Kyushu)
BAKER Arthur Edward - C/KX105783 - HMS Thracian - Held Hong Kong, Japan (Tokyo Area)
BAKER Edwin Douglas. - P/SSX30505 - Ship not known - Held Hong Kong, Japan (Osaka Area)
BAKER Herbert - D/J100625 - HMS Repulse - Held Sumatra (Palembang), Singapore
BAKER Jack - P/MX48263 - HMS Tamar - Held Hong Kong - Died Lisbon Maru 2.10.42 - Named Plymouth Memorial
BAKER John Richard - C/SSX33075 - HMS Electra - Held Java, Moluccas, Java
BAKER Robert Owen - HKRNVR - Act Sub Lt - Ship not known - Held Hong Kong
BAKER William Ernest - HKRNVR - Sub Lt - Ship not known - Held Hong Kong
BALDWIN Edward Arthur William - D/JX146429 - HMS Repulse - Held Sumatra (Medan), Burma, Thailand
BALL Clifford - C/SSX33491 - HMS Encounter - Held Celebes, Japan (Kyushu)
BALL Denis Ronald   RM - PLY/X2041 - HMS Tamar - Held Hong Kong, Japan (Osaka Area)   D i e d Japan 15.10.42 - Named Plymouth Memorial
BALL John William George - D/KX85251 - HMS Exeter - Held Celebes - Died Makassar 15.5.45 - Buried Ambon
BALL Richard Gregson - RM - PLY/X3682 - HMS Exeter - Held Celebes - Died Makassar 22.3.45 - Buried Ambon
BALLENTYNE John Craig Smith - P/JX258709 - HMS Exeter - Held Celebes, Japan (Kyushu)
BAMPFYLDE Reginald William - D/MX53207 - HMS Prince of Wales - Held Sumatra (Palembang), Singapore
BANCE Sidney Albert - RM - RMB/X68 - HMS Exeter - Held Celebes - Died Makassar 12.2.45 - Buried Ambon
BANKS Eric - C/JX169556 - HMS Encounter - Held Celebes - Died Makassar 12.7.45 - Buried Ambon
BANKS Gerald - C/JX208279 - HMS Tern - Held Hong Kong, Japan (Osaka Area)
BANKS Ronald Gray - MRNVR - Lt - HMS Laburnum - Held Sumatra (Palembang), Singapore, Thailand
BANNISTER Stephen - D/KX1280633 - HMS Sultan - Held Sumatra (Medan) - Died Harikiku Maru 26.6.44 - Named Plymouth Memorial
BANYARD Charles Edward - P/KX130632 - HMS Encounter - Held Celebes - Died Makassar 25.4.45 - Buried Ambon
BARBER Wilfred - see BLAKE Wilfred
BARKER Ivor - FAA/86731 - HMS Victorious - Held Sumatra (Palembang), Singapore Died   Singapore 15.8.45 - Named Lee-on-Solent Memorial
BARKER James Edwin - P/JX217617 - HMS Grasshopper - Held Sumatra (Medan, Atjeh, Railway)
BARNES Harold - C/JX262268 - Ship not known - Held Sumatra (Medan), Burma, Thailand
BARNES Leslie James - P/JX204017 - Ship not known - Held Hong Kong, Japan (Tokyo Area)
BARNES Ronald David - C/JX139814 - HMS Tern - Held Hong Kong, Japan (Osaka Area)

BARNES Victor Thomas - RM - PLY/X100152 - HMS Prince of Wales - Held Sumatra (Medan), Burma, Thailand

BARNETT William Charles - C/J104259 - HMS Encounter - Held Celebes

BARRETT Herbert - RM - PLY/X2184 - HMS Repulse - Held Singapore, Thailand

BARRICK Jack William - P/JX312688 - MV Empire Dawn - Held Java - captured in S Atlantic, Sumatra (Pangkalan Bali), Singapore

BARTEL Wallace Garnet Milliken - SANF - SA/68838 - HMS Exeter - Held Celebes, Japan (Kyushu)

BARTHOLOMEW Arthur William - D/KX1164162 - HMS Repulse - Held Singapore (from Bangka)

BARTHOLOMEW Gaythorne - D/JX188479 - HMS Exeter - Held Celebes, Japan (Kyushu)

BARTLETT Arthur Wheeler - P/J98569 - RN MTB - Held Hong Kong

BARTLETT Kingsley - P/JX131375 - Ship not known - Held Hong Kong, Japan (Tokyo Area)

BARTON George William - D/K67194 - HMS Tamar - Held Hong Kong, Japan (Osaka Area)

BARTON Sydney Allan - P/JX239537 - HMS Exeter - Held Celebes, Japan (Kyushu)

BARUGH Robert - P/SSX29240 - Ship not known - Held Sumatra (Medan), Burma, Thailand

BASHAM Walter James - D/JX276497 - HMS Fan Lin - Held Sumatra (Palembang)

BASTARD Arthur Leonard - P/MX53077 - HMS Dragonfly - Held Sumatra (Medan, Railway)

BATCHELOR William Arthur - C/KX92671 - HMS Exeter - Held Celebes

BATEMAN Robert William - Lt - Ship not known - Held Hong Kong

BATEMAN Sydney James - D/MX54936 - HMS Prince of Wales - Held Sumatra (Palembang)

BATER Harold Charles - D/M37318 - HMS Tamar - Held Hong Kong, Japan (Osaka Area) Died Japan 25.10.42 - Buried Yokohama

BATESON Morris - D/MX55105 - HMS Repulse - Held Singapore, Borneo

BATTEN William Henry - D/JX161400 - HMS Repulse - Held Java, Sumatra (Pangkalan Bali), Singapore

BAUKHAM Victor - HKRNVR - Act Sub Lt - Ship not known - Held Hong Kong

BAXTER Evan John - Lt (A) - HMS Illustrious - Held Sumatra (Palembang), Singapore - Died Singapore >15.8.45 - Named New Zealand Memorial

BAXTER Sidney Charles - D/JX182577 - HMS Repulse - Held Java, Singapore, Borneo

BAYFIELD Ernest Edward - C/JX156396 - HMS Encounter - Held Celebes, Japan (Kyushu)

BAYLISS Joseph Sidney - D/KX83110 - HMS Repulse - Held Sumatra (Palembang), Singapore

BAYRAM Allan George - D/MX52851 - HMS Redstart - Held Hong Kong, Japan (Osaka Area)

BEADLE Denis Mark - Lt - HMS Exeter - Held Celebes, Java

BEATTIE Laurence Duncan McNab - HKRNVR - Act Lt - HMS Cicala - Held Hong Kong

BEATTIE Richard George - P/SSX19359 - Ship not known - Held Sumatra (Palembang), Singapore

BEAUGIE Raymond George - D/SSX17064 - HMS Exeter - Held Celebes

BECKFORD William George - W O Mech - HMS Exeter - Held Celebes, Japan (Kyushu)

BEER Reginald Thomas - C/KX93925 - HMS Sultan - Held Singapore, Borneo

BELL Norman McLeod - D/JX194211 - Ship not known - Held Hong Kong, Japan (Osaka Area) - Died Japan 27.4.43 - Buried Yokohama

BELL Robert - C/SSX17158 - RN MTB - Held Hong Kong, Japan (Tokyo Area, Sendai Area)

BELL Stanley Hugh - D/JX188587 - HMS Exeter - Held Celebes

BELL Victor Robert - D/JX163790 - Stonecutters - Held Hong Kong, Japan (Osaka Area)

BELL Walter - D/JX154083 - Ship not known - Held Java, Singapore, Borneo

BENN Lewin Arthur - HKRNVR - Act Sub Lt - HMS Cornflower - Held Hong Kong

BENNETT George (19.12.93) - D/K16071 - HMS Exeter - Held Celebes, Japan (Kyushu)

BENNETT George (20.1.07) - L/JX315898 - MV Dalhousie - Held Japan (Osaka Area) - captured in S Atlantic

BENNETT Norman John Maurice - Sub Lt - HMS Exeter - Held Celebes, Japan (Kyushu), Manchuria

BENNETT William John - C/JX137473 - HMS Sultan - Held Sumatra (Palembang), Singapore

BENSON James Alan - RM - PLY/X100147 - HMS Prince of Wales - Held Singapore, Thailand - Died Toyofuku Maru 21.9.44 - Named Plymouth Memorial

BENSON Joseph Hugh - D/MX102740 - HMS Tamar - Held Hong Kong - Died Lisbon Maru 2.10.42 - Named Plymouth Memorial

BENTLEY William Arthur - RM - PLY/X100010 - HMS Repulse - Held Sumatra (Palembang)

BERRY Peter - D/MX72681 - HMS Exeter - Held Celebes, Japan (Kyushu)

BEST Arthur James - D/KX90350 - HMS Exeter - Held Celebes, Japan (Kyushu)

BEST Harold Ernest - D/JX169805 - HMS Tamar - Held Hong Kong - Died Lisbon Maru - 2.10.42 - Named Plymouth Memorial

BEST Richard - P/JX224187 - HMS Exeter - Held Celebes

BESWICK George Arthur - D/J54609 - HMS Exeter - Held Celebes

BETENSON Sidney Henry George - D/MX48570 - HMS Exeter - Held Celebes

UNSUNG HEROES of the ROYAL NAVY and ROYAL MARINES

BETTERTON Ernest Alfred - C/JX147240 - HMS Moth - Held Hong Kong, Japan (Tokyo Area, Sendai Area)

BEVAN Cecil - RM - PLY/X3127 - HMS Prince of Wales - Held Singapore, Thailand

BEVAN Granville Aubrey Mervyn - D/JX216195 - HMS Tamar - Held Hong Kong - Died Hong Kong 19.7.42 - Buried Stanley

BEVERIDGE Andrew D - RM - RMB/X1074 - HMS Exeter - Held Celebes

BEVIS Harry - Lt - Ship not known - Held Hong Kong, Japan (Osaka Area. Shikoku, Kyushu)

BEVIS Herbert Thomas - P/M22609 - HMS Tamar - Held Hong Kong - Died Lisbon Maru - 2.10.42 - Named Plymouth Memorial

BIBBINGS Kenneth John - D/JX163238 - HMS Sultan - Held Java, Sumatra (Pangkalan Bali) - Died Pangkalan Bali 27.8.45 - Buried Jakarta

BICKER Harold Stanley - C/KX76350 - HMS Encounter - Held Celebes, Japan (Kyushu)

BICKLE Kenneth James - D/LX25406 - HMS Exeter - Held Celebes - Died Makassar 2.6.45 - Buried Ambon

BICKMORE Ernest Alfred - C/JX174010 - HMS Tamar - Held Hong Kong - Died Lisbon Maru 2.10.42 Named Chatham Memorial

BIDDULPH Kenneth - P/SSX35695 - HMS Scorpion - Held Sumatra (Palembang)

BIGGS Arthur Leonard - HKRNVR - W O - HMS Tamar - Held Hong Kong - Died Lisbon Maru 2.10.42 - Named Plymouth Memorial

BIGNALL Gordon Howard - D/MX64067 - HMS Tamar - Held Hong Kong, Japan (Osaka Area)

BILLINGS Adrian Richardson - P/MX88331 - HMS Thracian - Held Hong Kong

BILTON Arthur - D/MX66814 - HMS Tamar - Held Hong Kong - Died Lisbon Maru 2.10.42 - Named Plymouth Memorial

BINNY John Graham - Lt Com - HMS Tamar - Held Hong Kong

BIRCH Arthur Edward - D/SSX22726 - HMS Tamar - Held Hong Kong - Died Lisbon Maru 2.10.42 Named Plymouth Memorial

BIRCUMSHAW Frederick - D/JX214712 - HMS Exeter - Held Celebes - Died Makassar 10.3.45 - Buried Ambon

BIRD James Campbell - D/JX181975 - HMS Exeter - Held Celebes - Died Makassar 2.10.43 - Buried Ambon

BIRKETT Ermald Prosser - Lt - HMS Thracian - Held Hong Kong

BISHOP Archibald Clarence James - D/JX139309 - HMS Exeter - Held Celebes, Japan (Kyushu)

BISHOP Leslie - D/SSX23703 - HMS Repulse - Held Sumatra (Palembang)

BLACK George - D/KX167039 - Ship not known - Held Java, Singapore, Japan (Hiroshima Area)

BLACK James Robert - D/MX64662 - HMS Exeter - Held Celebes

BLACK John Dalziel - D/KX89779 - HMS Exeter - Held Celebes, Japan (Kyushu)

BLACKADDER Robert Charles - D/JX190471 - HMS Pahlawan - Held Singapore (from Bangka)

BLACKBURN Joseph George - Pm Sub Lt - SS Nankin - Held Japan - captured in Indian Ocean (Tokyo Area, Shikoku, Tokyo Area)

BLACKMAN Alfred Henry - C/K66540 - HMS Encounter - Held Celebes, Japan (Kyushu)

BLACKWELL Edward Walter Joseph - P/JX136012 - HMS Exeter - Held Celebes

BLADES Alfred John - D/LX20212 - HMS Repulse - Held Sumatra (Medan, Railway)

BLAIN Robert Geoffrey - Lt Eng - HMS Exeter - Held Celebes, Japan (Kyushu), Manchuria

BLAINEY Laurence Henry - C/JX168293 - HMS Encounter - Held Celebes

BLAIR Frederick - D/JX267052 - MV Patella - Held Japan (Kyushu) - captured in S Atlantic - Died Japan 20.5.45 - Buried Yokohama

BLAKE Leslie John - RM - PLY/X2832 - HMS Sultan - Held Sumatra (Palembang)

BLAKE Wilfred - C/KX79226 - HMS Sultan - Held Sumatra (Palembang)

BLAKE William Levi - C/SSX28825 - Ship not known - Held Sumatra (Medan), Burma, Thailand

BLAKEMORE Thomas - D/MD/X2274 - HMS Jupiter - Held Java, Singapore, Japan (Osaka Area)

BLAKENEY Bertram Foulkes - Lt - HMS Cornflower - Held Hong Kong

BLAMIRE Edgar - P/JX87835 - RN MTB - Held Hong Kong, Japan (Osaka Area, Nagoya Area)

BLATHERWICK William James - D/JX237884 - HMS Exeter - Held Celebes

BLISS David Kenneth - D/J53499 - HMS Tamar - Held Hong Kong - Died Lisbon Maru 2.10.42 - Named Plymouth Memorial

BOGLE Robert Euwe - Pm Sub Lt - SS Nankin - Held Japan (Tokyo Area) - captured in Indian Ocean

BOLDERO John Christian - Lt Com - HMS Cicala - Held Hong Kong

BOLITHO William Symond - D/MX63503 - HMS Sultan - Held Sumatra (Palembang)

BOND Albert James - C/J109909 - HMS Encounter - Held Celebes, Japan (Kyushu)

BOND Alfred John - D/MX80266 - HMS Exeter - Held Celebes - Died Makassar 28.2.45 - Buried Ambon

BOND Ernest Alexander - D/JX125685 - HMS Exeter - Held Celebes
BOND William Horace - D/M36415 - HMS Tamar - Held Hong Kong - Died Lisbon Maru 2.10.42 - Named Plymouth Memorial
BONE John Henry - P/JX145591 - HMS Kung Wo - Held Sumatra (Medan), Burma, Thailand
BONFIELD Frank - D/M39742 - HMS Tamar - Held Hong Kong - Died Lisbon Maru 2.10.42 - Named Plymouth Memorial
BOOTE Harold - RM - PLY/X100930 - HMS Exeter - Held Celebes - Died Makassar 4.4.45 - Buried Ambon
BOOTHROYD George Herbert - P/SSX31937 - HMS Tamar - Held Hong Kong - Died Lisbon Maru 2.10.42 Named Plymouth Memorial
BORTON Richard Edward - Lt - HMS Vyner Brooke - Held Sumatra (Palembang), Singapore
BOSWARD Frederick - D/JX140525 - HMS Prince of Wales - Held Sumatra (Medan, Atjeh, Railway)
BOSWELL Cyril Lumley Lynn - P/J69622 - Mining Party - Held Hong Kong, Japan (Tokyo Area)
BOURNE Arthur Alexander - D/MX71562 - HMS Kung Wo - Held Sumatra (Medan), Burma, Thailand
BOW Stanley Henry - C/KX75164 - HMS Moth   Held Hong Kong, Japan (Osaka Area)
BOWDEN John William - D/JX134129 - HMS Exeter - Held Celebes
BOWELL Terence George - P/KX134343 - HMS Tapah - Held Singapore (from Bangka)
BOWEN Aubrey Alexander - D/J20512 - HMS Exeter - Held Celebes
BOWEN Hubert James - D/JX166631 - HMS Exeter - Held Celebes
BOWIE Andrew Malcolm Peter - RM - PLY/X3800 - HMS Prince of Wales - Held Sumatra (Palembang)
BOWLER Arthur William Spicer - RM - RMB/X1119 - HMS Exeter - Held Celebes
BOWLEY William Richard Lyon - Pm Lt - HMS Tamar - Held Hong Kong
BOYD John McAlister - D/J88011 - Boom Defence - Held Hong Kong, Japan (Nagoya Area)
BOYES Frank - D/JX188941 - HMS Sultan - Held Sumatra (Medan) - Died Harikiku Maru 26.6.44 - Named Plymouth Memorial
BOYES William James Lewis - D/M26910 - HMS Tamar - Held Hong Kong - Died Lisbon Maru 2.10.42 Named Plymouth Memorial
BOYNE Martin William Arthur - D/M36394 - HMS Tamar - Held Hong Kong - Died Lisbon Maru 2.10.42 Named Plymouth Memorial
BRACKENRIDGE William - D/MX66227 - HMS Mata Hari - Held Singapore (from Bangka)
BRADBURY John - P/M69963 - HMS Laburnum - Held Singapore (from Bangka)
BRADFORD Stanley Leonard - D/JX213065 - HMS Exeter - Held Celebes
BRADLEY Joseph Douglas - L/SFX435 - HMS Exeter - Held Celebes - Died Makassar 16.11.43 - Buried Ambon
BRADSHAW Reginald James - D/M39882 - HMS Exeter - Held Celebes
BRAKEWELL George - D/JX184097 - HMS Exeter - Held Celebes
BRANDER James McPherson - MRNVR - Lt - HMS Sin-Aik-Lee - Held Sumatra (Palembang), Singapore
BRANNEY William - D/SSX19734 - HMS Scorpion - Held Sumatra (Palembang)
BRANSON Alfred James William - P/JX23539 - SS Gemstone - Held Japan (Kyushu) - captured in S Atlantic
BRASH John Thomas - D/JX162910 - HMS Prince of Wales - Held Celebes - Died Makassar 21.8.45 Buried Ambon
BRAY Clarence Norman - D/JX133813 - HMS Repulse - Held Java, Singapore, Japan (Osaka Area)
BREAKSPEAR Edward James - P/J107280 - HMS Kedah - Held Singapore, Thailand
BREESE George Edwin RM - PLY/X539 - Stonecutters - Held Hong Kong, Japan (Osaka Area)
BRENNAN James Edward - SANF - SA/67417 - Ship not known - Held Java, Sumatra (Pangkalan Bali) - Died Pangkalan Bali 8.7.45 - Buried Jakarta
BREWER William George Henry - D/K63608 - HMS Exeter - Held Celebes - Died Makassar 11.1.45 - Buried Ambon
BRICE Cyril David - C/KX100722 - HMS Encounter - Held Celebes
BRICKER James - D/JX189724 - Ship not known - Held Hong Kong, Japan (Osaka Area, Nagoya Area)
BRIDGE Richard - D/SSX19922 - HMS Anking - Held Java, Singapore, Japan (Osaka Area)
BRIDGES Frederick Ronald - D/JX148812 - HMS Exeter - Held Celebes
BRIGHOUSE James - D/KX108775 - HMS Exeter - Held Celebes - Died Makassar 13.5.45 - Buried Ambon
BRIGHT Arthur William - P/K20823 - HMS Tamar - Held Hong Kong - Died Lisbon Maru 2.10.42 Named Plymouth Memorial
BRIGHTMAN Harold Lawrence - RM - PLY/X1874 - HMS Exeter - Held Celebes - Died Makassar 18.5.45 Buried Ambon
BRISTOW George Robert - P/KX121240 - HMS Tern - Held Hong Kong, Japan (Osaka Area, Nagoya Area)
BRITT Noel George - see JACKSON B Noel George
BRITTON Douglas - RM - PLY/1861 - HMS Exeter - Held Celebes

UNSUNG HEROES of the ROYAL NAVY and ROYAL MARINES

BROAD Donald - D/KX93306 - HMS Exeter - Held Celebes, Japan (Kyushu)
BROADWAY Alexander George - D/KX80238 - HMS Tapah - Held Singapore (from Bangka)
BROCK Thomas C - Lt - SS Nankin - Held Japan (Tokyo Area) - captured in Indian Ocean
BROMLEY Ythil Charles Lewis - 2nd Officer - SS Francol - Held Celebes, Java, Singapore - Died Singapore 3.8.45 - Named Tower Hill Memorial
BROOK Herbert Eric - D/JX212953 - HMS Exeter - Held Celebes - Died Makassar - 27.4.45 - Buried Ambon
BROOKE Bartholomew Joseph - P/J99019 - HMS Exeter - Held Celebes
BROOKES Munro Charles - C/JX139552 - HMS Encounter - Held Celebes, Japan (Kyushu)
BROOKS Terence Charles Frederick - RM - PLY/X1209 - HMS Prince of Wales - Held Singapore, Thailand
BROPHY John Ernest - P/JX226740 - HMS Sultan - Held Sumatra (Palembang) - Died Palembang 27.7.45 - Buried Jakarta
BROUGHAM Patrick - Lt - HMS Exeter - Held Celebes, Japan (Tokyo Area, Shikoku, Tokyo Area)
BROUGHTON Charles - D/JX200412 - HMS Exeter - Held Celebes
BROUGHTON William Edward D - P/JX299311 - HMS Exeter - Held Celebes
BROWN Arthur Robert - HKRNVR - Lt - Ship not known - Held Hong Kong
BROWN Cecil Edward Thomas - C/JX149041 - Ship not known - Held Sumatra (Medan), Burma, Thailand
BROWN David McNeilace - D/J194203 - HMS Tamar - Held Hong Kong - Died Lisbon Maru 2.10.42 Named Plymouth Memorial
BROWN Donald Stanley - RM - PLY/X3807 - HMS Prince of Wales - Held Sumatra (Palembang)
BROWN Frank - D/SSX17120 - HMS Cicala - Held Hong Kong, Japan (Osaka Area)
BROWN George Frederick - C/KX109342 - HMS Thracian - Held Hong Kong, Japan (Osaka Area)
BROWN George William Averillo - D/JX135011 - HMS Exeter - Held Celebes
BROWN Hugh - C/MX72244 - HMS Scorpion - Held Sumatra (Palembang) - Died Palembang 16.8.42 - Buried Jakarta
BROWN James Henry - D/JX237707 - HMS Jupiter - Held Java, Moluccas, Java
BROWN James Thomas - HKRNVR - Lt - HMS Margaret - Held Hong Kong
BROWN John - RM - PLY/X2140 - HMS Prince of Wales - Held Singapore, Thailand - Died Thailand 8.7.43 - Buried Kanchanaburi
BROWN John Cedric - HKRNVR - Pm Lt - HMS Tamar - Held Hong Kong
BROWN John S H CUNYNGHAM- see CUNYINGHAM-BROWN John S H
BROWN Kenneth George - D/SSX23154 - HMS Exeter - Held Celebes, Japan (Kyushu)
BROWN Reginald - D/SSX23791 - HMS Exeter - Held Celebes, Japan (Kyushu)
BROWN Robert William Charles - RM - PLY/X3812 - HMS Prince of Wales - Held Singapore, Thailand
BROWN William Edward - RM - CH/X3377 - HMS Tapah - Held Sumatra (Palembang)
BROWN William Oddy - C/LDX2504 - HMS Encounter - Held Celebes - Died Makassar 24.2.45 - Buried Ambon
BROWNING Robert - D/K63072 - Ship not known - Held Singapore, Thailand
BRUFORD Rowland Charles Henry - D/JX153457 - HMS Repulse - Held Singapore (from Bangka Strait)
BRYAN Sydney - D/JX166463 - HMS Exeter - Held Celebes - Died Makassar 14.2.45 - Buried Ambon
BRYANT John Henry - D/KX120645 - Ship not known - Held Sumatra (Palembang)
BRYANT Vivian Gwyn Escott - D/KX108485 - HMS Exeter - Held Celebes, Japan (Kyushu)
BRYDIE Cecil Corstorphine - D/MX54814 - HMS Tamar - Held Hong Kong - Died Lisbon Maru 2.10.42 - Named Plymouth Memorial
BUCHANAN Andrew Mair - Lt - Ship not known - Held Hong Kong
BUCK Harry - D/KX108774 - HMS Exeter - Held Celebes
BUCKLE Frank - HKRNVR - Lt - HMS Ho Shing - Held Hong Kong
BUCKLE John Terence - RM - RMB/X693 - HMS Exeter - Held Celebes - Died Pomelaa 3.9.43 - Buried Ambon
BUCKLEY James - P/ESD/X1401 - HMS Thracian - Held Hong Kong, Japan (Osaka Area, Hiroshima Area)
BUCKLEY Victor - RM - PLY/X2099 - HMS Repulse - Held Singapore, Thailand - Died Thailand 29.7.43 Buried Kanchanaburi
BUCKWELL Selwyn Robert Leighton - MRNVR - Sub Lt - HMS Scorpion - Held Sumatra (Palembang)
BULBECK James George Richard - C/J107654 - HMS Encounter - Held Celebes, Japan (Kyushu)
BULL Francis Charles - D/JX165781 - HMS Tamar - Held Hong Kong, Japan (Osaka Area) - Died Japan 17.12.42 - Buried Yokohama
BULLEN Jack - C/KX133623 - HMS Stronghold - Held Celebes
BULLOCK Edwin - C/J97973 - Boom Defence - Held Hong Kong, Japan (Nagoya Area)
BURBIDGE Robert William - D/KX113261 - HMS Sultan - Held Sumatra (Medan), Burma, Thailand - Died Thailand 11.3.44 - Buried Kanchanaburi
BURCH Arthur James - D/J28741 - HMS Exeter - Held Celebes - Died Makassar 24.5.45 - Buried Ambon

BURFORD Frederick James - P/JX201141 - HMS Tamar - Held Hong Kong, Japan (Osaka Area) - Died Japan 15.10.42 - Buried Yokohama
BURGESS Geoffrey Haden - RM - PLY/X3772 - HMS Repulse - Held Sumatra (Palembang)
BURGESS Stanley Joseph - D/JX191056 - Ship not known - Held Sumatra (Palembang)
BURGIN Ernest - D/SSX20669 - HMS Thracian - Held Hong Kong, Japan (Osaka Area) - Died Japan 14.2.45 - Buried Yokohama
BURKE William J - C/SSX17768 - SS Nankin - Held Japan (Tokyo Area) - captured in Indian Ocean
BURLING William John - HKRNVR - Act Sub Lt - Ship not known - Held Hong Kong
BURNETT Ernest - D/KX134337 - HMS Sultan - Held Java, Singapore, Borneo - Died Labuan 16.2.45 - Named Plymouth Memorial
BURNS John Robert - Sub Lt (A) - HMS Victorious - Held Sumatra (Palembang), Singapore - Died Singapore >15.8.45 - Named Lee-on-Solent Memorial
BURRENSTON Kenneth Morgan - Lt (A) - HMS Victorious - Held Sumatra (Palembang), Singapore - Died Singapore >15.8.45 - Named Lee-on-Solent Memorial
BURROUGHS Bertram Ernest - C/JX158918 - HMS Jarak   Held Sumatra (Medan), Burma, Thailand
BURROWS Edgar George - C/KX83472 - Boom Defence - Held Hong Kong - Died Lisbon Maru 2.10.42 - Named Chatham Memorial
BURROWS Geoffrey - RM - PLY/X3103 - HMS Prince of Wales - Held Singapore, Thailand - Died Rakuyo Maru 12.9.44 - Named Plymouth Memorial
BURROWS Kenneth George - P/J102981 - HMS Tamar - Held Hong Kong, Japan (Osaka Area) - Died Japan 5.12.42 - Buried Yokohama
BURROWS William George Ladbrook - D/J32682 - HMS Exeter - Held Celebes - Died Makassar 20.5.45 - Buried Ambon
BURTON Edward Scott - Pm Com - HMS Tamar - Held Hong Kong
BURTON Vere Ansted - MRNVR - Lt - HMS Tapah - Held Sumatra (Palembang)
BUSH Lewis - Sub Lt - Ship not known - Held Hong Kong, Japan (Tokyo Area)
BUSSEL Albert Edward - D/J105398 - HMS Stronghold - Held Celebes
BUTCHER David - D/SSX19914 - HMS Exeter - Held Celebes - Died Pomelaa 14.5.43 - Buried Ambon
BUTCHER Eric Robert - HKRNVR - W O - Ship not known - Held Hong Kong - Died Shanghai after sinking of Lisbon Maru 9.10.42 - Buried Yokohama
BUTLER Harry - D/SSX22668 - HMS Thracian - Held Hong Kong, Japan (Osaka Area)
BUTLER Ivor - D/KX129480 - HMS Sultan - Held Singapore, Taiwan, Japan (Tokyo Area, Sendai Area)
BUTTERFIELD Dennis - D/MX64878 - HMS Exeter - Held Celebes
BUTTERWORTH John - C/KX105640 - Ship not known - Held Hong Kong, Japan (Osaka Area)
BYFORD Herbert James - C/JX128533 - HMS Encounter - Held Celebes
BYRNE Patrick (13.9.19) - D/MX62989 - HMS Repulse - Held Sumatra (Palembang)
BYRNE Patrick (8.8.20) - D/MX61963 - HMS Prince of Wales - Held Sumatra (Medan), Burma, Thailand
BYWORTH George John - C/JX278529 - HMS Repulse - Held Sumatra (Palembang)
CABLE Arthur Roy - D/JX166359 - HMS Exeter - Held Celebes
CADGER John B - D/JX188580 - HMS Exeter - Held Celebes
CAHALANE Cornelius - P/JX131439 - HMS Tamar - Held Hong Kong, Japan (Tokyo Area)
CAIN Reginald - P/JX311382 - MV Patella - Held Japan (Kyushu) - captured in S Atlantic
CAIN Timothy John - W O - SS Nankin - Held Japan (Tokyo Area) - captured in Indian Ocean
CAKE Wallace Vivian - D/JX211542 - HMS Vyner Brooke - Held Sumatra (Palembang)
CALDWELL Hugh Cochrane - Sub Lt - Ship not known - Held Sumatra (Palembang), Singapore, Taiwan, Japan (Tokyo Area) - Died Japan - 12.12.42 - Named Liverpool Memorial
CALLCUT Robert Ernest - P/SSX33274 - HMS Moth - Held Hong Kong, Japan (Nagoya Area)
CALLEJA Ugo - E/L14949 - HMS Exeter - Held Celebes
CALVERT Hans - D/JX229549 - HMS Tamar - Held Hong Kong - Died Lisbon Maru 2.10.42 - Named Plymouth Memorial
CALVERT Joseph Norman - D/K61013 - HMS Stronghold - Held Celebes
CAMBRIDGE William Edward - C/KX104701 - HMS Redstart - Held Hong Kong, Japan (Tokyo Area)
CAMPBELL Allan - RM - PLY/X100369 - HMS Exeter - Held Celebes - Died Makassar 23.3.45 - Buried Ambon
CAMPBELL John Alexander - SANF - SA/68214 - HMS Exeter - Held Celebes
CAMPBELL Leveson Granville Byron A - Capt - HMS Tamar - Held Hong Kong, Taiwan, Manchuria
CAMPBELL William - D/MX80127 - HMS Tamar - Held Hong Kong - Died Lisbon Maru 2.10.42 - Named Plymouth Memorial
CAMPION Albert - RM - PLY/X100431 - HMS Prince of Wales - Held Singapore, Thailand
CAMPION Bernard Gerald - D/JX134274 - HMS Prince of Wales - Held Singapore, Thailand, Singapore
CARDEW Harry - D/J113542 - HMS Stronghold - Held Celebes

CARDWELL Reginald Richard Edward - D/MX80508 - HMS Exeter - Held Celebes - Died Makassar 15.2.45 - Buried Ambon

CAREY Francis Roydon Lamiter - HKRNVR - Act Lt - Ship not known - Held Hong Kong

CARMICHAEL Hugh - C/JX169389 - HMS Encounter - Held Celebes

CARNE Arthur Morris - D/MX53061 - HMS Exeter - Held Celebes, Japan (Kyushu)

CARR Charles Donald - D/SSX24465 - HMS Exeter - Held Celebes - Died Makassar 6.4.45 - Buried Ambon

CARR George Joseph - C/MX45294 - HMS Encounter - Held Celebes

CARR John Patrick - D/JX204210 - HMS Siang Wo - Held Sumatra (Palembang), Singapore

CARROLL Joseph - P/KX106341 - HMS Rahman - Held Java, Singapore

CARSON William Henry - D/JX188467 - HMS Exeter - Held Celebes

CARSTON Albert Charles - Lt - HMS Mata Hari - Held Sumatra (Palembang), Singapore, Taiwan, Japan (Hiroshima Area)

CARTER Charles Walter - P/K62608 - HMS Cicala - Held Hong Kong, Japan (Osaka Area)

CARTER John Douglas Haig - C/SSX16249 - HMS Tern - Held Hong Kong, Japan (Osaka Area)

CARTER John Edward - D/JX156962 - Ship not known - Held Sumatra (Medan), Burma, Thailand

CARTER John Hall - D/JX140262 - HMS Exeter - Held Celebes

CARTWRIGHT William - RM - PLY/X734 - HMS Exeter - Held Celebes

CASE John Henry - D/JX176593 - HMS Exeter - Held Celebes, Japan (Kyushu)

CASEY Jeremiah - D/K57916 - HMS Tamar - Held Hong Kong, Japan (Osaka Area)

CASEY Patrick John - D/JX171765 - HMS Giang Bee - Held Sumatra (Palembang), Singapore

CASSEL Kenneth - D/JX154797 - HMS Exeter - Held Celebes

CASSIDY John McFerran - P/UDX1320 - HMS Tamar - Held Hong Kong, Japan (Osaka Area) - Died Japan 29.6.43 Buried Yokohama

CASSIN Francis - D/JX153144 - HMS Tamar - Held Hong Kong - Died Lisbon Maru 2.10.42 - Named Plymouth Memorial

CASTLE Raymond Douglas - P/JX236193 - HMS Exeter - Held Celebes - Died Makassar 22.3.45 - Buried Ambon

CASTLETON Reginald Gaze - HKRNVR - Snr Gnr - HMS Cornflower - Held Hong Kong, Japan (Osaka Area)

CASTRO George William - D/JX147705 - HMS Exeter - Held Celebes - Died Makassar 31.5.45 - Buried Ambon

CASWELL Charles Alfred - P/JX164941 - HMS Tamar - Held Hong Kong - Died Hong Kong 22.9.42 - Buried Stanley

CATHERWOOD Thomas George - D/SSX28442 - HMS Exeter - Held Celebes

CAVENEY James J - C/JX208282 - SS Nankin - Held Japan (Tokyo Area) - captured in Indian Ocean

CAWLEY Patrick Joseph - D/KX110157 - HMS Exeter - Held Celebes

CAWTHORNE James Francis - C/JX160343 - SS Nankin - Held Japan (Tokyo Area) - captured in Indian Ocean

CAYZER Albert Edward George - RM - RMB/X1581 - HMS Exeter - Held Celebes, Java

CHAFFE Leonard - NAAFI - HMS Exeter - Held Celebes

CHALCRAFT George Louis - P/MX53758 - HMS Dragonfly - Held Sumatra (Medan), Singapore, Sumatra (Railway)

CHAMBERLAIN Frank William - RM - CH/X1198 - Stonecutters - Held Hong Kong

CHAMBERS Charles Ernest - C/MX56624 - HMS Encounter - Held Celebes - Died Pomelaa 23.8.43 - Buried Ambon

CHAMBERS James - C/SSX28512 - HMS Tamar - Held Hong Kong, Japan (Osaka Area) - Died Japan 14.11.43 - Buried Yokohama

CHAMBERS James Wilfred - P/MX71505 - HMS Moth - Held Hong Kong

CHANDLER Alfred - RM - PLY/X3387 - HMS Prince of Wales - Held Singapore, Thailand

CHANDLER Richard Charles Frederick - D/MX48549 - HMS Exeter - Held Celebes

CHANNON Gordon Allan - L/FX79055 - HMS Exeter - Held Celebes - Died Makassar 20.4.45 - Buried Ambon

CHAPMAN Arthur Thomas - D/KX111127 - HMS Exeter - Held Celebes, Japan (Kyushu)

CHAPMAN Harry - RM - PLY/X1710 - HMS Exeter - Held Celebes, Japan (Kyushu)

CHAPMAN Roland Paul - Capt - RN Base Singapore - Held Sumatra (Palembang), Singapore, Taiwan, Manchuria

CHAPPELL Aubrey Bertram - RM - EX4371 - RM Special Service - Held Burma

CHAPPELL Francis Henry - P/J31979 - HMS Pelandok - Held Sumatra (Palembang)

CHAPPLE Thomas Henry - D/JX217236 - HMS Scorpion - Held Sumatra (Palembang)

CHARD Eric Athelstan - MRNVR - Lt - HMS Sultan - Held Sumatra (Palembang), Singapore

CHARLES John Francis William - P/272331 - Ship not known Held Singapore (from Bangka)

CHARLES Reginald James - C/JX182021 - HMS Jupiter - Held Java, Moluccas, Java

CHATFIELD Alfred Charles - P/JX276477 - HMS Sultan - Held Sumatra (Medan), Burma, Thailand - Died Thailand 16.3.44 - Buried Kanchanaburi

CHATFIELD Arthur Bailey - C/MX50361 - HMS Scorpion - Held Singapore (from Bangka Strait)

CHATTOCK Thomas Rawdon - Lt Com - HMS Tamar - Held Hong Kong

CHEEK George Henry - P/J30260 - HMS Tamar - Held Hong Kong - Died Lisbon Maru 2.10.42 - Named Plymouth Memorial

CHENNELLS Graham George - RNZN - NZ/W3763 - HMS Sultan - Held Sumatra (Palembang)

CHESWORTH George - D/MX70122 - HMS Prince of Wales - Held Sumatra (Palembang)

CHEYNE Richard Warren - RM - PLY/X2132 - HMS Exeter - Held Celebes, Japan (Kyushu)

CHILCRAFT Robert Albert A - C/JX198043 - HMS Tamar - Held Hong Kong - Died Lisbon Maru 2.10.42 - Named Chatham Memorial

CHILDS George Montague - C/JX147246 - HMS Tern - Held Hong Kong, Japan (Osaka Area) - Died Japan 9.11.42 - Buried Yokohama

CHILDS William Edward - D/SSX28855 - Ship not known - Held Singapore, Thailand, Japan (Kyushu)

CHISHOLME Frederick Noel - D/SSX31770 - HMS Exeter - Held Celebes - Died Makassar 28.3.42 - Buried Ambon

CHISWELL Reginald Clarence George - D/M28197 - HMS Tamar - Held Hong Kong, Japan (Osaka Area) - Died Japan 11.10.42 - Buried Yokohama

CHOWN John Charles Herbert - Lt - Ship not known - Held Hong Kong

CHRISTIAN Albert Edward - D/JX200409 - HMS Exeter - Held Celebes, Java

CHRISTIE David Hamilton - MRNVR - Lt - HMS Tapah - Held Sumatra (Palembang)

CHRISTIE Sydney - D/MX65008 - HMS Exeter - Held Celebes, Japan (Kyushu)

CHRISTOPHER Ronald Francis - D/KX84047 - HMS Exeter - Held Celebes - Died Makassar 11.3.45 - Buried Ambon

CHRISTOPHER William - P/KX81363 - HMS Grasshopper - Held Sumatra (Medan) - Died Harikiku Maru 26.6.44 - Named Plymouth Memorial

CHRISTOPHERSON Harold Ashley - D/JX149189 - HMS Exeter - Held Celebes

CHUBB David William Early - Lt - HMS Exeter - Held Celebes, Java

CHUBB Edwin Joseph - Lt Com - HMS Exeter - Held Celebes, Japan (Kyushu), Manchuria

CHUBB Leonard John - D/SSX35815 - HMS Exeter - Held Celebes, Japan (Kyushu)

CHURCHWARD Cyril James - D/MX55726 - HMS Exeter - Held Celebes

CLAMP Joseph William - D/JX144510 - HMS Exeter - Held Celebes - Died Pomelaa 8.9.43 - Buried Ambon

CLARBOUR Leslie Richard - C/JX262357 - HMS Encounter - Held Celebes, Japan (Kyushu)

CLARE Harry - D/KX110154 - HMS Exeter - Held Celebes

CLARIDGE Frederick James - C/JX131015 - HMS Pelandok - Held Sumatra (Palembang)

CLARK Douglas - C/SSX16957 - HMS Encounter - Held Celebes, Japan (Kyushu)

CLARK Harold - Lt - Ship not known - Held Hong Kong

CLARK James Bruce - Sub Lt - HMS Dragonfly - Held Sumatra (Medan), Singapore, Thailand

CLARK Keith Hood Fergusson - MidShipman - HMS Exeter - Held Celebes, Java

CLARK Leonard Stanley - D/SSX28450 - HMS Exeter - Held Celebes, Japan (Kyushu)

CLARK Victor Cecil Froggatt - Lt Com - HMS Repulse - Held Sumatra (Palembang), Singapore

CLARKE Alfred Horatio James - C/J105465 - HMS Moth - Held Hong Kong, Japan (Osaka Area)

CLARKE Arthur Charles - P/MX68048 - RN MTB - Held Hong Kong

CLARKE Wilfred Allan - D/JX138843 - HMS Tamar - Held Hong Kong - Died Lisbon Maru 2.10.42 - Named Plymouth Memorial

CLASBY John William - D/SSX21179 - HMS Exeter - Held Celebes

CLAXTON Frank Allan RM - PLY/X3725 - HMS Repulse - Held Sumatra (Palembang)

CLAY Norman Leslie - RM - PLY/X2918 - HMS Exeter - Held Celebes

CLAYTON George - RM - PLY/X1542 - HMS Exeter - Held Celebes

CLAYTON William Charles - RM - PLY/X1855 - HMS Tamar - Held Hong Kong, Japan (Tokyo Area, Sendai Area)

CLEARY George - RM - PLY/X2589 - HMS Prince of Wales - Held Singapore, Taiwan, Japan (Tokyo Area)

CLEAVE Hugh Latimer - Surg Com - RN Hospital - Held Hong Kong, Japan (Tokyo Area)

CLEAVER Frederick - C/JX262356 - HMS St Breock - Held Sumatra (Medan), Burma, Thailand

CLEGG James Stansfield - D/KX115754 - HMS Siang Wo - Held Singapore (from Bangka)

CLEMENS Llewellyn - D/J102215 - HMS Tapah - Held Sumatra (Palembang), Singapore

CLEMENTS Frank Edwin - Cant Man - HMS Exeter - Held Celebes

CLIFTON Ernest - D/KX102768 - HMS Repulse - Held Sumatra (Medan), Burma, Thailand

CLIMIE William - D/JX166495 - HMS Exeter - Held Celebes
CLINTON Hugh Stevenson - P/JX248649 - MV Dalhousie - Held Japan (Osaka Area) - captured in S Atlantic
CLOKE Charles James - D/K64458 - HMS Exeter - Held Celebes, Japan (Kyushu)
CLUNE Norman Walter - D/JX238266 - HMS Exeter - Held Celebes
COATES William Henry Everest - HKRNVR - W O - Ship not known - Held Hong Kong, Japan (Nagoya Area)
COBB Arthur Henry Kingston - Pm Lt - Ship not known - Held Hong Kong
COBB Roy William - D/MX80267 - HMS Prince of Wales - Held Sumatra (Medan, Railway)
COCKBURN William Gordon - D/JX175921 - HMS Prince of Wales - Held Java, Singapore, Borneo
COCKER John William - D/K64796 - HMS Jupiter - Held Java
COCKERELL Walter George - D/J103652 - HMS Exeter - Held Celebes
COCKLE Harry Maughan - HKRNVR - Lt - Ship not known - Held Hong Kong
COFFEY Norman Wilfred - RM - PO/22448 - HMS Sultan - Held Sumatra (Palembang), Singapore
COILS James - C/JX158359 - SS Nankin - Held Japan (Tokyo Area) - captured in Indian Ocean - Died Japan 31.7.44 Named Chatham Memorial
COITE Reginald John William - D/JX137331 - HMS Thracian Held Hong Kong, Japan (Osaka Area)
COLE Daniel Rex - D/J46239 - HMS Prince of Wales - Held Singapore (from Bangka Strait)
COLE Ernest George - C/SSX32571 - HMS Encounter - Held Celebes - Died Makassar 8.4.45 - Buried Ambon
COLE Frank - RM - PLY/X946 - HMS Tamar - Held Hong Kong, Japan (Osaka Area)
COLEMAN Albert French - P/JX135448 - HMS Moth - Held Hong Kong
COLLARD Charles Walter - D/J109695 - HMS Cicala - Held Hong Kong, Japan (Osaka Area)
COLLEN Henry Walter - C/SSX17769 - HMS Moth - Held Hong Kong, Japan (Tokyo Area, Sendai Area)
COLLIER Nelson Leslie Bailey - RM - PLY/X100037 - HMS Exeter - Held Celebes
COLLINS Herbert James - C/JX126928 - HMS Encounter - Held Celebes
COLLINS John - C/JX213598 - HMS Jupiter - Held Java, Sumatra (Railway) - Died Sumatra Railway 11.7.45 - Buried Jakarta
COLLINS Kenneth - D/MX71932 - HMS Exeter - Held Celebes, Japan (Kyushu)
COLLINSON Alfred Creighton - Com - Ship not known - Held Hong Kong, Taiwan, Manchuria
COLQUHOUN David - C/K62803 - HMS Sultan - Held Sumatra (Medan, Railway) - Died Sumatra Railway - 16.7.45 - Buried Jakarta
COLQUHOUN Robert - D/SSX35707 - HMS Repulse - Held Sumatra (Palembang)
CONIBEAR Robert John Murdock - Lt - HMS Encounter - Held Celebes, Japan (Tokyo Area, Shikoku, Tokyo Area)
CONNOR Herbert Howard - C/MX48637 - HMS Tamar - Held Hong Kong, Japan (Osaka Area)
CONWAY Philip Thomas - C/JX185987 - HMS Dragonfly - Held Sumatra (Medan) - Died Harikiku Maru 26.6.44 - Named Chatham Memorial
CONWELL Cornelius - D/SSX17323 - HMS Exeter - Held Celebes - Died Makassar 29.3.45 - Buried Ambon
COOK Clifford Montague - D/MX60856 - HMS Tamar - Held Hong Kong, Japan (Osaka Area)
COOK Norman - Lt - HMS Fuh Wo - Held Sumatra (Palembang) - Died Palembang 21.10.43 - Buried Jakarta
COOK Thomas - D/MX73727 - HMS Exeter - Held Celebes
COOKE William Joseph - C/KX94969 - RN MTB - Held Hong Kong, Japan (Tokyo Area)
COOKMAN James - D/SSX19376 - Ship not known - Held Singapore, Thailand
COOMB Francis Alfred - P/KX121350 - HMS Thracian - Held Hong Kong, Japan (Osaka Area, Nagoya Area)
COOPER Frederick - D/MX61459 - HMS Sultan - Held Celebes, Japan (Kyushu)
COOPER George Tyndale - Lt Com - HMS Exeter - Held Celebes, Java
COOPER Jack Andrew - P/JX261367 - SS Wellpark - Held Japan (Tokyo Area) - captured in S Atlantic
COOPER Leonard Lawton - MRNVR - Lt Com - HMS Rahman - Held Java, Singapore, Japan (Hiroshima Area, Shikoku, Tokyo Area)
COOPER Leslie - D/JX184615 - HMS Exeter - Held Celebes
COOPER William Edward - C/SSX27716 - HMS Kung Wo - Held Sumatra (Medan), Burma, Thailand
COPLEY David Judd - Pm Lt - HMS Sultan - Held Sumatra (Palembang)
COPPING Norman - P/KX86161 - HMS Grasshopper - Held Sumatra (Medan), Burma - Died Burma (Railway) 25.10.43 - Buried Thanbyuzayat
CORCORAN John Patrick - Surg - HMS Sultan - Held Sumatra (Palembang), Singapore
CORDON John Henry - P/SSX123495 - HMS Moth - Held Hong Kong, Japan (Osaka Area)
CORK Philip Dorian - MRNVR - Lt - HMS Pahlawan - Held Sumatra (Palembang)

CORK Samuel Henry - D/K19253 - HMS Exeter - Held Celebes - Died Makassar 1.2.45 - Buried Ambon

CORLETT Thomas Arnold - D/KX108559 - HMS Exeter - Held Celebes

CORNELL R W - MRNVR - Pm Sub Lt - HMS Mata Hari - Held Sumatra (Palembang), Singapore

CORNEY Clarence Henry - RM - PLY/X1870 - HMS Prince of Wales - Held Sumatra (Palembang) - Died Palembang 11.3.45 - Buried Jakarta

CORNFORD Donald Edward - D/SSX32762 - HMS Repulse - Held Singapore, Thailand

CORRIGAN John - C/JX207930 - HMS Stronghold - Held Celebes

CORY William Edward - D/K21680 - HMS Exeter - Held Celebes - Died Pomelaa 18.5.43 - Buried Ambon

COSTA Peter David - RM - PLY/X1831 - HMS Prince of Wales - Held Sumatra (Medan, Atjeh, Railway)

COSTIN Stephen John - RM - PLY/X1122 - HMS Repulse - Held Sumatra (Palembang)

COTTLE Reginald William - D/JX137349 - HMS Repulse - Held Sumatra (Palembang)

COTTON Frank - D/JX150686 - HMS Jupiter - Held Java, Moluccas, Celebes - Died Muna 24.2.45 - Buried Ambon

COTTON Walter Donald - P/JX205143 - HMS Stronghold - Held Celebes

COWAN James Miller - D/MX75466 - HMS Sultan - Held Sumatra (Medan, Atjeh, Railway)

COWDALL Leslie - RM - PLY/X2462 - HMS Exeter - Held Celebes - Died Makassar 31.1.45 - Buried Ambon

COWELL Stanley Phillip - D/SSX31346 - HMS Exeter - Held Celebes - Died Makassa 11.4.45 - Buried Ambon

COWLING John Hartley - Capt - HMS Aldgate - Held Hong Kong, Japan (Osaka Area. Shikoku, Kyushu)

COWSER Hugh - P/JX146257 - HMS Encounter - Held Celebes

COX Albert Henry - D/J23871 - HMS Tamar - Held Hong Kong

COX John - D/JX174256 - HMS Prince of Wales - Held Sumatra (Medan) - Died Harikiku Maru 26.6.44 - Named Plymouth Memorial

COX Lawrence - P/J76801 - HMS Sultan - Held Singapore, Thailand

COX Norman - RM - PLY/X1510 - HMS Tamar - Held Hong Kong, Japan (Osaka Area)

COX Percy - P/JX207801 - SS Willesden - Held Japan (Tokyo Area) - captured in S Atlantic

COX Robert William - C/JX145403 - HMS Encounter - Held Celebes, Japan (Kyushu)

CRABBE William Gordon - HKRNVR - W O - Ship not known - Held Hong Kong, Japan (Osaka Area) - Died Japan 20.10.42 - Buried Yokohama

CRABTREE Allan - D/SSX30457 - HMS Tamar - Held Hong Kong - Died Lisbon Maru 2.10.42 - Named Plymouth Memorial

CRAIG George - D/SSX23071 - HMS Exeter - Held Celebes

CRAIG John Harcourt - MRNVR - Lt - HMS Hung Jao - Held Sumatra (Medan), Singapore, Thailand

CRANE Herbert William - FAA/FX75095 - HMS Exeter - Held Celebes

CRANEFIELD Philip Garton - Sub Lt - HMS Exeter - Held Celebes, Java, Singapore, Japan (Kyushu), Manchuria

CRANGLE John Raphael - P/UDX1399 - HMS Tamar - Held Hong Kong - Died Lisbon Maru 2.10.42 - Named Plymouth Memorial

CRANWELL Wilfred Benedict - D/MX45442 - HMS Exeter - Held Celebes - Died Makassar 12.1.44 - Buried Ambon

CRAPPER Arnold - C/JX176436 - Ship not known - Held Sumatra (Palembang), Singapore, Taiwan, Japan (Tokyo Area, Sendai Area)

CRAVEN Cyril Hector - D/SSX31768 - HMS Exeter - Held Celebes - Died Makassar 15.4.45 - Buried Ambon

CRAVEN Douglas Hugh Stewart - Com - Ship not known - Held Hong Kong

CRAWFORD George William - C/KX107328 - HMS Stronghold - Held Celebes, Japan (Kyushu) - Died Japan 20.1.43 - Buried Yokohama

CRAWLEY Cyril Ernest - Lt - HMS Fuh Wo - Held Sumatra (Palembang), Singapore

CRIGHTON James - D/JX180649 - HMS Prince of Wales - Held Sumatra (Medan, Atjeh, Railway)

CROCKER George Isaac - D/K62163 - HMS Exeter - Held Celebes

CROCKER William Harry - D/K57382 - HMS Exeter - Held Celebes

CROFT Sidney - RM - PLY/X753 - Stonecutters - Held Hong Kong, Shanghai, Japan (Hokkaido)

CROMPTON Peers - RM - PLY/X100723 - HMS Prince of Wales - Held Sumatra (Palembang), Singapore

CRONIN John Patrick - D/MX73027 - HMS Exeter - Held Celebes

CROOKHAM Charles Leslie - D/KX82067 - HMS Stronghold - Held Celebes

CROSS Denis Herbert - P/JX173809 - Ship not known - Held Sumatra (Palembang)

CROSS Hugh - D/JX149477 - HMS Exeter - Held Celebes, Japan (Kyushu)

CROSS Ivor George Harry - D/SSX823702 - HMS Repulse - Held Singapore (from Bangka Strait)

CROSSLEY Charles William - HKRNVR - W O - Ship not known - Held Hong Kong - Died Lisbon Maru 2.10.42 - Named Plymouth Memorial

CROSSLEY Thomas Anderson - MRNVR - Lt - Ship not known - Held Sumatra (Palembang), Singapore, Taiwan, Japan (Tokyo Area, Shikoku, Tokyo Area)
CROSSMAN James - Lt - HMS Indefatigable - Held Japan (Tokyo Area)
CROWLE Leslie James - D/KX57375 - HMS Blumut - Held Singapore (from Bangka)
CROWTHER Francis William - Com - Ship not known - Held Hong Kong
CRUDEN Stewart Hunter - Sub Lt - HMS Electra - Held Java
CRUMLIN James - D/JX153513 - Ship not known - Held Singapore, Thailand, Japan (Kyushu)
CRUMP Ronald Charles - FAA/FX77822 - HMS Exeter - Held Celebes
CULLUM Harold - D/J96876 - HMS Tamar - Held Hong Kong - Died Hong Kong 27.9.42 - Buried Stanley
CUMBERLIN Arthur - D/SSX19122 - HMS Jupiter - Held Java
CUMMINGS Thomas - RM - PLY/X3416 - HMS Repulse - Held Sumatra (Palembang)
CUNYNGHAM-BROWN John S H - MRNVR - Sub Lt - HMS Hung Jao - Held Sumatra (Medan), Singapore, Sumatra (Railway)
CURNICK Ronald Robert - C/KX100719 - HMS Encounter - Held Celebes - Died Makassar 10.2.45 - Buried Ambon
CURRUTHER Leonard Gordon - SANF - SA68828 - HMS Exeter - Held Celebes
CURTIN Augustine Peter - Surg Lt - SS Nankin - Held Japan (Tokyo Area) - captured in Indian Ocean
CUTHBERT John - D/JX211672 - HMS Exeter - Held Celebes
CUTHBERTSON James - D/MX74081 - HMS Repulse - Held Sumatra (Palembang)
DADDS Thomas Frederick - RM - PLY/X2261 - HMS Exeter - Held Celebes
DALGLEISH William - D/MX53213 - HMS Exeter - Held Celebes
DALLEY George Alexanda - RM - PLY/X3821 - HMS Prince of Wales - Held Singapore, Thailand - Died Thailand 13.5.43 - Buried Chungkai
DANCE Ernest Arthur - P/SSX21186 - HMS Stronghold - Held Celebes, Java
DANGER Richard Henry - Lt - HMS Thanet - Held Singapore (from Saigon), Thailand
DANIELS Russell Humphrey - D/K13613 - HMS Exeter - Held Celebes, Java
DARK Sidney Gordon - RM - PLY/X797 - HMS Tamar - Held Hong Kong
DARLEY George A R - D/KX111329 - HMS Exeter - Held Celebes
DARNELL John William - D/K66763 - HMS Exeter - Held Celebes, Japan (Kyushu)
DARRIGAN Walter Henry - C/JX181411 - Ship not known - Held Sumatra (Medan), Burma, Thailand
DARRIGAN William Stanley - C/JX181409 - Ship not known - Held Sumatra (Medan), Burma, Thailand
DART Ernest George - RM - PLY/22558 - HMS Prince of Wales - Held Sumatra (Palembang), Singapore
DAVENPORT Jack - RM - PLY/X100127 - HMS Prince of Wales - Held Singapore, Thailand - Died Toyofuku Maru 21.9.44 - Named Plymouth Memorial
DAVIDSON David - P/MX52321 - HMS Sultan - Held Singapore - Died Singapore 29.8.45 - Buried Kranji
DAVIES Evan Hywel - D/MX67611 - HMS Exeter - Held Celebes
DAVIES Glyn - D/KX113792 - HMS Exeter - Held Celebes, Japan (Kyushu)
DAVIES Glyn Elwyn - D/LX25053 - HMS Exeter - Held Celebes
DAVIES Granville - D/MX75369 - HMS Kuala - Held Sumatra (Medan, Atjeh, Railway)
DAVIES Harry Graham - D/JX188735 - HMS Cicala - Held Hong Kong, Japan (Tokyo Area, Sendai Area)
DAVIES Hedley Walters - P/MX56369 - RN MTB - Held Hong Kong, Japan (Osaka Area)
DAVIES Henry G - D/JX153156 - HMS Thracian Held Hong Kong, Japan (Osaka Area) - Died Japan 10.3.43 - Buried Yokohama
DAVIES Herbert F - D/JX232369 - Ship not known - Held Sumatra (Palembang), Singapore, Taiwan, Japan (Tokyo Area, Sendai Area)
DAVIES Joseph Edward - C/K65720 - HMS Electra - Held Java, Moluccas - Died Maros Maru 29.9.44 - Named Chatham Memorial
DAVIES Kenneth Vernon - D/MX82684 - HMS Tamar - Held Hong Kong - Died Hong Kong 23.7.42 - Buried Stanley
DAVIES Richard John - RM - PLY/21977 - HMS Repulse - Held Singapore, Thailand
DAVIES Roy Malcolm - RM - PLY/X2573 - HMS Prince of Wales - Held Sumatra (Palembang) - Died Palembang 30.11.42 - Buried Jakarta
DAVIES Stanley Gordon - RM - PLY/X3829 - HMS Exeter - Held Celebes - Died Makassar 19.4.45 - Buried Ambon
DAVIES Thomas Glyndwr - C/LDX3569 - HMS Encounter - Held Celebes, Japan (Kyushu)
DAVIES William - D/KX114818 - HMS Blumut - Held Singapore (from Bangka Strait)
DAVIS Claude Trenchard - HKRNVR - Lt - Ship not known - Held Hong Kong
DAVIS Edward Thomas Alexander - C/M37678 - HMS Tern - Held Hong Kong, Japan (Osaka Area)
DAVIS Henry - D/KX77895 - HMS Prince of Wales - Held Sumatra (Medan, Railway)
DAVIS Reginald G - D/JX148878 - HMS Tamar - Held Hong Kong, Japan (Osaka Area, Hiroshima Area)
DAVIS Richard James Lance - RM - Lt - HMS Repulse - Held Singapore, Thailand

DAVIS Walter Frank - Lt - HMS Cicala - Held Hong Kong
DAVIS William Richard - D/JX139971 - HMS Repulse - Held Sumatra (Palembang)
DAWBER William - D/SSX19538 - HMS Prince of Wales - Held Java, Singapore, Borneo
DAWES Hugh Campbell Frederick - Lt Com - Ship not known - Held Hong Kong
DAWSON Alfred John - D/MX67584 - HMS Anking - Held Celebes, Java
DAWSON George Thomas - D/JX206185 - HMS Exeter - Held Celebes, Java
DAWSON John - D/JX225316 - Ship not known - Held Hong Kong, Japan (Osaka Area)
DAWSON-GROVE Antony Warren - HKRNVR - Surg Lt - HMS Cornflower - Held Hong Kong, Japan (Tokyo Area)
DAY Charles William - RM - CH/X2170 - HMS Sultan - Held Singapore (from Jibbia), Thailand, Singapore
DAY Harry Joseph - D/JX158862 - HMS Exeter - Held Celebes, Java
DAYMAN Frederick J - C/JX186830 - HMS Encounter - Held Celebes
DEAN Reginald Ernest - P/JX149860 - HMS Tamar - Held Hong Kong - Died Hong Kong 15.8.42 - Buried Stanley
DEAN Wilfred Eric - D/JX237927 - HMS Exeter - Held Celebes
DEE David John - D/JX188472 - HMS Exeter - Held Celebes
DEEGAN Michael Ronald - D/MX53856 - Ship not known - Held Hong Kong
DEERE Denis Peters - D/JX142301 - HMS Exeter - Held Celebes - Died Makassar 11.4.45 - Buried Ambon
DEERING William - C/JX247292 - HMS Thracian - Held Hong Kong, Japan (Osaka Area)
DELBRIDGE Leslie - D/JX138282 - HMS Repulse - Held Sumatra (Medan), Singapore, Sumatra (Railway)
DENHAM Peter Arthur Henry - C/JX143630 - HMS Encounter - Held Celebes - Died Makassar 12.5.45 - Buried Ambon
DENMARK Robert Arthur - P/JX311303 - SS Kirkpool - Held Japan (Tokyo Area) - captured in S Atlantic
DENT Eric Sydney - C/SSX17873 - HMS Encounter - Held Celebes
DENT Frederick - P/JX290039 - SS Gemstone - Held Japan (Kyushu) - captured in S Atlantic
DENT William Henry - D/SSX23802 - HMS Sultan - Held Singapore (from Bangka Strait), Thailand, Japan (Kyushu)
DENTITH Thomas R - D/JX162944 - HMS Repulse - Held Singapore (from Bangka), Borneo
DERRICK Michael - P/SSX19527 - HMS Scorpion - Held Sumatra (Palembang)
DESTE Frank Duncombe - P/K60218 - HMS Grasshopper - Held Sumatra (Medan) - Died Harikiku Maru 26.6.44 - Named Plymouth Memorial
DESVERGEZ Francis Pierre Louis - D/J87016 - HMS Exeter - Held Celebes - Died Makassar 16.4.44 - Buried Ambon
DEVANEY Robert - C/JX262385 - HMS Dragonfly - Held Sumatra (Medan, Railway)
DEVIS Sidney Arthur Joseph - D/JX106125 - HMS Repulse - Held Sumatra (Palembang) - Died Palembang 1.9.45 - Buried Jakarta
DEVLIN George - D/JX162145 - HMS Exeter - Held Celebes
DEVLIN John - D/K85087 - HMS Exeter - Held Celebes, Japan (Kyushu)
DICKENSON Peter - Sub Lt - HMS Sultan - Held Singapore, Thailand - Died Thailand 11.11.42 - Buried Kanchanaburi
DICKER Richard Skelton - D/JX175795 - HMS Prince of Wales - Held Sumatra (Medan, Atjeh, Railway)
DICKEY Walter Hugh - P/SSX19718 - HMS Moth - Held Hong Kong, Japan (Tokyo Area)
DIGGLE Herbert - D/J105375 - HMS Exeter - Held Celebes
DIMECH Maurice - Cant Asst - HMS Encounter - Held Celebes
DINES Joe - Lt - HMS Thracian - Held Hong Kong
DIRKS Fredrick Leonard - D/JX135795 - HMS Prince of Wales - Held Java, Singapore, Japan (Kyushu)
DITCHBURN John - 3rd Officer - SS Francol - Held Celebes, Java, Singapore
DIVETT Geoffrey Edward Ross - HKRNVR - W O - APV Stanley - Held Hong Kong, Japan (Osaka Area, Nagoya Area)
DIXIE Frederick - D/SSX22929 - HMS Exeter - Held Celebes
DIXON Christopher - RM - PLY/X1409 - HMS Prince of Wales - Held Sumatra (Palembang), Singapore
DIXON Frederick - P/MX50109 - HMS Exeter - Held Celebes
DIXON Herbert Charles - RNZN - Lt - Ship not known - Held Hong Kong
DIXON Joseph - C/JX201675 - SS Kirkpool - Held Japan (Tokyo Area) - captured in S Atlantic
DIXON Walter - D/JX239586 - HMS Exeter - Held Celebes
DOBSON Charles Rennie Cowil - Sub Lt - HMS Thracian - Held Hong Kong
DOBSON John - RNZN - NZ/D2939 - HMS Exeter - Held Celebes
DOBSON Kenneth Roland - C/SSX28042 - HMS Encounter - Held Celebes - Died Makassar 20.3.45 - Buried Ambon
DODD John Bell - D/SSX17029 - HMS Jupiter - Held Java, Moluccas, Java
DODDS Allan - RM - RMB/X3045 - HMS Exeter - Held Celebes, Japan (Kyushu)

DODDS Andrew Kenneth - RM - PLY/X3885 - HMS Exeter - Held Celebes

DODDS Harry - D/FX81148 - HMS Exeter - Held Celebes

DODGSON Arthur - RM - PLY/X3698 - HMS Repulse - Held Sumatra (Palembang)

DODSON Charles Henry - C/230594 - HMS Tamar - Held Hong Kong - Died Lisbon Maru 2.10.42 - Named Chatham Memorial

DODSWORTH Joseph Henry - C/JX278236 - HMS Mata Hari - Held Sumatra (Palembang), Singapore, Taiwan, Japan (Tokyo Area, Sendai Area)

DODSWORTH Philip Albert - D/JX166777 - HMS Exeter - Held Celebes

DOHERTY Thomas - D/JX15968 - Boom Defence - Held Hong Kong, Japan (Tokyo Area)

DONALDSON Thomas Ritchie - D/SSX35809 - HMS Exeter - Held Celebes, Japan (Kyushu)

DONEY Vernard Archie - D/KX77613 - HMS Sultan - Held Java, Singapore - Died Tamahoko Maru 24.6.44 - Named Plymouth Memorial

DONISTHORPE Anthony Russell Bradshaw - D/JX188480 - HMS Exeter - Held Celebes

DONNELLY Thomas - D/KX89838 - HMS Exeter - Held Celebes, Japan (Kyushu)

DOUGHTY Frederick Arthur - D/MX50925 - HMS Repulse - Held Sumatra (Palembang)

DOUGLAS Dould Cameron - Lt - HM Sub. Stratagem - Held Singapore (from Malacca Strait), Japan (Tokyo Area)

DOW Robert - C/KX90980 - HMS Tern - Held Hong Kong, Japan (Osaka Area) - Died Japan 19.10.42 - Buried Yokohama

DOWLING Maurice - P/SSX117816 - HMS Cicala - Held Hong Kong, Japan (Osaka Area) - Died Japan 21.10.42 - Buried Yokohama

DOWNING Frank - C/SSX17129 - HMS Moth - Held Hong Kong

DOWNING Frank Howard - D/J81746 - HMS Fuh Wo - Held Sumatra (Palembang) - Died Palembang 20.12.44 - Buried Jakarta

DOWNS Leslie - D/JX311180 - MV Dalhousie - Held Japan (Osaka Area) - captured in S Atlantic

DOWSETT Samuel - C/JX156068 - HMS Tamar - Held Hong Kong, Japan (Osaka Area) - Died Japan 22.3.43 - Buried Yokohama

DOYLE Francis Ronald - D/JX204339 - HMS Stronghold - Held Celebes, Japan (Kyushu)

DRAKE Arthur Hamiton - Com - HMS Exeter - Held Celebes, Japan (Tokyo Area, Shikoku, Tokyo Area)

DRAKE Elfred Charles - D/JX145132 - Ship not known - Held Sumatra (Medan, Railway) - Died Sumatra Railway 15.9.45 - Buried Jakarta

DRAKE William Stanley - HKRNVR - W O - Ship not known Held Hong Kong - Died Lisbon Maru 2.10.42 - Named Plymouth Memorial

DRINKWATER William - D/MX47092 - HMS Exeter - Held Celebes, Japan (Kyushu)

DRISCOLL John Featherstone - D/MX67653 - HMS Exeter - Held Celebes - Died Makassar 8.4.45 - Buried Ambon

DRUCE Frank George - C/JX106522 - HMS Encounter - Held Celebes

DRUMMOND John - D/JX155219 - HMS Repulse - Held Sumatra (Palembang)

DRYDALE George - D/SSX24738 - HMS Exeter - Held Celebes

DUCKER Neville James - D/MX59150 - HMS Tamar - Held Hong Kong - Died Lisbon Maru 2.10.42 - Named Plymouth Memorial

DUDLEY Guildford Charles - Lt - HMS Cornflower - Held Hong Kong

DUFFY Charles Joseph - RM - PLY/X906 - HMS Tamar - Held Hong Kong, Japan (Osaka Area)

DUFFY James Edwin - HKRNVR - W O - Ship not known - Held Hong Kong, Japan (Osaka Area)

DUFFY John - D/JX134983 - HMS Thracian - Held Hong Kong, Japan (Osaka Area) - Died Japan 20.10.42 - Buried Yokohama

DUFFY Thomas - D/SSX21382 - HMS Exeter - Held Celebes

DUNBAR Thomas Fraser - D/MX49426 - HMS Exeter - Held Celebes

DUNCAN Daniel - D/JX214789 - HMS Repulse - Held Sumatra (Palembang)

DUNCAN Samuel George - RM - PLY/X3717 - HMS Repulse Held Singapore, Thailand - Died Thailand 19.7.42 - Buried Kanchanaburi

DUNFORD Alfred Joseph - P/K62043 - HMS Grasshopper - Held Sumatra (Medan) - Died Harikiku Maru 26.6.44 - Named Plymouth Memorial

DUNLEVEY William Richard - D/JX147895 - HMS Exeter - Held Celebes, Japan (Kyushu)

DUNMORE Maurice Norman - D/JX213509 - HMS Grasshopper - Held Sumatra (Medan), Burma, Thailand

DUNN John - RM - PLY/X101176 - HMS Prince of Wales - Held Singapore, Taiwan - Died Taiwan 22.6.44 - Buried Sai Wan Bay

DUNN Percy Albert Holmes - P/KX132616 - ML 311 - Held Java, Singapore, Thailand, Singapore

DUNSMORE John - D/MDX2758 - HMS Prince of Wales - Held Sumatra (Palembang), Singapore, Taiwan, Japan (Tokyo Area)

DUNSTAN Peter George - RM - PLY/X3813 - HMS Prince of Wales - Held Singapore, Thailand

DURRAND James Garvie - P/SSX29072 - HMS Sultan - Held Singapore, Thailand
DUTHIE Charles John - D/JX169296 - HMS Sultan - Held Sumatra (Medan), Burma, Thailand - Died Thailand 19.3.44 - Buried Kanchanaburi
DWYER Thomas Francis - RM - PLY/100762 - HMS Tapah - Held Sumatra (Palembang)
DYKE Leslie Edward - C/M39586 - HMS Tamar - Held Hong Kong, Japan (Osaka Area) - Died Japan 13.10.42 - Buried Yokohama
DYKES John - D/KX101694 - HMS Tapah - Held Singapore (from Bangka)
DYOS Walter John - RM - PLY/X3802 - HMS Exeter - Held Celebes
EADES Thomas - D/JX167277 - HMS Tern - Held Hong Kong, Japan (Osaka Area)
EAGLESTONE Sydney Thomas - C/KX108862 - HMS Electra - Held Java, Moluccas - Died Maros Maru 19.9.44 - Named Chatham Memorial
EAKINS Eric - RM - PLY/X3128 - HMS Prince of Wales - Held Sumatra (Palembang), Singapore
EARDLEY Henry Charles - HKRNVR - Act Lt - Ship not known - Held Hong Kong
EARLAM Donald - RM - PLY/X3816 - HMS Exeter - Held Celebes - Died Makassar 9.3.44 - Buried Ambon
EARP Denis Godfrey - P/MX47982 - HMS Tamar - Held Hong Kong, Japan (Tokyo Area, Sendai Area)
EASTERBROOK William George Ronald - Boatswain - HMS Tamar - Held Hong Kong - Died Lisbon Maru 2.10.42 - Named Plymouth Memorial
EAVES Reginald Greeaert - P/SSX20084 - HMS Redstart - Held Hong Kong, Japan (Nagoya Area)
EBURN William John - P/JX262539 - MV Tantalus - Held Philippines, Japan (Kyushu)
ECCLES George - D/J38314 - HMS Prince of Wales - Held Sumatra (Palembang)
ECCLES Thomas - D/JX190984 - HMS Anking - Held Java, Singapore, Japan (Osaka Area)
ECCLESTON Thomas James - D/MX55623 - HMS Tamar - Held Hong Kong, Japan (Osaka Area)
ECKLEY Vincent Maurice - D/JX186982 - HMS Sultan - Held Sumatra (Palembang)
EDDY William Arthur - D/M38490 - HMS Exeter - Held Celebes
EDEN Byron - D/J101619 - HMS Sultan - Held Sumatra (Palembang) - Died Palembang 30.6.45 - Buried Jakarta
EDEN Henry - D/K63031 - Ship not known - Held Singapore (from Bangka)
EDGE Ellis Taylor - P/M6033 - HMS Tamar - Held Hong Kong, Japan (Osaka Area) - Died Japan 7.7.43 - Buried Yokohama
EDINBOROUGH Kenneth Henry - D/MX61746 - HMS Mata Hari - Held Singapore (from Bangka)
EDMUNDS Martin - P/KX82325 - HMS Dragonfly - Held Sumatra (Medan, Railway) - Died Sumatra Railway 17.4.45 - Named Plymouth Memorial
EDWARDS Charles Hugh - RM - PLY/X3669 - HMS Repulse - Held Sumatra (Palembang)
EDWARDS Douglas William - P/J111512 - Ship not known - Held Sumatra (Medan), Burma, Thailand
EDWARDS Eric - D/JX188049 - HMS Exeter - Held Celebes, Japan (Kyushu)
EDWARDS Glyn - D/JX199768 - MV Tantalus - Held Philippines, Japan (Kyushu)
EDWARDS Guildford Ronald - C/JX151594 - Stonecutters - Held Hong Kong
EDWARDS John Edward Devenport - D/JX132038 - HMS Tamar - Held Hong Kong - Died Lisbon Maru 2.10.42 - Named Plymouth Memorial
EDWARDS John Reginald - D/JX237610 - HMS Exeter - Held Celebes
EDWARDS Maurice Francis George - RM - PLY/X3810 - HMS Prince of Wales - Held Singapore, Thailand
EDWARDS Norman John - D/JX166603 - HMS Repulse - Held Sumatra (Palembang)
EDWARDS Richard John Gilbert - D/JX213102 - HMS Sultan - Held Singapore, Thailand
EDWARDS Wilfred John - D/MX52632 - HMS Exeter - Held Celebes
EDWARDS William George - D/K65827 - HMS Jupiter - Held Java, Moluccas - Died Maros Maru 26.9.44 - Named Plymouth Memorial
EDWORTHY Douglas James - NAFFI - HMS Exeter - Held Celebes, Japan (Kyushu)
EGAN P - 4th Eng - SS Francol - Held Celebes, Japan (Kyushu), Manchuria
ELDRIDGE Harry Norman - P/J110399 - HMS Redstart - Held Hong Kong, Japan (Osaka Area) - Died Japan 23.5.43 - Buried Yokohama
ELKINS Arthur John - C/J111704 - HMS Encounter - Held Celebes
ELLIOTT David Mons Lorrain - RM - PLY/X101537 - HMS Repulse - Held Singapore, Thailand - Died Thailand 29.6.43 - Buried Kanchanaburi
ELLIS Albert - C/JX158166 - HMS Sultan - Held Sumatra (Medan, Atjeh, Railway)
ELLIS Alfred Louis - D/MX3125 - HMS Prince of Wales - Held Sumatra (Palembang)
ELLIS Christopher - C/KX104449 - HMS Encounter - Held Celebes
ELLIS Ivor - MRNVR - Sub Lt - HMS Laburnum - Held Sumatra (Palembang), Singapore
ELLIS James Stewart - D/MX74876 - HMS Sultan - Held Sumatra (Medan) - Died Sumatra 20.1.44 - Buried Jakarta
ELLIS Sydney - D/KX90730 - HMS Exeter - Held Celebes

ELLISON Raymond - C/SSX20123 - HMS Encounter - Held Celebes
ELLISON William - D/SSX21006 - HMS Sultan - Held Sumatra (Palembang)
ELMS David Kenneth - P/JX225181 - HMS Tamar - Held Hong Kong - Died Lisbon Maru 2.10.42 - Named Plymouth Memorial
ELSMORE Clifford Basil - D/JX144065 - HMS Prince of Wales - Held Sumatra (Medan), Burma, Thailand
ELSWORTH William James - P/J49352 - HMS Thracian - Held Hong Kong, Japan (Osaka Area)
EMMETT Stephen A - D/KX138646 - HMS Exeter - Held Celebes
ENDACOTT Frank William - RM - PLY/X1236 - HMS Repulse - Held Singapore
ENDICOTT Joe - D/JX161815 - HMS Exeter - Held Celebes
ENDRES Francis Walter - P/JX152255 - HMS Redstart - Held Hong Kong, Japan (Osaka Area)
ENNIFER Arthur Vincent Blackbourn - P/JX127920 - Stonecutters - Held Hong Kong, Japan (Osaka Area)
ERRIDGE Percy Albert - C/KX120402 - HMS Exeter - Held Celebes, Java
ESBESTER Reginald - RM - PLY/X101191 - HMS Prince of Wales - Held Sumatra (Medan), Burma, Thailand
ESCOTT John William - D/JX167278 - Ship not known - Held Sumatra (Medan), Burma, Thailand
ETHERIDGE Arthur - C/L3410 - HMS Encounter - Held Celebes - Died Makassar 16.3.45 - Buried Ambon
EUSTACE Owen Henry - MRNVR - Lt - HMS Kuala - Held Sumatra (Medan), Singapore, Thailand
EUSTACE Reginald Herbert - D/JX237973 - HMS Exeter - Held Celebes, Japan (Kyushu)
EUSTACE Sydney Joseph Garfield - D/LX21632 - HMS Sultan - Held Sumatra (Palembang) - Died Palembang 22.5.42 - Buried Jakarta
EVANS Alun Meryod - D/JX165291 - HMS Kung Wo - Held Sumatra (Medan), Burma, Thailand
EVANS Arthur Jack William - HKRNVR - AB - Ship not known - Held Hong Kong - Evaded recapture after sinking of Lisbon Maru
EVANS Bernard William - RM - PLY/X3969 - HMS Exeter - Held Celebes, Java
EVANS Gordon Meredith - RM - PLY/X100272 - HMS Exeter - Held Celebes, Java
EVANS James - D/MDX2200 - Ship not known - Held Singapore (from Bangka)
EVANS John Gwynne - RNZN - NZ/2162 - HMS Sultan - Held Sumatra (Palembang)
EVANS Ronald John - D/MX45260 - HMS Prince of Wales - Held Singapore, Thailand
EVANS Samuel Leonard - D/KX111275 - HMS Exeter - Held Celebes, Japan (Kyushu)
EVANS Thomas Horace - D/JX165215 - HMS Exeter - Held Celebes, Japan (Kyushu)
EVANS Walter Keating - RM - PLY/X1700 - HMS Exeter - Held Celebes, Japan (Kyushu)
EVANS William Edwin - D/K18412 - HMS Exeter - Held Celebes
EVERARD Henry Joseph - C/JX188399 - HMS Tern - Held Hong Kong, Japan (Osaka Area)
EYNON William John - D/J110720 - HMS Exeter - Held Celebes
FABIAN Harold George - MRNVR - Lt - HMS Scorpion - Held Singapore (from Bangka Strait), Thailand
FACER William James - C/J48822 - HMS Tamar - Held Hong Kong, Japan (Osaka Area)
FAGE Charles Edward - D/JX168086 - HMS Tamar - Held Hong Kong - Died Lisbon Maru 2.10.42 - Named Plymouth Memorial
FAINT Norman Kenneth - RM - PLY/X100099 - HMS Repulse - Held Sumatra (Palembang)
FAIRBURN Thomas Campbell - Lt - Ship not known - Held Hong Kong
FAIRBURN William - C/JX247183 - HMS Tern - Held Hong Kong, Taiwan
FAIRHURST Henry - D/KX94484 - HMS Exeter - Held Celebes, Japan (Kyushu)
FALLACE James Wilfred - HKRNVR - W O - Ship not known - Held Hong Kong - Evaded recapture after sinking of Lisbon Maru
FALLE Samuel - Lt - HMS Encounter - Held Celebes, Java
FALLICK Ronald Edgar - D/KX78194 - HMS Exeter - Held Celebes
FALLON Bernard William - D/SSX18168 - HMS Jupiter - Held Java, Moluccas, Java
FALLOW Alexander - D/SSX14298 - HMS Exeter - Held Celebes
FARLEY Wilfred John - C/KX97618 - HMS Dragonfly - Held Sumatra (Medan), Singapore, Sumatra (Railway)
FARMERY John Bennett - D/SMX230 - HMS Stronghold - Held Celebes
FARNSWORTH Paul Hildreth - P/JX182182 - Ship not known - Held Singapore, Japan (Hokkaido)
FARR William Charles - C/J81525 - HMS Encounter - Held Celebes
FARRELL Henry William - RM - PLY/X1865 - HMS Repulse - Held Singapore, Thailand, Japan (Kyushu)
FARREN Charles Edmund - W O Eng - HMS Exeter - Held Celebes, Japan (Kyushu)
FARRIE John Reid - D/MX69160 - HMS Tamar - Held Hong Kong - Died Lisbon Maru 2.10.42 - Named Plymouth Memorial
FARRINGTON George B O - RM - Major - HMS Tamar - Held Hong Kong
FARRON Frederick - D/KX127093 - HMS Prince of Wales - Held Sumatra (Palembang)
FAULKNER William Frederick Barnett - Sub Lt - HMS Exeter - Held Celebes, Java
FEAR Frank - D/JX200305 - HMS Exeter - Held Celebes

FEARN George Edwin - D/KX133492 - HMS Siang Wo - Held Singapore (from Bangka)
FEATHER James William - RM - PLY/X1819 - HMS Tamar - Held Hong Kong - Died Hong Kong 29.9.42 - Buried Sai Wan Bay
FELSTED George James - C/JX240272 - HMS Tern - Held Hong Kong
FENNELL Eric Rodney - D/JX237939 - HMS Exeter - Held Celebes
FENTON Douglas - D/JX137097 - HMS Tamar - Held Hong Kong
FERRIER Vivian Edmund - HKRNVR - W O - Ship not known - Held Hong Kong
FERRY Peter - D/JX158414 - HMS Exeter - Held Celebes
FEVER James - D/KX110265 - HMS Jupiter - Held Java
FIELD Walter Harold - C/J95443 - HMS Moth - Held Hong Kong, Japan (Osaka Area, Nagoya Area)
FIELD William Valentine - HKRNVR - C Yeo - Ship not known - Held Hong Kong
FIELDHOUSE John Thomas - P/KX93901 - HMS Tamar - Held Hong Kong, Japan (Osaka Area) - Died Japan 3.1.44 - Buried Yokohama
FIENNES David Eustace Martindale - MRNVR - Lt - HMS Sultan - Held Sumatra (Palembang)
FINCH Harold - P/K61634 - HMS Tamar - Held Hong Kong - Died Lisbon Maru 2.10.42 - Named Plymouth Memorial
FINCH Harry - C/JX229871 - Boom Defence - Held Hong Kong, Japan (Nagoya Area)
FINCH Jack - P/J27023 - HMS Pelandok - Held Sumatra (Palembang) - Died Palembang 24.1.45 - Buried Jakarta
FINCH Richard Howell - D/JX153328 - HMS Tamar - Held Hong Kong - Died Lisbon Maru 2.10.42 - Named Plymouth Memorial
FINCH Victor John Russell - RM - PLY/X2381 - HMS Repulse - Held Sumatra (Palembang), Singapore
FINN Thomas HILTON- see HILTON-FINN Thomas
FINNIE George Marshal - D/MX73028 - HMS Exeter - Held Celebes
FIRBANK Charles Frederick - D/JX136884 - HMS Prince of Wales - Held Singapore (from Jibbia)
FISH John - P/SSX20040 - HMS Redstart - Held Hong Kong, Japan (Tokyo Area, Sendai Area)
FISHER Albert Louis - D/JX150282 - HMS Tamar - Held Hong Kong - Died Lisbon Maru 2.10.42 - Named Plymouth Memorial
FISHER George Francis - C/JX183998 - HMS Encounter - Held Celebes
FITCHETT Donald William Alliston - P/JX205689 - HMS Stronghold - Held Celebes - Died Makassar 10.3.45 - Buried Ambon
FITCHETT Raymond Horace - D/JX237882 - HMS Exeter - Held Celebes, Japan (Kyushu)
FITZGERALD Gerald O'Connor - Chaplain - HMS Exeter - Held Celebes
FITZPATRICK Bernard Joseph - C/K66366 - HMS Tapah - Held Singapore (from Bangka)
FITZPATRICK John - D/KX86212 - HMS Stronghold - Held Celebes - Died Makassar 16.4.45 - Buried Ambon
FLETCHER Frank - P/SSX29023 - HMS Repulse - Held Java, Sumatra (Pangkalan Bali), Singapore
FLETCHER Richard George - RM - PLY/22344 - HMS Prince of Wales - Held Sumatra (Palembang), Singapore
FLETCHER William Henry - D/J107182 - HMS Jupiter - Held Java, Moluccas, Java
FLETT Andrew - Chief Boom Skipper - Boom Defence - Held Hong Kong - Died Lisbon Maru 2.10.42 - Named Plymouth Memorial
FLOOD John - P/JX218135 - HMS Scorpion - Held Sumatra (Palembang), Singapore
FLUCK Reginald Walter John - RM - PLY/X962 - HMS Prince of Wales - Held Singapore, Thailand - Died Rakuyo Maru 12.9.44 - Named Plymouth Memorial
FLYNN Patrick Joseph - D/MX48649 - HMS Tamar - Held Hong Kong, Japan (Osaka Area)
FOGG William - Lt - Boom Defence - Held Hong Kong
FOGG William Charles - C/JX131350 - HMS Encounter - Held Celebes - Died Makassar 26.7.45 - Buried Ambon
FOGWILL William - HKRNVR - Act Sub Lt - Ship not known - Held Hong Kong
FORBES Alexander Samuel - D/JX170913 - HMS Exeter - Held Celebes
FORBES Ian Dudley Stewart - Lt - HMS Prince of Wales - Held Celebes, Java
FORD Alfred Charles - HKRNVR - Lt - Ship not known - Held Hong Kong
FORDHAM George Alfred - RM - PLY/X100445 - HMS Exeter - Held Celebes, Java
FORMHALS Frederick William - D/MX46523 - HMS Exeter - Held Celebes, Japan (Kyushu)
FORRESTER William - C/DX2202 - HMS Sultan - Held Sumatra (Palembang)
FORSTER Robert M - D/JX237601 - HMS Exeter - Held Celebes
FORSTER Stanley Arnold - D/JX184645 - HMS Prince of Wales - Held Sumatra (Medan), Burma - Died Burma (Railway - 22.12.43 - Buried Thanbyuzayat
FORSTER Thomas - D/MX49187 - HMS Prince of Wales - Held Sumatra (Palembang)
FORSYTH James Leslie Wilson - P/JX146260 - HMS Tamar - Held Hong Kong - Died Lisbon Maru - 2.10.42

UNSUNG HEROES of the ROYAL NAVY and ROYAL MARINES

- Named Plymouth Memorial

FORTUNE Ivan Lawrence - RNZN - NZD/2934 - HMS Exeter - Held Celebes

FORTUNE John Park - D/J105049 - HMS Prince of Wales - Held Singapore, Thailand - Died Thailand - 14.2.43 - Buried Kanchanaburi

FOSTER James Albert - FAA/FX82418 - HMS Exeter - Held Celebes, Japan (Kyushu)

FOSTER William Bernard Denton - P/MX68046 - RN MTB - Held Hong Kong

FOWLER George William - RM - PLY/X703 - HMS Exeter - Held Celebes

FOX Robert Horace Irwin - D/JX137514 - HMS Exeter - Held Celebes, Japan (Kyushu)

FRANCIS Evan Charles - D/JX156024 - HMS Tamar - Held Hong Kong - Died Lisbon Maru 2.10.42 - Named Plymouth Memorial

FRANCIS Martin William - D/JX237950 - HMS Exeter - Held Celebes - Died Makassar - 5.3.45 - Buried Ambon

FRANCIS Thomas Henry Eric - D/J108664 - HMS Exeter - Held Celebes - Died Makassar - 30.9.42 - Buried Ambon

FRANCIS William Thomas - D/KX138647 - HMS Exeter - Held Celebes

FRANKCOM Graham - D/MX65188 - RN Hospital - Held Hong Kong, Japan (Nagoya Area)

FRANKLIN Harry Tudor - RNZN - NZ/1846 - HMS Tamar - Held Hong Kong, Japan (Osaka Area)

FRASER Joseph - HKRNVR - Act Sub Lt - Ship not known - Held Hong Kong

FREEMAN Derek Gailard - MRNVR - Sub Lt - HMS Rahman - Held Java, Moluccas, Java

FRENCH Joseph William - C/JX240157 - HMS Thracian - Held Hong Kong

FRENCH Stanley James - P/MX47314 - HMS Moth - Held Hong Kong, Japan (Osaka Area)

FRIEND Harry Lancelot - C/JX236947 - HMS Electra - Held Java, Moluccas - Died Muna - 31.5.43 - Buried Ambon

FRYERS Dennis Beresford - C/JX314491 - SS Nancy Moeller - Held Singapore (from Indian Ocean)

FULFORD Leonard John - P/JX286923 - HMS Exeter - Held Celebes - Died Makassar 16.3.45 - Buried Ambon

FULLER John Robert Cannon - D/KX82864 - HMS Stronghold - Held Celebes

FURNEAUX Edwin George - W O Gunner - HMS Jupiter - Held Java

FURNEVILL Jack C - P/SSX19351 - Ship not known - Held Singapore

FURZER Donald Frank - D/MX58728 - HMS Tamar - Held Hong Kong, Japan (Osaka Area)

GALLAGHER Frank Joseph - P/UDX1094 - HMS Sultan - Held Singapore (from Bangka)

GAME George V - D/MX65891 - HMS Prince of Wales - Held Sumatra (Palembang), Singapore

GAMMON James Henry - RM - PLY/X409 - HMS Repulse - Held Singapore, Thailand

GANDER Ronald William - P/SSX20272 - HMS Peterel - Held Shanghai, Japan (Hokkaido)

GARDINER George Alexander - RM - PLY/X1933 - HMS Prince of Wales - Held - Sumatra (Palembang), Singapore

GARDINER Leslie John - D/K56061 - HMS Thracian - Held Hong Kong, Japan (Osaka Area) - Died Japan 9.4.43 - Buried Yokohama

GARRATT William Thomas - C/J84534 - HMS Encounter - Held Celebes - Died Makassar - 9.8.43 - Buried Ambon

GARRETT Arthur Thomas - P/J106280 - HMS Tamar - Held Hong Kong - Died Lisbon Maru 2.10.42 - Named Plymouth Memorial

GARRIOCH Robert - RM - PLY/X2672 - HMS Exeter - Held Celebes, Japan (Kyushu)

GARRITY John - D/MDX2379 - HMS Exeter - Held Celebes, Japan (Kyushu)

GARTON Frank Kekewich - HKRNVR - Sen Gnr - Ship not known - Held Hong Kong, Japan (Osaka Area)

GASKELL George - D/KX111337 - HMS Exeter - Held Celebes

GASPER Arthur Clarence Lamb - Lt - Ship not known - Held Hong Kong

GATES Edwin William - C/J105411 - HMS Tamar - Held Hong Kong - Died Lisbon Maru 2.10.42 - Named Chatham Memorial

GATES Stuart - D/JX184675 - HMS Exeter - Held Celebes, Japan (Kyushu)

GATTY William Ernest - C/JX172488 - HMS Encounter - Held Celebes - Died Makassar 27.2.45 - Buried Ambon

GAY Harry - C/MX58799 - HMS Moth - Held Hong Kong, Japan (Osaka Area) - Died Japan - 2.6.43 - Buried Yokohama

GEACH Bevil John - D/KX78171 - HMS Exeter - Held Celebes, Japan (Kyushu)

GEAKE Donald William - D/MX53362 - HMS Exeter - Held Celebes

GEORGE Frederick Charles Granville - Boom Engineer - HMS Robin - Held Hong Kong, Japan (Osaka Area) - Died Japan 6.4.43 - Buried Yokohama

GERRY Frederick - D/KX130662 - Ship not known - Held Sumatra (Medan), Burma, Thailand

GESS Francis - C/KX75268 - HMS Encounter - Held Celebes - Died Makassar - 27.7.45 - Buried Ambon

GIBBONS Reginald Thomas - D/JX208386 - HMS Exeter - Held Celebes, Java

GIBBS Francis George - D/K56955 - HMS Exeter - Held Celebes

GIBBS Sidney - D/JX154510 - HM Sub. Stratagem - Held Singapore (from Malacca Strait), Japan (Tokyo Area)

GIBBS William A - D/J98245 - Ship not known - Held Java, Singapore, Borneo

GIBSON Albert George - C/JX144449 - RN MTB - Held Hong Kong, Japan (Tokyo Area, Sendai Area)

GIBSON Edwin Elder - P/UDX1314 - HMS Grasshopper - Held Sumatra (Medan), Burma, Thailand

GIBSON Robert - D/JX164194 - HMS Exeter - Held Celebes

GIBSON Robert Alderson - C/JX152147 - Stonecutters - Held Hong Kong, Japan (Osaka Area)

GIFFIN George Arthur - P/KX110177 - HMS Sultan - Held Java, Singapore, Thailand - Died Thailand - 21.7.43 - Buried Kanchanaburi

GILES Robert Clement - RM - Major - Ship not known - Held Hong Kong

GILLBANKS Harold - D/MX71344 - HMS Exeter - Held Celebes - Died Makassar - 13.6.45 - Buried Ambon

GILLETT Thomas H - C/JX192088 - HMS Encounter - Held Celebes, Japan (Kyushu)

GILLILAND John Walter - D/JX150357 - HMS Repulse - Held Sumatra (Palembang)

GILLINGHAM Edward Henry - D/JX273017 - HMS Sultan - Held Singapore (from Bangka Strait)

GILLMAN Rex Hubert - C/JX130608 - HMS Grasshopper - Held Sumatra (Medan), Singapore, Taiwan, Japan (Tokyo Area, Sendai Area)

GINDERS Bruce - RNZN - NZ/D2929 - HMS Exeter - Held Celebes

GIRLING Victor Frederick - D/MX74558 - HMS Sultan - Held Sumatra (Palembang) - Died Palembang 3.8.45 - Buried Jakarta

GISSING Charles Newman - D/M38681 - HMS Prince of Wales - Held Sumatra (Palembang)

GLASS David Reuben - RM - PLY/X1062 - HMS Prince of Wales - Held Sumatra (Palembang)

GLAYZER Harold Thomas - P/JX251288 - HMS Scorpion - Held Singapore (from Bangka Strait)

GLOVER Allbert Tudor RM - PLY/100035 - HMS Exeter - Held Celebes

GLOVER Basil - RM - PLY/X1272 - HMS Tamar - Held Hong Kong, Japan (Osaka Area)

GLOVER Henry Claude - HKRNVR - Sub Lt - APV Indira - Held Hong Kong

GLOVER Kenneth Gordon - RM - PLY/X1070 - HMS Prince of Wales - Held Singapore, Thailand, Singapore

GLOVER Raymond Arthur - P/MX70430 - HMS Grasshopper - Held Sumatra (Medan, Railway)

GLOVER William Charles - D/J88112 - HMS Sultan - Held Singapore, Thailand - Died Thailand 24.7.43 Buried Kanchanaburi

GLOVER William Mark - P/J101471 - Ship not known - Held Hong Kong

GODDARD Alfred Gruncell - P/JX130147 - HMS Redstart - Held Hong Kong, Japan (Osaka Area)

GODFREE Ronald Frank - C/KX88260 - HMS Tamar - Held Hong Kong - Died Lisbon Maru 2.10.42 - Named Chatham Memorial

GODFREY George Anthony - D/MX53951 - HMS Repulse - Held Sumatra (Palembang)

GOFF George Henry - D/JX143304 - HMS Exeter - Held Celebes

GOFF Harold Sidney - C/JX190324 - HMS Scorpion - Held Sumatra (Palembang), Singapore

GOMERY Charles James - RM - PLY/X101425 - HMS Repulse - Held Sumatra (Palembang), Singapore

GOODE John Henry - D/JX161816 - HMS Repulse - Held Sumatra (Medan), Burma, Thailand

GOODLIFF Frederick Henry - RM - PLY/X1013 - HMS Prince of Wales - Held Sumatra (Palembang)

GOODMAN Lawrence James - D/J106065 - HMS Exeter - Held Celebes - Died Makassar - 4.5.45 - Buried Ambon

GOODWIN Albert - C/JX147931 - Stonecutters - Held Hong Kong, Japan (Osaka Area)

GOODWIN Ralph Burton - Lt - RN MTB - Held Hong Kong - Escaped 17.7.44

GORDON Oliver Loudon - Capt - HMS Exeter - Held Celebes, Japan (Tokyo Area, Shikoku, Tokyo Area)

GORDON Thomas Richard - Sub Lt - HMS Mata Hari - Held Singapore (from Bangka), Thailand

GORE Dudley Eric - HKRNVR - W O - Ship not known - Held Hong Kong, Japan (Osaka Area, Nagoya Area)

GORMAN Roy John - C/JX152406 - HMS Prince of Wales - Held Sumatra (Palembang)

GOSDEN Alan - P/MX53953 - HMS Scorpion - Held Sumatra (Palembang) - Died Palembang 26.6.45 - Buried Jakarta

GOSDEN Horace Martin - D/JX184063 - HMS Repulse - Held Sumatra (Palembang)

GOSS Alfred John - D/JX139497 - HMS Grasshopper - Held Sumatra (Medan), Singapore, Sumatra (Railway)

GOSS Frederick Arthur - D/K60844 - HMS Exeter - Held Celebes, Japan (Kyushu)

GOSSAGE Clifford Norman - C/LX23915 - HMS Encounter - Held Celebes, Japan (Kyushu)

GOSSET Ronald Leonard - C/SSX31237 - HMS Encounter - Held Celebes - Died Makassar 9.4.45 - Buried Ambon

GOUGH Samuel - C/SSX18144 - HMS Moth - Held Hong Kong, Japan (Osaka Area)

UNSUNG HEROES of the ROYAL NAVY and ROYAL MARINES

GOULD Sidney Arthur - D/MX46433 - HMS Exeter - Held Celebes
GOULD William John Arthur - D/MX45844 - HMS Tamar - Held Hong Kong, Japan (Osaka Area)
GRAHAM Duncan - D/MX55900 - HMS Tamar - Held Hong Kong - Died Lisbon Maru 2.10.42 - Named Plymouth Memorial
GRAHAM Robert - D/JX226951 - HMS Exeter - Held Celebes
GRAHAM Thomas - D/MX62672 - HMS Repulse - Held Sumatra (Palembang)
GRANDIDGE George Kelsall Waterton - D/JX218091 - HMS Sultan - Held Sumatra (Palembang), Singapore, Taiwan - Died Taiwan 11.1.43 - Buried Sai Wan Bay
GRANSDEN John Collier - MRNVR - Lt - HMS Tapah - Held Sumatra (Palembang), Singapore, Taiwan
GRANT Douglas Gordon - C/MX76523 - HMS Exeter - Held Celebes, Japan (Kyushu)
GRANT Frederick Cyril - HKRNVR - Act Sub Lt - Ship not known - Held Hong Kong
GRANT Walter Ramsey - Lt - HMS Siang Wo - Held Sumatra (Palembang), Singapore, Taiwan, Japan (Tokyo Area)
GRATTAN Alexander George - HKRNVR - W O Gnr - Ship not known - Held Hong Kong - Died Hong Kong 10.12.42 - Buried Stanley
GRAVES Leonard William - C/JX155828 - HMS Electra - Held Java
GRAY Cecil Jesse Austen - Lt - HMS Tamar - Held Hong Kong
GRAY Colin Alexander - RM - PLY/X3148 - HMS Prince of Wales - Held Singapore
GRAY David - D/SSX23815 - HMS Thracian - Held Hong Kong
GRAY David Patterson - P/MX81848 - HMS Sultan - Held Sumatra (Palembang)
GRAY Norman William Hoskyn - HKRNVR - Sub Lt - HMS Cornflower - Held Hong Kong
GREEN Alexander - C/JX158642 - HMS Encounter - Held Celebes
GREEN Alfred Edward - D/J96728 - HMS Exeter - Held Celebes, Japan (Kyushu) - Died after release 16.12.45 - Buried Sydney
GREEN Denis Spencer - P/MX84307 - HMS Sultan - Held Sumatra (Palembang)
GREEN Henry De Wet - D/K55094 - HMS Exeter - Held Celebes - Died Makassar 27.6.45 - Buried Ambon
GREEN Herbert - P/JX187137 - HMS Tamar - Held Hong Kong - Died Lisbon Maru - 2.10.42 Named Portsmouth Memorial
GREEN Jack - D/JX167280 - HMS Thracian - Held Hong Kong, Japan (Osaka Area)
GREEN Kenneth A TOWNSEND- see TOWNSEND-GREEN Kenneth A
GREEN Samuel - D/JX238072 - HMS Exeter - Held Celebes, Japan (Kyushu)
GREEN William Henry - RM - PO/22388 - HMS Tamar - Held Hong Kong - Died Lisbon Maru 2.10.42 - Named Plymouth Memorial
GREENHILL John David - RM - PLY/X1374 - HMS Exeter - Held Celebes - Died Makassar 23.4.42 - Buried Ambon
GREENWOOD Joseph - D/SSX213628 - HMS Exeter - Held Celebes
GREENWOOD Norman Thomas John - Com Tel - HMS Tamar - Held Hong Kong - Died Lisbon Maru 2.10.42 - Named Plymouth Memorial
GREGG James - D/JX184635 - HMS Exeter - Held Celebes
GREGORY Herbert Frederick - C/K64771 - HMS Encounter - Held Celebes - Died Makassar 23.3.45 - Buried Ambon
GREGORY John Joseph - D/M3246 - Ship not known - Held Hong Kong
GREGORY William - D/SSX3577 - HMS Exeter - Held Celebes, Japan (Kyushu)
GRENFELL Cyril Donovan - SANF - SA/68831 - HMS Exeter - Held Celebes
GRENHAM John Charles - Lt Com - HMS Cornflower - Held Hong Kong
GREY William Edward - D/J106392 - HMS Tamar - Held Hong Kong - Died Lisbon Maru 2.10.42 - Named Plymouth Memorial
GRIFFIN Anthony - D/JX126597 - HMS Exeter - Held Celebes, Japan (Kyushu)
GRIFFITH Robert Alexander Skilling - RM - PLY/X684 - Stonecutters - Held Hong Kong, Japan (Osaka Area)
GRIFFITH Robert Thomas - D/MX65858 - HMS Cicala - Held Hong Kong, Japan (Osaka Area) - Died Japan 16.10.42 - Buried Yokohama
GRIFFITHS James - D/KX95755 - HMS Exeter - Held Celebes

GRIFFITHS Kenneth Cecil - P/MX71272 - HMS Tamar - Held Hong Kong, Shanghai, Japan (Hokkaido)
GRIFFITHS Morris William Charles - D/KX80191 - HMS Exeter - Held Celebes
GRIFFITHS Walter Leonard - P/JX185951 - MV Behar - Held Java - captured in Indian Ocean
GRIFFITHS William Edward - D/JX237954 - HMS Exeter - Held Celebes
GRIMA Paul - E/KX117530 - HMS Exeter - Held Celebes
GRIMSHAW Herbert - D/SSX13733 - HMS Exeter - Held Celebes - Died Makassa 14.9.42 - Buried Ambon
GROCOCK Charles - D/KX76291 - HMS Tamar - Held Hong Kong, Japan (Osaka Area)

GROVE Antony W DAWSON - see DAWSON-GROVE Antony W

GUIVER Frederick George - P/J80264 - HMS Mata Hari - Held Sumatra (Palembang), Singapore

GULLEY William George - D/JX127688 - HMS Stronghold - Held Celebes

GUNN Leslie - D/KX96295 - Ship not known - Held Sumatra (Medan), Burma, Thailand

GUNN William Donald - Surg Lt Com - Ship not known - Held Hong Kong - Died Hong Kong 8.9.44 - Buried Stanley

GUNTHER Robert Michael - Sub Lt - HMS Illustrious - Held Andaman Is., Japan (Tokyo Area)

GUPPY Reginald Albert - RM - PLY/22197 - HMS Tamar - Held Hong Kong - Died Hong Kong 8.8.42 - Buried Stanley

GUTTERIDGE Cecil Charles - MRNVR - Sub Lt - HMS Giang Bee - Held Singapore (from Bangka Strait)

GUTTERIDGE John - P/JX273041 - HMS Trang - Held Sumatra (Medan), Burma, Thailand

GUY William Stanley - D/JX229762 - HMS Exeter - Held Celebes

GWILLIAMS David John - D/JX188485 - HMS Exeter - Held Celebes, Japan (Kyushu)

HABERFIELD John Kerle Tipaho - Lt (A) - HMS Indomitable - Held Sumatra (Palembang), Singapore Died Singapore >15.8.45 - Named New Zealand Memorial

HACKING Harry - RM - PLY/X100122 - HMS Prince of Wales - Held Singapore, Thailand

HADDEN Harry Raymond - P/SSX28628 - HMS Sultan - Held Sumatra (Palembang)

HADDOCK Joseph Robert - HKRNVR - Sub Lt - Ship not known - Held Hong Kong

HADLEY James Bruce Douglas - D/JX142890 - HMS Li Wo - Held Sumatra (Palembang) - Died Palembang 26.4.42 - Buried Jakarta

HAGGER Kenneth Leslie - P/JX184270 - HMS Cicala - Held Hong Kong, Japan (Osaka Area)

HAGGETT Douglas Charles - RM - PLY/3458 - HMS Exeter - Held Celebes

HAIGH Wilfred Harru - P/JX289883 - SS Gemstone - Held Japan (Kyushu) - captured in S Atlantic

HAINES Stanley John - C/JX126907 - HMS Tern Held Hong Kong, Japan (Osaka Area)

HALEY Ronald - D/SSX33923 - HMS Exeter - Held Celebes, Japan (Kyushu)

HALFYARD Robert Edward - D/J105831 - HMS Tamar - Held Hong Kong - Died Hong Kong 2.6.43 - Buried Stanley

HALL Albert William - D/KX129654 - HMS Encounter - Held Celebes, Japan (Kyushu)

HALL Douglas Henry Stuart - RM - PLY/X101190 - HMS Prince of Wales - Held Sumatra (Palembang)

HALL Edward - RM - PLY/X3250 - HMS Prince of Wales - Held Sumatra (Palembang)

HALL Roy - D/KX112273 - HMS Exeter - Held Celebes

HALL Thomas - D/JX151649 - HMS Exeter - Held Celebes - Died Makassar 27.2.45 - Buried Ambon

HALLAM Aubrey - D/JX349583 - SS Empire March - Held Japan (Hokkaido) - captured in Indian Ocean

HALLETT Benjamin Melville - D/JX188715 - HMS Grasshopper - Held Sumatra (Medan, Railway)

HALLS John - D/JX229544 - Ship not known - Held Java, Sumatra (Railway)

HAMBLEY Garfield Edward - D/JX157528 - HMS Jupiter - Held Java, probably Moluccas, Java, Singapore

HAMER William - RM - PLY/X2121 - HMS Tamar - Held Hong Kong

HAMILTON William Henry - D/JX154261 - HMS Exeter - Held Celebes

HAMLYN James Pendleton - D/SSX22673 - HMS Exeter - Held Celebes

HAMMOND Francis Sidney - P/JX204605 - HMS Jupiter - Held Java, Moluccas, Java

HAMMOND Frank - D/KX91967 - HMS Tamar - Held Hong Kong - Died Lisbon Maru 2.10.42 - Named Plymouth Memorial

HAMMOND Percy John - C/K63298 - HMS Encounter - Held Celebes

HANCOCK Edwin Frederick - D/MX53365 - Ship not known - Held Sumatra (Palembang)

HANCOCK Frank William - RM - PLY/X1628 - HMS Tamar - Held Hong Kong, Japan (Osaka Area)

HANCOCK John Neil Coulter - MRNVR - Lt - HMS Tapah - Held Sumatra (Palembang), Singapore

HANCOCK William Duncan - P/J104280 - Boom Defence - Held Hong Kong, Japan (Tokyo Area)

HAND James Cyril - D/J104503 - HMS Exeter - Held Celebes - Died Makassar 10.5.45 - Buried Ambon

HAND Stanley - P/JX273670 - HMS Exeter - Held Celebes, Japan (Kyushu)

HANDSLEY Henry Sidney - RM - PLY/X35vHMS Tamar - Held Hong Kong, Japan (Osaka Area)

HANMAN John Patrick - D/JX237633 - HMS Exeter - Held Celebes

HANNAFORD Frederick John - D/K63027 - HMS Exeter - Held Celebes - Died Makassar 31.3.45 - Buried Ambon

HANNAFORD Frederick Joseph George - RM - PLY/20209 - HMS Prince of Wales - Held Singapore, Thailand - Died Thailand 6.7.43 - Buried Kanchanaburi

HANNAFORD Victor Frederick - D/MX51885 - HMS Exeter - Held Celebes

HANWELL Henry Sidney - D/KX77874 - HMS Encounter - Held Celebes - Died Makassar 14.3.45 - Buried Ambon

HARBRON Albert - P/MX78047 - HMS Tapah - Held Singapore (from Bangka)

HARDING James William Frank - D/MX46533 - HMS Exeter - Held Celebes, Japan (Kyushu)

HARDING Laurence Sidney - C/SSX32205 - HMS Encounter - Held Celebes, Japan (Kyushu)

UNSUNG HEROES of the ROYAL NAVY and ROYAL MARINES

HARDING Sydney George - C/JX173891 - HMS Encounter - Held Celebes - Died Makassar 16.4.45 - Buried Ambon

HARDING William Edwin - W O Swright - HMS Exeter - Held Celebes, Japan (Kyushu)

HARDMAN Wilfred - C/MX50190 - HMS Laburnum - Held Sumatra (Palembang)

HARDY Francis Gordon - C/JX138044 - HMS Tamar - Held Hong Kong - Died Lisbon Maru 2.10.42 - Named Chatham Memorial

HARE Alexis Alfred - MRNVR - Lt - HMS Siang Wo - Held Sumatra (Palembang)

HARKNESS James Percy Knowles - Lt Com - HMS Exeter - Held Celebes, Java

HARPER Ronald George - C/KX79052 - HMS Tamar - Held Hong Kong - Died Lisbon Maru 2.10.42 - Named Chatham Memorial

HARRIMAN Gilbert Alexander - HKRNVR - Act Sub Lt - Ship not known - Held Hong Kong

HARRINGTON William Lock - C/MX54944 - HMS Tamar - Held Hong Kong, Japan (Tokyo Area)

HARRIS Frank - RM - RMB/X1445 - HMS Exeter - Held Celebes - Died Makassar 6.7.45 - Buried Ambon

HARRIS George Arthur - P/SSX19802 - HMS Tamar - Held Hong Kong - Died Lisbon Maru 2.10.42 - Named Plymouth Memorial

HARRIS Sidney John - D/MX64147 - HMS Exeter - Held Celebes - Died Makassar 26.4.44 - Buried Ambon

HARRIS Vernon - D/KX120988 - HMS Sultan - Held Java, Singapore, Borneo

HARRIS Wilfred (23.12.16) - D/JX237664 - HMS Exeter - Held Celebes

HARRIS Wilfred (14.7.18) - D/KX95750 - HMS Prince of Wales - Held Singapore, Thailand - Died Thailand 30.12.43 - Buried Kanchanaburi

HARRISON Ernest - D/JX238419 - HMS Jupiter - Held Java, Moluccas, Java, Singapore

HARRISON Joseph - D/JX195007 - HMS Jupiter - Held Java, Moluccas, Java

HARRISON Richard Stuart - HKRNVR - W O - Ship not known - Held Hong Kong - Died Lisbon Maru 2.10.42 - Named Plymouth Memorial

HARRISON Wilfred Hugh Lane - Com - Ship not known - Held Hong Kong

HART Charles Felix - P/KX121305 - HMS Exeter - Held Celebes, Japan (Kyushu)

HARTLEY William Arthur - RM - RMB/X500 - HMS Exeter - Held Celebes

HARVERSON Charles John - D/J75160 - HMS Tamar - Held Hong Kong

HARVEY Harry - D/KX94225 - HMS Exeter - Held Celebes - Died Makassar 14.4.45 - Buried Ambon

HARWOOD Thomas - D/X73319 - HMS Exeter - Held Celebes

HASKELL Frederick William - P/JX168974 - HMS Stronghold - Held Celebes, Japan (Kyushu)

HASLEHURST William Joseph - Lt - Ship not known - Held Hong Kong

HASLETT Maurice John - D/JX154320 - Ship not known - Held Sumatra (Medan), Burma, Thailand

HASTINGS Wallace George Melton - C/MX53017 - HMS Tamar - Held Hong Kong, Japan (Osaka Area)

HATFIELD George - D/KX134503 - HMS Mata Hari - Held Singapore (from Bangka Strait)

HATFIELD Thomas - MRNVR - Sub Lt - HMS Sultan - Held Sumatra (Palembang), Singapore

HATHERALL Ian John - RM - PLY/X101562 - HMS Repulse - Held Sumatra (Palembang)

HAVELOCK William - C/J80251 - HMS Aldgate - Held Hong Kong, Japan (Osaka Area) - Died Japan 22.10.42 - Buried Yokohama

HAVILAND Charles Stephen - C/J53451 - Stonecutters - Held Hong Kong - Died Lisbon Maru 2.10.42 - Named Chatham Memorial

HAWES Malcolm - P/JX335297 - SS Gloucester Castle - Held Singapore (from South Atlantic)

HAWKEY Albert - D/MX61434 - HMS Exeter - Held Celebes

HAWKINS Arthur - C/JX130757 - HMS Moth   Held Hong Kong, Japan (Osaka Area)

HAWKINS Horace - C/KX119575 - HMS Encounter - Held Celebes, Japan (Kyushu)

HAWKINS Richard - MRNVR - Lt - HMS Mata Hari - Held Sumatra (Palembang), Singapore

HAWKRIDGE Arthur Edward - RM - PLY/22283 - HMS Repulse - Held Sumatra (Palembang)

HAWKSWORTH William Edward John - C/JX136629 - HMS Tamar - Held Hong Kong - Died Lisbon Maru 2.10.42 - Named Chatham Memorial

HAWORTH Norman - D/JX204169 - HMS Exeter - Held Celebes

HAYBALL William George - D/J84579 - HMS Jupiter - Held Java, Moluccas - Died Haruku 9.9.43 - Buried Ambon

HAYES Francis Edward - D/M32794 - HMS Exeter - Held Celebes - Died Makassar 3.10.44 - Buried Ambon

HAYES George - RM - PLY/100419 - HMS Giang Bee - Held Java, Singapore, Borneo

HAYES John - RM - PLY/2059 - HMS Repulse - Held Sumatra (Palembang)

HAYLOCK William Robert - C/JX140502 - HMS Moth - Held Hong Kong, Japan (Osaka Area, Hiroshima Area)

HAYNE Ronald Francis - P/MX52003 - HMS Peterel - Held Shanghai, Japan (Hokkaido)

HAYNES Harold William K - C/KX75401 - HMS Encounter - Held Celebes

HAZELL Denis Henry - Pm Lt - Ship not known - Held Hong Kong

HAZELL Francis Charles - D/MX46980 - HMS Exeter - Held Celebes
HAZELL Frank Edward - D/JX151843 - HMS Exeter - Held Celebes, Japan (Kyushu)
HAZELTON David Carson - Sub Lt - HMS Encounter - Held Celebes, Java - Died Junyo Maru 18.9.44 - Named Chatham Memorial
HEADFORD John Henry - P/MX69779 - HMS Tamar - Held Hong Kong, Japan (Nagoya Area)
HEALE Reginald William - MRNVR - Lt - HMS Sultan - Held Sumatra (Medan), Singapore, Thailand
HEALEY Gordon Allenby - RM - PLY/X2213 - HMS Repulse - Held Sumatra (Palembang) - Died Palembang 27.5.45 - Buried Jakarta
HEALY Dennis - C/JX228518 - HMS Cicala - Held Hong Kong - Died Lisbon Maru 2.10.42 - Named Chatham Memorial
HEAP George - C/JX184002 - HMS Encounter - Held Celebes - Died Makassar 23.12.44 - Buried Ambon
HEELEY Harry - P/JX200173 - HMS Sultan - Held Sumatra (Palembang) - Died Palembang 8.2.45 - Buried Jakarta
HEFFERMAN Nelson Joseph - SANF - SA/68576 - HMS Encounter - Held Celebes - Died Makassar 11.2.45 - Buried Ambon
HEGNEY James Henry - C/JX172684 - HMS Exeter - Held Celebes
HELEN Robert John - C/KX89963 - HMS Cicala - Held Hong Kong, Japan (Nagoya Area)
HELM John Fredrick - C/L13393 - HMS Encounter - Held Celebes
HENDERSON John McLean - P/MX65207 - HMS Sultan - Held Sumatra (Palembang)
HENDRIE John Albert - RM - PLY/X3804 - HMS Prince of Wales - Held Sumatra (Palembang)
HENDY Norman - D/MX48101 - HMS Tamar - Held Hong Kong - Died Lisbon Maru 2.10.42 - Named Plymouth Memorial
HENLEY James - C/K57125 - HMS Moth - Held Hong Kong, Japan (Osaka Area)
HENMAN Owen Robin Templer - MRNVR - Lt - HMS Hung Jao - Held Sumatra (Medan, Atjeh, Railway)
HENNESSEY Ronald James - D/MX64103 - HMS Exeter - Held Celebes
HENSON Arthur Peter - D/JX198553 - HMS Exeter - Held Celebes - Died Pomelaa 8.9.43 - Buried Ambon
HENWOOD Harry - RM - PLY/X3083 - HMS Exeter - Held Celebes, Japan (Kyushu)
HERD Lancelot Hugh - RNZN - Lt - ML 432 - Held Sumatra (Palembang), Singapore
HERMAN Albert Frank - P/KX125726 - HMS Redstart - Held Hong Kong, Japan (Osaka Area)
HERMAN Harold George - D/MX48144 - Ship not known - Held Singapore, Thailand
HERON Harry - D/JX289930 - SS Gemstone - Held Japan (Kyushu) - captured in S Atlantic
HERON Richard Victor - C/MX62404 - HMS Encounter - Held Celebes
HERRAGHTY Owen - C/DX2537 - HMS Sultan - Held Sumatra (Palembang)
HERRIMAN John Oswald James - D/JX233491 - ML 432 - Held Sumatra (Palembang)
HEWETT Edward Tucker - RM - CH/X458 - HMS Tamar - Held Hong Kong, Japan (Osaka Area) - Died Japan 11.10.42 - Buried Yokohama
HEYWOOD Robert James - D/JX143423 - HMS Prince of Wales - Held Sumatra (Palembang) - Died Palembang 10.7.45 - Buried Jakarta
HIBBERT Donald - D/JX184629 - HMS Exeter - Held Celebes, Japan (Kyushu)
HICKLEY John Allen Victor - Lt - HMS Encounter - Held Celebes, Java, Singapore, Japan (Kyushu), Manchuria
HICKMAN Cecil Stanhope Blair - Pm Com - Ship not known - Held Hong Kong
HICKMAN Harold - C/KX84961 - HMS Moth - Held Hong Kong, Japan (Nagoya Area)
HICKS John Arthur - D/MX51414 - HMS Exeter - Held Celebes
HIGGINS Douglas Ewart - RM - PLY/X2002 - HMS Prince of Wales - Held Singapore, Thailand - Died Thailand 28.6.43 - Buried Chungkai
HIGGINSON Hyram - D/MX7651 - HMS Prince of Wales - Held Sumatra (Palembang), Singapore
HIGMAN Mark Edward - W O Gunner - HMS Exeter - Held Celebes
HILL Albert Lester - C/J97164 - HMS Encounter - Held Celebes
HILL Felix George - D/MX51662 - HMS Tamar - Held Hong Kong
HILL Francis - D/JX130880 - HMS Exeter - Held Celebes
HILL George - D/JX194218 - HMS Tamar - Held Hong Kong - Died Lisbon Maru 2.10.42 - Named Plymouth Memorial
HILL George Richard - RM - PLY/X2758 - HMS Repulse - Held Singapore, Thailand, Japan (Kyushu)
HILL Herbert - D/KX119576 - HMS Exeter - Held Celebes, Java
HILL Jack Alfred - RM - PLY/X100190 - HMS Prince of Wales - Held Sumatra (Palembang) - Died Palembang 9.8.45 - Buried Jakarta
HILL John Rupert Edwards - MRNVR - SE/XE6 - HMS Pahlawan - Held Sumatra (Palembang)
HILLMAN Stanley Maginess - C/KX74748 - HMS Encounter - Held Celebes
HILLS Thomas - C/J48902 - HMS Encounter - Held Celebes - Died Makassar 22.4.45 - Buried Ambon
HILTON Frederick Charles - C/LDX2573 - HMS Encounter - Held Celebes

HILTON-FINN Thomas - Sub Lt - HMS Exeter - Held Celebes, Java
HINDMARCH Leslie - C/MX56389 - HMS Cicala - Held Hong Kong, Japan (Osaka Area)
HINDMARSH Desmond Ernest - HKRNVR - Lt - APV Indira Held Hong Kong
HINGE Frank Charles - P/J97839 - HMS Tamar - Held Hong Kong - Died Lisbon Maru 2.10.42 - Named Plymouth Memorial
HINTON George - P/J32954 - HMS Tamar - Held Hong Kong - Died Hong Kong 14.10.42 Buried Stanley
HIRD Ellis - C/J72894 - Boom Defence - Held Hong Kong, Japan (Nagoya Area)
HIRST Eric - C/SSX28293 - Ship not known - Held Sumatra (Medan, Railway)
HISSEY Alfred George - D/JX185059 - HMS Sultan - Held Sumatra (Palembang) - Died Palembang 26.7.45 - Buried Jakarta
HITCHEN Thomas Harry Stanley - D/M39835 - Ship not known - Held Sumatra (Palembang), Singapore
HITCHENS Richard McClure - D/JX147680 - HMS Exeter - Held Celebes
HOBBS Joseph William - C/KX85442 - HMS Dragon - Held Java
HOBBS Thomas E - D/M36562 - HMS Repulse - Held Sumatra (Medan, Railway)
HOCKING Leonard James - D/JX94495 - HMS Exeter - Held Celebes - Died Makassar 26.5.45 - Buried Ambon
HOCKLEY Fred - Sub Lt - HMS Indefatigable - Held Japan - Died Japan >15.8.45 - Buried Yokohama
HODDER Kenneth Richard - D/MX73329 - HMS Exeter - Held Celebes
HODGE Christopher Gwynne - D/JX208658 - HMS Exeter - Held Celebes
HODGSON Charles James - P/MX64902 - HMS Sultan - Held Sumatra (Palembang)
HODGSON Frank - P/KX121764 - HMS Cicala - Held Hong Kong, Japan (Osaka Area)
HODGSON James - C/JX213450 - HMS Dragonfly - Held Sumatra (Medan), Burma, Thailand
HODGSON Richard - C/KX111674 - HMS Sultan - Held Sumatra (Palembang)
HODGSON Robert - P/K65270 - HMS Tamar - Held Hong KongvDied Lisbon Maru 2.10.42 - Named Plymouth Memorial
HODGSON Thomas - D/MX53865 - Ship not known - Held Hong Kong, Japan (Osaka Area)
HOGARTH William - D/JX147973 - HMS Repulse - Held Sumatra (Palembang), Singapore
HOGGE Arthur Henry - Sub Lt - HMS Mata Hari - Held Singapore (from Bangka Strait)
HOLBORN Robert - D/KX93522 - HMS Exeter - Held Celebes - Died Makassar 14.5.45 - Buried Ambon
HOLEHOUSE George Frederick - D/JX147322 - HMS Prince of Wales - Held Sumatra (Medan), Singapore, Sumatra (Railway)
HOLLAND Frank - D/JX239979 - HMS Tapah - Held Singapore (from Bangka)
HOLLIER James - C/JX162087 - HMS Encounter - Held Celebes
HOLLIS George Walter - D/KX118120 - HMS Exeter - Held Celebes, Java
HOLLOWAY Reginald Albert - MRNVR - Lt - HMS Grasshopper - Held Singapore (from Indian Ocean), Thailand
HOLMAN Harold David - P/J93002 - HMS Peterel - Held Shanghai, Japan (Hokkaido)
HOLT James Samuel - P/JX201158 - HMS Tamar - Held Hong Kong - Died Lisbon Maru 2.10.42 - Named Plymouth Memorial
HOLT John Walter - D/JX238069 - HMS Exeter - Held Celebes, Java
HOMER Leonard Gordon - D/J110705 - HMS Repulse - Held Sumatra (Palembang)
HONEYWELL Reginald John - RM - PLY/X101171 - HMS Exeter - Held Celebes, Japan (Kyushu)
HONYWILL Jack - D/JX138723 - HMS Peterel - Held Shanghai, Japan (Hokkaido)
HOOD Thomas Hanson - HKRNVR - Sub Lt - APV Han Wo - Held Hong Kong
HOOKER James William - P/SSX21736 - RN MTB - Held Hong Kong, Japan (Osaka Area) - Died Japan 22.4.45 - Buried Yokohama
HOOPER Cecil Wallace - D/JX154784 - HMS Jupiter - Held Java, Moluccas - Died Sugi Maru 6.9.44 - Named Plymouth Memorial
HOOPER Edmund Albert - MRNVR - Lt - HMS Jarak - Held Singapore (from Indian Ocean), Thailand
HOPKINS Francis Yonge - C/J59399 - HMS Tamar - Held Hong Kong - Died Lisbon Maru 2.10.42 - Named Chatham Memorial
HOPKINS Norman Ellis - D/JX233149 - HMS Encounter - Held Celebes
HOPKINS Reginald Horace - P/KX78613 - HMS Grasshopper - Held Sumatra (Medan), Burma - Died Burma (Railway) 22.11.43 - Buried Thanbyuzayat
HORDER Douglas George - P/MX67988 - HMS Tamar - Held Hong Kong - Died Shanghai after sinking of Lisbon Maru 16.10.42 - Buried Yokohama
HOREY Gerald Mansell - Lt - HMS Tern - Held Hong Kong
HORKINS James - D/SS958568 - Ship not known - Held Singapore
HORN Robert - D/SSX33614 - HMS Exeter - Held Celebes, Java
HORN William Henry - C/J112019 - HMS Encounter - Held Celebes - Died Makassar 5.3.45 - Buried Ambon

HORNBY Ian Whitfield - MRNVR - Sub Lt - HMS Dymas - Held Singapore (from Bangka)
HORSFALL Leo Herbert - D/LX24534 - HMS Exeter - Held Celebes
HORSLEY Bernard - P/KX90369 - HMS Prince of Wales - Held Sumatra (Medan), Burma, Thailand
HORSLEY Eric - RM - PO/X2159 - HMS Tamar - Held Hong Kong - Died Lisbon Maru 2.10.42 - Named Plymouth Memorial
HORWELL Victor Albert - P/JX239654 - HMS Exeter - Held Celebes
HOSFORD Robert - D/JX139032 - HMS Tamar - Held Hong Kong - Died Lisbon Maru 2.10.42 - Named Plymouth Memorial
HOUGHTON Jack - P/JX219794 - HMS Grasshopper - Held Sumatra (Medan, Railway) - Died Sumatra Railway 5.2.45 - Named Plymouth Memorial
HOUSE Kenneth Lawrence Oliver - P/K61408 - HMS Scorpion - Held Sumatra (Palembang), Singapore
HOUSLEY Clifford - RM - PLY/X2798 - HMS Prince of Wales - Held Singapore, Thailand
HOWARD John A - D/SSX23404 - HMS Exeter - Held Celebes, Java
HOWELL Edward - C/J38055 - HMS Encounter - Held Celebes
HOWELL John Noel - D/JX213211 - HMS Prince of Wales - Held Sumatra (Palembang)
HOWELLS Leslie Edward - D/KX86625 - HMS Jupiter - Held Java, Moluccas, Java
HOWLETT Reginald Charles - D/KX164938 - HM Sub. Stratagem - Held Singapore (from Malacca Strait) - Died Singapore 31.12.44 - Named Plymouth Memorial
HOWSON Ronald - D/MX53857 - HMS Tamar - Held Hong Kong - Died Lisbon Maru 2.10.42 - Named Plymouth Memorial
HUDSON Edward Alexander - C/JX258728 - HMS Prince of Wales - Held Sumatra (Medan, Atjeh, Railway)
HUDSON Frank - P/JX291294 - HMS Exeter - Held Celebes
HUDSON Mark - D/SSX20588 - HMS Exeter - Held Celebes - Died Makassar 1.5.45 - Buried Ambon
HUDSON Roland Keith - Lt Com - HMS Exeter - Held Celebes, Japan (Tokyo Area, Shikoku, Tokyo Area)
HUDSON Sydney - D/KX116626 - HMS Exeter - Held Celebes, Japan (Kyushu)
HUGGON David Edmund - D/SMX95 - HMS Exeter - Held Celebes
HUGHES Benjamin Ronald - C/J114923 - HMS Encounter - Held Celebes, Japan (Kyushu)
HUGHES Caradol Morgan - D/KX121359 - HMS Prince of Wales - Held Sumatra (Palembang)
HUGHES John Edward - P/M36795 - HMS Encounter - Held Celebes
HUGHES John Henry - P/JX203496 - HMS Dragonfly - Held Sumatra (Medan), Burma, Thailand
HUGHES John Joseph - P/KX103487 - HMS Grasshopper - Held Sumatra (Medan, Atjeh, Railway)
HUGHES Kenneth Wynford - D/JX167282 - HMS Thracian - Held Hong Kong, Japan (Osaka Area)
HUGHES Lycargus G - HKRNVR - 2nd Eng - Ship not known - Held Hong Kong
HUGHES Michael James - D/SSX23515 - HMS Repulse - Held Sumatra (Palembang)
HUGHES Owen Noel - D/JX158320 - HMS Exeter - Held Celebes, Japan (Kyushu)
HUGHES Philip Charles - D/KX129173 - HMS Stronghold - Held Celebes
HUGHES Sidney Powell - D/MX71895 - HMS Sultan - Held Sumatra (Palembang) - Died Palembang 12.8.45 - Buried Jakarta
HUGHIESON Jack H - P/WRX456 - RN MTB - Held Hong Kong, Japan (Osaka Area)
HUGH-JONES Graeme Sisson - Lt Com - Ship not known - Held Hong Kong
HULIN Donald Llewellyn - D/JX217190 - HMS Exeter - Held Celebes
HULL George James Parsons - D/MX55902 - HMS Tamar - Held Hong Kong - Died Lisbon Maru 2.10.42 - Named Plymouth Memorial
HULL Richard - D/JX196766 - HMS Prince of Wales - Held Sumatra (Medan), Burma, Thailand - Died Thailand 22.1.44 - Buried Kanchanaburi
HULLAND Frederick James - C/KX97322 - HMS Dragon - Held Java, Singapore, Japan (Osaka Area)
HULME Samuel - RM - PLY/22188 - HMS Tamar - Held Hong Kong
HULONCE Thomas Henry - D/KX113086 - HMS Encounter - Held Celebes, Japan (Kyushu)
HULTON Geoffrey Alan - RM - Lt - HMS Repulse - Held Singapore, Thailand
HUMBY Percy Kenneth George - RM - PLY/X3031 - HMS Prince of Wales - Held Sumatra (Palembang)
HUMPHREY Frederick Harold - D/X18167 - HMS Li Wo - Held Singapore (from Bangka)
HUMPHREY Thomas James - D/J111246 - HMS Exeter - Held Celebes, Japan (Kyushu)
HUMPHREYS James - RM - PLY/X100359 - HMS Exeter - Held Celebes - Died Makassar 28.4.45 - Buried Ambon
HUMPHRY Bert D'Arcy Langford - P/J42027 - HMS Tamar - Held Hong Kong, Japan (Osaka Area) - Died Japan 29.2.44 - Buried Yokohama
HUNT Alfred Dennis - D/JX143929 - RN MTB - Held Hong Kong, Japan (Osaka Area)
HUNT Arthur James - C/JX262409 - MV Tantalus - Held Philippines, Japan (Osaka Area)
HUNT Donald Kenneth - C/SSX14778 - HMS Encounter - Held Celebes, Japan (Kyushu)
HUNT Patrick Derek - D/JX169736 - HMS Jupiter - Held Java, Moluccas, Java

HUNT Ronald Albert - D/JX136310 - HMS Encounter - Held Celebes, Japan (Tokyo Area)

HUNTING Basil Eric - HKRNVR - Cadet - Ship not known - Held Hong Kong, Japan (Tokyo Area)

HURD John W - P/KX99165 - HMS Sultan - Held Sumatra (Palembang)

HURDEN Reginald Samuel - D/MX48316 - HMS Exeter - Held Celebes, Japan (Kyushu)

HURLEY Edward Frank - HKRNVR - Cadet - Ship not known - Held Hong Kong

HURST Edward William - C/SSX22017 - HMS Encounter - Held Celebes

HURST William Arthur - C/SSX32200 - HMS Encounter - Held Celebes

HUTCHESON Hugh Anthony - Lt - HMS Exeter - Held Celebes, Java

HUTCHINSON George Harold - D/J111178 - HMS Tamar - Held Hong Kong - Died Hong Kong 5.9.42 - Buried Stanley

HUTCHINSON George Thomas Cormack - C/JX278153 - HMS Anking - Held Java, Singapore, Japan (Osaka Area)

HUTCHINSON George William - C/JX126731 - HMS Tamar - Held Hong Kong - Died Lisbon Maru 2.10.42 - Named Chatham Memorial

HUTLER John - P/SSX18302 - HMS Scorpion - Held Sumatra (Palembang) - Died Palembang 4.8.45 - Buried Jakarta

HUTTON Edmund Feltham - D/MX66831 - HMS Tamar - Held Hong Kong - Died Lisbon Maru 2.10.42 - Named Plymouth Memorial

HUTTON-POTTS Jack Yuan - HKRNVR - Lt - APV Minnie - Held Hong Kong

HYDE Albert James - D/JX232345 - HMS Exeter - Held Celebes, Java

HYDE Harold William Raymond - MRNVR - Sub Lt - HMS Pahlawan - Held Sumatra (Palembang), Singapore

HYDE Reginald George - D/J115535 - HMS Repulse - Held Sumatra (Medan), Singapore, Sumatra (Railway)

ILLINGWORTH John Henry George - C/LDX3258 - HMS Encounter - Held Celebes, Japan (Kyushu)

INGS John Rupert - D/SSX15096 - HMS Exeter - Held Celebes - Died Makassar 20.3.45 - Buried Ambon

INNES David McGillivray - D/JX136256 - RN MTB - Held Hong Kong, Japan (Tokyo Area, Sendai Area)

INNES Harry - D/KX87378 - HMS Exeter - Held Celebes

IRELAND Michael Norman - P/MX70045 - HMS Tamar - Held Hong Kong, Japan (Osaka Area) - Died Japan 24.2.43 - Buried Yokohama

IRVINE George Robert - C/JX132780 - RN MTB - Held Hong Kong, Japan (Osaka Area)

IRVINE George William Harry - D/JX166444 - HMS Exeter - Held Celebes, Japan (Kyushu)

IRWIN Martin Adair - D/JX184636 - HMS Exeter - Held Celebes

JACK Robert Reid - RM - PLY/X1043 - HMS Tamar - Held Hong Kong

JACKSON Albert - P/JX167285 - MV Dalhousie - Held Japan (Osaka Area) - captured in S Atlantic

JACKSON Alfred Samuel - D/MX53219 - HMS Exeter - Held Celebes, Japan (Kyushu)

JACKSON B Noel George - C/JX132622 - HMS Thanet - Held Sumatra (Palembang)

JACKSON Charles Antony - Surg Lt HMS Tamar - Held Hong Kong, Japan (Osaka Area, Nagoya Area)

JACKSON Richard Thomas - D/KX107258 - HMS Exeter - Held Celebes, Java

JACKSON Thomas - P/KX130580 - HMS Exeter - Held Celebes

JACKSON William Arthur - Lt - RNLMS De Ruyter - Held Celebes, Japan (Tokyo Area, Shikoku, Tokyo Area)

JACQUES John Myers - P/JX205696 - HMS Tamar - Held Hong Kong, Japan (Osaka Area) - Died Japan 2.3.43 - Buried Yokohama

JAFFE Nathan - RNZN - NZD/2412 - HMS Exeter - Held Celebes

JAGGER Herbert William - RM - PLY/22566 - HMS Exeter - Held Celebes - Died Makassar 8.5.45 - Buried Ambon

JAGO Leslie Gordon - MRNVR - Lt - HMS Pengawal - Held Sumatra (Palembang), Singapore

JALLAND Jack Edward - C/JX125501 - HMS Tamar - Held Hong Kong - Died Lisbon Maru 2.10.42 - Named Chatham Memorial

JAMES Albert John - D/KX75814 - HMS Tamar - Held Hong Kong

JAMES Cecil Howard - Asst Surg - Ship not known - Held Singapore, Thailand, Singapore

JAMES Ernest Walter - C/JX278589 - HMS Repulse - Held Sumatra (Palembang)

JAMES Wilfred Harold - D/JX176334 - HMS Thracian - Held Hong Kong

JAMES William Arthur - Seaman - MV Empire Dawn - Held Java - captured in S Atlantic, Sumatra (Pangkalan Bali), Singapore

JARVIS William G R - D/JX126416 - HMS Grasshopper - Held Sumatra (Medan, Railway)

JEFFEREYS Frank Edward - D/JX745267 - HMS Exeter - Held Celebes

JEFFERSON George - D/KX111146 - HMS Exeter - Held Celebes - Died Makassar 29.1.45 - Buried Ambon

JEFFERY Frederick Alfred - D/X7929C - HMS Exeter - Held Celebes - Died Makassar - 15.4.45 - Buried Ambon

JEFFERY Garfield Harry - D/SSX18944 - HMS Thracian - Held Hong Kong, Japan (Osaka Area)
JEFFERY Ralph - D/KX83143 - HMS Exeter - Held Celebes
JEFFREY Richard - RM - PLY/X2411 - HMS Tamar - Held Hong Kong - Died Hong Kong 9.9.42 - Buried Stanley
JEFFS Harold Thomas French - D/SSX20620 - HMS Exeter - Held Celebes, Japan (Kyushu) - Died Japan 3.5.43 - Buried Yokohama
JEFFS Sydney Hill - C/MX46760 - HMS Tamar - Held Hong Kong, Japan (Osaka Area) - Died Japan 21.4.43 - Buried Yokohama
JENKINS Albert Clifford - D/MX58231 - HMS Exeter - Held Celebes, Japan (Kyushu)
JENKINS Charles John - D/KX132352 - HMS Mata Hari - Held Singapore (from Bangka)
JENKINS Francis Roy - D/JX161821 - HMS Exeter - Held Celebes - Died Makassar 15.2.45 - Buried Ambon
JENKINS Frederick - D/KX111145 - HMS Exeter - Held Celebes
JENKINS William Alfred - RM - PLY/X941 - HMS Exeter - Held Celebes, Japan (Kyushu)
JENKINS Willliam Gerald - Sub Lt - RNLMS Java - Held Celebes, Japan (Kyushu), Manchuria
JEREMIAH Daniel - D/JX195017 - HMS Exeter - Held Celebes
JOB Harry Cornelius - C/JX133425 - HMS Encounter - Held Celebes, Japan (Kyushu)
JOHN James Edward - W O Gnr - HMS Exeter - Held Celebes
JOHNCOCK Thomas Henry Samuel - C/MX77482 - HMS Laburnum - Held Singapore (from Jibbia)
JOHNS William Edward - D/MX45581 - HMS Exeter - Held Celebes
JOHNSON Frederick William - C/MX53641 - HMS Tamar - Held Hong Kong - Died Lisbon Maru 2.10.42 - Named Chatham Memorial
JOHNSON James Burt Openshaw - D/JX188535 - HMS Sultan - Held Sumatra (Palembang) - Died after release 15.10.45 - Buried Kranji
JOHNSON John - P/JX139841 - HMS Encounter - Held Celebes
JOHNSON Montague Victor Reginald - P/MX78657 - HMS Hung Jao - Held Sumatra (Medan), Singapore
JOHNSON Ronald Arthur - D/JX254816 - HMS Laburnum - Held Singapore (from Jibbia), Japan (Hokkaido)
JOHNSTON Eric - D/JX256569 - HMS Encounter - Held Celebes
JOHNSTONE James Gordon - RM - Lt Col - Ship not known - Held Singapore
JOHNSTONE James McLudoc - D/KX81489 - HMS Exeter - Held Celebes, Japan (Kyushu)
JOHNSTONE Joseph G - P/KX130581 - HMS Exeter - Held Celebes
JOHNSTONE William Charles - HKRNVR - W O - Ship not known - Held Hong Kong - Evaded - recapture after sinking of Lisbon Maru
JOLLEY Sidney William - P/JX264860 - HMS Encounter - Held Celebes
JOLLY James Henry - D/SSX32899 - HMS Jupiter - Held Java, Singapore, Japan (Osaka Area)
JONES Alan Henry - D/KX127937 - HMS Jarak - Held Sumatra (Medan), Burma, Thailand
JONES Benjamin Glyndor - C/JX209672 - HMS Exeter - Held Celebes, Japan (Kyushu)
JONES Charles William - D/MX70302 - HMS Exeter - Held Celebes
JONES Cynlas C - C/JX187387 - HMS Encounter - Held Celebes, Japan (Kyushu)
JONES Daniel Thomas - C/JX168586 - HMS Trang - Held Sumatra (Medan), Singapore
JONES Douglas Harold - D/KX100056 - HMS Exeter - Held Celebes
JONES Edmund Francis - D/JX171074 - HMS Prince of Wales - Held Sumatra (Medan, Railway)
JONES Edward Cecil - RM - RMB/X1179 - HMS Exeter - Held Celebes, Java
JONES Emrys Rowland - C/JX176621 - HMS Encounter - Held Celebes
JONES Evan David - D/SSX33535 - HMS Repulse - Held Singapore (from Bangka)
JONES Frederick - D/KX117188 - HMS Exeter - Held Celebes, Japan (Kyushu)
JONES Frederick James - Chargeman - Ship not known - Held Hong Kong
JONES George Victor - RM - PLY/X2443 - HMS Prince of Wales - Held Singapore (from Bangka), Thailand, Singapore
JONES Gonville Royce - D/JX138348 - HMS Tamar - Held Hong Kong - Died Lisbon Maru 2.10.42 - Named Plymouth Memorial
JONES Graeme Sisson HUGH- see HUGH-JONES Graeme Sisson
JONES Herbert Cyril - RM - PLY/X48 - HMS Tamar - Held Hong Kong - Died Lisbon Maru 2.10.42 - Named Plymouth Memorial
JONES Hugh William - D/JX136832 - HMS Repulse - Held Sumatra (Palembang), Singapore
JONES James Thomas Alban - D/JX232518 - HMS Tamar - Held Hong Kong - Died Lisbon Maru 2.10.42 - Named Plymouth Memorial
JONES John - C/KX104964 - HMS Sultan - Held Singapore - Died Singapore 12.11.42 - Buried Kranji
JONES John Glyn - RM - PLY/22393 - HMS Prince of Wales - Held Singapore, Thailand
JONES John James - D/MX73313 - HMS Repulse - Held Sumatra (Palembang), Singapore

JONES Kenneth - D/JX238976 - HMS Kung Wo - Held Sumatra (Medan), Burma, Thailand
JONES Kenneth Robert - P/JX157892 - HMS Sultan - Held Sumatra (Medan) - Died Harikiku Maru 26.6.44 - Named Plymouth Memorial
JONES Leonard - D/KX132652 - HMS Encounter - Held Celebes, Japan (Kyushu)
JONES Lewis Denzil - D/KX111328 - HMS Exeter - Held Celebes
JONES Maurice - D/MX64726 - HMS Tamar - Held Hong Kong, Japan (Nagoya Area)
JONES Nicholas James - RM - PLY/X101539 - HMS Repulse - Held Singapore, Thailand, Taiwan
JONES Rees Lloyd - D/KX111150 - HMS Exeter - Held Celebes - Died Makassar 14.3.45 - Buried Ambon
JONES Robert - D/MX64267 - HMS Exeter - Held Celebes
JONES Robert Brown - C/JX249015 - SS Empire March - Held Japan (Hokkaido) - captured in Indian Ocean
JONES Robert Douglas - D/JX188585 - HMS Exeter - Held Celebes
JONES Robert Mathew - D/JX237957 - HMS Exeter - Held Celebes
JONES Ronald Percival - RM - PLY/X668 - HMS Exeter - Held Celebes, Japan (Kyushu)
JONES Stanley Frederick - D/JX261822 - HMS Prince of Wales - Held Sumatra (Medan, Railway)
JONES Thomas Edward - P/KX130422 - HMS Exeter - Held Celebes, Japan (Kyushu)
JONES Thomas Theodore - P/SR8222 - HMS Tamar - Held Hong Kong, Japan (Osaka Area)
JORDAN Reginald Henry - D/BDX1593 - HMS Exeter - Held Celebes
JOSEY Geoffrey Louis - P/J98353 - RN MTB - Held Hong Kong, Japan (Tokyo Area)
JOWETT Sydney - D/SSX22738 - HMS Exeter - Held Celebes
JUPP John Edmund - HKRNVR - W O - Ship not known - Held Hong Kong, Japan (Osaka Area) - Died Japan - 12.10.42 - Buried Yokohama
KAVANAGH Henry - D/JX147274 - HMS Exeter - Held Celebes
KAYE George Henry - RM - PLY/22411 - HMS Exeter - Held Celebes, Japan (Kyushu)
KEARLEY Ernest James - D/JX130881 - HMS Prince of Wales - Held Sumatra (Palembang)
KEARNEY Timothy - D/KX88638 - HMS Thracian - Held Hong Kong, Japan (Osaka Area, Nagoya Area)
KEARNS James Bruce - C/MX55895 - HMS Tamar - Held Hong Kong - Died Lisbon Maru 2.10.42 - Named Chatham Memorial
KEAST Reginald - D/KX97045 - HMS Hung Jao - Held Sumatra (Medan), Burma, Thailand
KEATS Arthur Charles - D/JX272242 - HMS Exeter - Held Celebes
KEELAN John - P/JX111154 - HMS Exeter - Held Celebes
KEENAN Joseph - D/K56888 - HMS Exeter - Held Celebes - Died Makassar 20.3.45 - Buried Ambon
KEFFORD Arthur John - P/JX274355 - HMS Sultan - Held Sumatra (Medan, Atjeh, Railway)
KELLEHER James - D/KX87258 - HMS Thracian - Held Hong Kong, Japan (Osaka Area)
KELLY Henry Arthur - D/JX188454 - HMS Exeter - Held Celebes
KELLY John Miller - D/J110554 - HMS Sultan - Held Sumatra (Palembang) - Died Palembang 31.10.42 - Buried Jakarta
KELSALL Samuel - D/KX92345 - HMS Exeter - Held Celebes
KEMP John Cresswell Wallace - MRNVR - Lt - HMS Scorpion - Held Sumatra (Palembang), Singapore
KEMP Stanley - D/JX167288 - HMS Tamar - Held Hong Kong - Died Lisbon Maru 2.10.42 - Named Plymouth Memorial
KENDRICK Thomas John - D/KX89700 - HMS Exeter - Held Celebes, Japan (Kyushu)
KENNARD Herbert Walter Godfrey - C/J18821 - HMS Tamar - Held Hong Kong - Died Lisbon Maru 2.10.42 - Named Chatham Memorial
KENNY Aubrey Brian Huruata - RNZN - NZ/D3017 - HMS Stronghold - Held Celebes
KENSHOLE Frederick George - D/KX84745 - HMS Prince of Wales - Held Singapore (from Bangka) remaining on HMS Tapah until release
KENT John Arthur - RM - PLY/X100014 - HMS Prince of Wales - Held Sumatra (Palembang), Singapore, Taiwan, Japan (Tokyo Area, Sendai Area)
KENWORTHY Lawrence - RM - PO/19018 - HMS Tamar - Held Hong Kong
KENYON Herbert - D/JX267054 - SS Lylepark - Held Japan (Osaka Area) - captured in S Atlantic
KERMODE William R - Lt - SS Francol - Held Celebes, Java
KERR Alexander William - Pm Lt - HMS Exeter - Held Celebes, Java
KERR David - D/KX90605 - HMS Repulse - Held Java, Singapore, Borneo
KERR Mark William Brownrigg - Lt - HMS Exeter - Held Celebes, Java
KERSHAW Charles P H - D/JX187567 - MV Behar - Held Java - captured in Indian Ocean
KERSLAKE Norman Alexander - C/MX76353 - HMS Sultan - Held Singapore (from Bangka Strait)
KETTLE Frederick Lawrence - P/JX274433 - HMS Hung Jao - Held Sumatra (Medan, Atjeh, Railway)
KEW Henry Charles - HKRNVR - Seaman - Ship not known - Held Hong Kong - Died Lisbon Maru 2.10.42 - Named Plymouth Memorial
KEY Robert McCulloch - D/JX232688 - HMS Exeter - Held Celebes

KIDD John - P/MX78833 - HMS Exeter - Held Celebes
KIDGER Walter - P/JX193392 - HMS Sultan - Held Sumatra (Palembang)
KILBEE Laurence Dudley - HKRNVR - Lt - RN MTB - Held Hong Kong
KILROY John - RM - PO/17132 - HMS Tamar - Held Hong Kong
KIM George Victor - HKRNVR - Ldg Sgm - Ship not known - Held Hong Kong, Japan (Osaka Area)
KIMBER Walter William - P/MX67981 - HMS Tamar - Held Hong Kong - Died Lisbon Maru 2.10.42 - Named Plymouth Memorial
KING Alfred - D/KX89693 - HMS Exeter - Held Celebes, Japan (Kyushu)
KING Alfred Thomas - RM - RMB/X1136 - HMS Exeter - Held Celebes
KING Ernest Alfred - P/JX178899 - HMS Tamar - Held Hong Kong - Died Lisbon Maru 2.10.42 - Named Plymouth Memorial
KING Frederick - P/JX131021 - HMS Rahman - Held Java, Sumatra (Pangkalan Bali), Singapore
KING John - D/MX62918 - HMS Exeter - Held Celebes, Japan (Kyushu)
KING John - RM - PLY/X773 - HMS Prince of Wales - Held Sumatra (Palembang)
KING John Kenneth - C/MX54645 - HMS Tamar - Held Hong Kong - Died Lisbon Maru 2.10.42 - Named Chatham Memorial
KING Leonard - D/K66543 - HMS Jupiter - Held Java, Moluccas - Died Taiwan Maru 23.8.44 - Named Plymouth Memorial
KING Nigel Harle - D/JX159940 - HMS Repulse - Held Sumatra (Medan), Singapore, Sumatra (Railway)
KING Peter McKendrick - C/JX171654 - SS Nankin - Held Japan (Tokyo Area) - captured in Indian Ocean
KING Reginald Arthur - D/MX45853 - HMS Tamar - Held Hong Kong, Japan (Osaka Area)
KING Victor Stanley - RM - PLY/21254 - HMS Exeter - Held Celebes
KINGSTON Frank Edward William - P/M18451 - HMS Tamar - Held Hong Kong - Died Hong Kong 26.1.42 - Buried Stanley
KINNEAR Duncan George Robertson - MRNVR - Sub Lt - HMS Siang Wo - Held Java, Singapore, Japan (Hiroshima Area), Shikoku, Kyushu)
KINSEY William Ronald - C/SX278600 - HMS Repulse - Held Sumatra (Palembang)
KIRBY George Edward - D/JX184693 - HMS Prince of Wales - Held Sumatra (Palembang)
KIRBY Kenneth Woodburn - Lt Com - Ship not known - Held Hong Kong
KIRK Harold - P/JX248739 - HMS Exeter - Held Celebes
KIRKHAM Louis - D/KX81171 - HMS Exeter - Held Celebes - Died Makassarm 3.6.45 - Buried Ambon
KIRTON Stanley Stuart - MRNVR - Pm Lt - Ship not known - Held Singapore (from Bangka), Thailand
KIRTON William Watt - HKRNVR - 2nd Eng - Ship not known - Held Hong Kong, Japan (Osaka Area)
KITCHEN Harry - D/SSX18660 - HMS Prince of Wales - Held Sumatra (Palembang), Singapore
KITCHEN William - D/MX72663 - HMS Encounter - Held Celebes - Died Makassar 11.2.45 - Buried Ambon
KITTO Charles Edwin Brian W S - NAAFI - HMS Exeter - Held Celebes - Died Makassar 24.3.45 - Buried Ambon
KNIGHT Brian William Sidney - C/JX172664 - HMS Encounter - Held Celebes - Died Makassar 25.5.45 - Buried Ambon
KNIGHT William Charles Hubert - MRNVR - Lt - HMS Sultan - Held Sumatra (Medan), Singapore
KNOWLES Alexander - D/MX59223 - HMS Exeter - Held Celebes
KNOX Charles Francis - HKRNVR - Sub Lt - HMS Cornflower - Held Hong Kong
KNOX David - HKRNVR - Seaman Gnr - Ship not known - Held Hong Kong - Died Lisbon Maru 2.10.42 - Named Plymouth Memorial
LALOE Michael Francis - HKRNVR - Cadet - Ship not known - Held Hong Kong, Japan (Osaka Area)
LAMB Harry - D/JX198576 - HMS Exeter - Held Celebes, Japan (Kyushu)
LAMBERT Albert Theodore - D/MX50346 - HMS Exeter - Held Celebes
LAMBLE Roger Dryck - HKRNVR - Sub Lt - Ship not known - Held Hong Kong
LAMPARD Victor George - P/MX68682 - RN MTB - Held Hong Kong, Japan (Osaka Area)
LAND Reginald Charles Rex - MRNVR - Sub Lt - HMS Siang Wo - Held Sumatra (Palembang)
LANDSBERT Albert Leslie - HKRNVR - Sub Lt - HMS Cornflower - Held Hong Kong
LANE William John - D/KX82190 - HMS Exeter - Held Celebes
LANG Robert Cage Somers - RM - Capt - HMS Repulse - Held Singapore, Thailand
LANG Thomas Fuller - D/JX196867 - HMS Exeter - Held Celebes
LANGDEN Arthur - D/J107492 - HMS Jupiter - Held Java, Sumatra (Railway)
LANGDON Ernest Patrick Carlton - MRNVR - Lt - HMS Sultan - Held Sumatra (Palembang), Singapore, Thailand
LANGFORD Elwyn - D/SSX18216 - HMS Exeter - Held Celebes, Java
LANGMEAD Percival John Hines - D/KX85316 - HMS Exeter - Held Celebes
LANGRIDGE Basil Frederick Jack - D/JX165725 - HMS Exeter - Held Celebes - Died Pomelaa 12.5.43

- Buried Ambon
LANSLEY Alan Edward James - P/L13064 - HMS Exeter - Held Celebes - Died Makassar 19.4.45 - Buried Ambon
LAPWORTH Leslie - C/JX210031 - HMS Tamar - Held Hong Kong - Died Hong Kong 26.8.42 - Buried Stanley
LARCINA Hermilio M - HKRNVR - Ldg Sgm - Ship not known - Held Hong Kong, Japan (Tokyo Area, Sendai Area)
LAST Frederick James - D/JX38154 - HMS Exeter - Held Celebes, Java
LAUGHTON Charles William George - C/MX48489 - HMS Encounter - Held Celebes
LAUTERBACK Frank - C/JX212925 - HMS Exeter - Held Celebes, Japan (Kyushu)
LAVER Ronald - RM - PLY/X990 - HMS Tamar - Held Hong Kong, Japan (Osaka Area)
LAWRENCE Frank - P/MX64475 - HMS Tamar - Held Hong Kong, Japan (Osaka Area)
LAWRENCE Peter Edwin - D/JX175812 - HMS Prince of Wales - Held Sumatra (Palembang)
LAWRENCE Thomas Edgar - C/J106784 - HMS Encounter - Held Celebes
LAWRENCE William Robert - P/JX201264 - HMS Thracian - Held Hong Kong
LEACH Jack - D/JX128300 - Ship not known - Held Sumatra (Medan), Singapore, Sumatra (Railway)
LEADBETTER Harold - RM - PLY/X100140 - HMS Prince of Wales - Held Sumatra (Palembang)
LEADBITTER Arthur - D/SSX32277 - HMS Scorpion - Held Singapore (from Bangka)
LEARY Harry - C/JX262298 - Ship not known - Held Hong Kong, Japan (Osaka Area)
LEE Frederick George - D/MX47790 - HMS Tamar - Held Hong Kong - Died Lisbon Maru 2.10.42 - Named Plymouth Memorial
LEE Leonard Lionel - C/JX143545 - HMS Exeter - Held Celebes, Japan (Kyushu)
LEEHAN Maurice - P/MX55532 - HMS Sin-Aik-Lee - Held Sumatra (Palembang), Singapore
LEES Alexander - D/MX51876 - HMS Tamar - Held Hong Kong - Died Lisbon Maru 2.10.42 - Named Plymouth Memorial
LEGGATT William - MRNVR - Lt - Ship not known - Held Sumatra (Palembang) - Died Palembang 23.9.42 - Buried Jakarta
LEICESTER Reginald - P/SSX19710 - HMS Tern - Held Hong Kong, Japan (Tokyo Area, Sendai Area)
LEIPER John Victor - W O Gnr - HMS Encounter - Held Celebes, Japan (Tokyo Area)
LEIR Richard Hugh - RCN - MidShipman - HMS Exeter - Held Celebes, Java
LEMON James Gifford - D/JX151845 - HMS Thracian - Held Hong Kong, Japan (Tokyo Area, Sendai Area)
LEMON Sydney Alfred - D/SSX13030 - HMS Siang Wo - Held Singapore (from Bangka)
LENNY Sydney George - RM - PLY/X3809 - HMS Prince of Wales - Held Singapore, Thailand, Japan (Kyushu)
LETHEBY William Arthur - RM - PLY/X2178 - HMS Exeter - Held Celebes
LEVI Charles Henry - C/JX238059 - HMS Cicala - Held Hong Kong, Japan (Osaka Area)
LEWINGTON Harry S - C/J113939 - HMS Exeter - Held Celebes
LEWIS Albert George - D/KX83383 - HMS Thracian - Held Hong Kong, Japan (Tokyo Area)
LEWIS Alfred Leslie - D/MD/X2420 - HMS Exeter - Held Celebes
LEWIS Arthur George - D/KX87928 - HMS Exeter - Held Celebes
LEWIS Arthur Stanley - Lt - Ship not known - Held Hong Kong
LEWIS Daniel - D/MX49903 - HMS Tamar - Held Hong Kong - Died Lisbon Maru 2.10.42 - Named Plymouth Memorial
LEWIS Ernest - RM - PLY/X892 - HMS Exeter - Held Celebes, Japan (Kyushu)
LEWIS Francis Herbert - D/JX127878 - HMS Exeter - Held Celebes, Japan (Kyushu)
LEWIS Kenneth Thomas - D/JX177494 - HMS Exeter - Held Celebes
LEWIS Ronald John - Cant Asst - HMS Anking - Held Java, Singapore - Died Tamahoko Maru 24.6.44 - Named Plymouth Memorial
LEWIS William Philip - D/JX149343 - HMS Exeter - Held Celebes
LIDBURY Oswald Spencer - P/MX67373 - HMS Sultan - Held Sumatra (Palembang)
LIDINGTON William Henry - P/J80117 - HMS Peterel - Held Shanghai, Japan (Osaka Area) - Died Japan 26.7.45 - Buried Yokohama
LIFTON Cyril Alfred Bateman - C/M27929 - HMS Tern - Held Hong Kong - Died Lisbon Maru 2.10.42 - Named Chatham Memorial
LILBURN Alistair James - MRNVR - Lt - HMS Blumut - Held Sumatra (Palembang), Singapore
LILLEY Bernard Charles - D/M40029 - HMS Tamar - Held Hong Kong, Japan (Osaka Area)
LILLYWHITE Sidney Frederick - C/J107065 - HMS Encounter - Held Celebes
LINDSAY James - D/JX155802 - HMS Jupiter - Held Java, Moluccas - Died Maros Maru 12.10.44 - Named Plymouth Memorial
LINDSAY William - D/JX137251 - HMS Exeter - Held Celebes, Java
LINDSAY William Gillespie - D/JX148055 - ML 432 - Held Sumatra (Palembang), Singapore, Taiwan, Japan

(Tokyo Area)

LINDSLEY John - C/KX129629 - HMS Rahman - Held Java, Sumatra (Pangkalan Bali), Singapore

LINDSLEY Mervyn Ewart SCOTT- see SCOTT-LINDLEY Mervyn Ewart

LINN Ernest Boswell - C/SSX27519 - HMS Sultan - Held Sumatra (Palembang)

LINSCOTT Leonard James - D/MX47993 - HMS Exeter - Held Celebes

LINTERN William Edwin John - Sub Lt (A) - HMS Victorious - Held Sumatra (Palembang), Singapore - Died Singapore>15.8.45 - Named Lee-on-Solent Memorial

LIPSCOMB Eric Streetfield - Lt Com - HMS Exeter - Held Celebes, Japan (Tokyo Area, Shikoku, Tokyo Area)

LISTER Robert Stephenson - D/JX191095 - HMS Prince of Wales - Held Java, Singapore, Borneo

LITTLE Frederick C - D/J97309 - HMS Exeter - Held Celebes

LIVERMORE Charles Francis Bowman - D/MX63672 - HMS Sultan - Held Sumatra (Medan), Burma - Died Burma (Railway) 3.1.44 - Buried Thanbyuzayat

LIVESEY Ellis Norman - P/SSX17109 - Ship not known - Held Hong Kong, Japan (Osaka Area)

LIVSEY Reginald F - P/JX273728 - Ship not known - Held Singapore, Borneo

LLOYD Ernest Alexander - C/KX86448 - HMS Prince of Wales - Held Sumatra (Palembang)

LLOYD John - D/SSX15748 - HMS Thracian - Held Hong Kong, Japan (Osaka Area)

LOADMAN Leslie Holland - C/MX51538 - HMS Laburnum - Held Sumatra (Palembang)

LOCK Harold Edward - C/JX163108 - HMS Jupiter - Held Java, Moluccas, Java

LOCKER George Henry - RM - PLY/22510 - HMS Prince of Wales - Held Sumatra (Palembang)

LOCKLIN Thomas - RM - PLY/X669 - HMS Prince of Wales - Held Singapore, Thailand

LOCKWOOD Russell Garthwaite - D/JX188698 - HMS Cicala - Held Hong Kong

LOMAX Samuel - RM - PLY/X3254 - HMS Prince of Wales - Held Sumatra (Palembang) - Died Palembang 4.8.45 Buried Jakarta

LONERGAN Harry Ronald - P/JX155100 - HMS Repulse - Held Sumatra (Palembang)

LONG George Lloyd - C/JX146271 - Ship not known - Held Hong Kong, Japan (Osaka Area)

LONG William John - D/JX167693 - HMS Dragonfly - Held Sumatra (Medan, Atjeh, Railway)

LONGHURST Edward Henry - P/JX147099 - HMS Danae - Held Singapore

LONGWORTH Eric - D/MX704159 - HMS Exeter - Held Celebes

LORD Walter - C/JX212825 - SS Gloucester Castle - Held Singapore (from South Atlantic)

LOVESEY William - D/JX140918 - HMS Dragonfly - Held Sumatra (Medan, Railway) - Died Sumatra Railway 10.1.45 - Named Plymouth Memorial

LOWE Thomas - P/KX122439 - HMS Encounter - Held Celebes

LOYAL Joseph A - D/J108681 - HMS Exeter - Held Celebes

LUCKES Raymond Fredrick - D/LX20400 - HMS Repulse - Held Sumatra (Palembang), Singapore

LUCKHURST Ernest Albert - P/KX121819 - HMS Grasshopper - Held Sumatra (Medan), Burma, Thailand

LUDFORD Arthur Herbert - D/M39771 - HMS Tamar - Held Hong Kong - Died Lisbon Maru 2.10.42 - Named Plymouth Memorial

LUDLOW Owen Eric John - RNZN - NZ/2396 - HMS Encounter - Held Celebes

LUMLEY Francis John - Lt - HMS Mata Hari - Held Singapore (from Bangka Strait)

LYLE Claud Workman - MRNVR - Sub Lt - HMS Siang Wo - Held Sumatra (Palembang)

LYNN Robert - D/SSX30082 - HMS Jupiter - Held Java, Moluccas, Celebes, Java

LYNNEBERG Ross - RNZN - NZ/3669 - HMS Tamar - Held Hong Kong, Japan

LYONS George - MRNVR - Sub Lt - HMS Mata Hari - Held Sumatra (Palembang), Singapore

McAFEE David - P/UDX575 - HMS Tamar - Held Hong Kong, Japan (Osaka Area)

McAFEE James George - D/KX138902 - HMS Sultan - Held Sumatra (Medan), Burma, Thailand - Died Thailand - 24.1.44 - Buried Kanchanaburi

McALANEY Bernard - C/JX262316 - HMS Sin-Aik-Lee - Held Java, Singapore, Borneo

McALLAN William Primrose - Lt - HMS Moth - Held Hong Kong

McANULTY James - D/JX221238 - HMS Exeter - Held Celebes, Japan (Kyushu)

McARDLE John - D/JX167248 - HMS Sultan - Held Sumatra (Palembang)

McCAFFERTY Joseph Patrick - P/SSX19139 - HMS Sultan - Held Singapore, Thailand

McCAFFERY Ralph Chapman - P/SSX32349 - HMS Sultan - Held Sumatra (Medan), Burma - Died Burma (Railway) 21.5.43 - Buried Thanbyuzayat

McCAHON John Hamilton - Lt Com - HMS Exeter - Held Celebes, Java

McCALL James Alexander - D/SSX32998 - HMS Prince of Wales - Held Sumatra (Medan), Burma, Thailand

McCALL Thomas Garvin - C/JX175266 - HMS Thracian - Held Hong Kong, Japan (Osaka Area, Nagoya Area)

McCANN Thomas - P/ESD/X1851 - HMS Thracian - Held Hong Kong, Japan (Tokyo Area)

McCARTHY Denis - D/JX208187 - Ship not known - Held Sumatra (Palembang)

McCARTHY Francis Henry - D/JX135117 - HMS Exeter - Held Celebes
McCARTNEY Patrick - C/KX123546 - HMS Ying Pin - Held Singapore (from Bangka Strait)
McCLURE George Richmond - D/MX273 - HMS Exeter - Held Celebes
McCOMB Malcolm Patrick - D/SSX24324 - HMS Sultan - Held Singapore, Borneo
McCONVILLE John - RM - PLY/X609 - HMS Exeter - Held Celebes
McCONVILLE John - P/KX119660 - SS Nankin - Held Japan (Tokyo Area) - captured in Indian Ocean
McCOURTY Wilfred Black - D/SSX29275 - HMS Stronghold - Held Celebes
McCREADY Thomas - D/MX49148 - RN Hospital - Held Hong Kong, Japan (Osaka Area)
McCREERY Sydney - D/KX96013 - HMS Siang Wo - Held Sumatra (Palembang), Singapore, Taiwan, Japan (Tokyo Area, Sendai Area)
McCRORIE William - Sub Lt - HMS Mata Hari - Held Singapore (from Bangka Strait)
McCUE Rees Morgan - C/KX79483 - HMS Grasshopper - Held Sumatra (Medan) - Died Harikiku Maru 26.6.44 - Named Chatham Memorial
McDONALD Ernest Arthur - D/JX184684 - HMS Exeter - Held Celebes - Died Makassar 13.4.45 - Buried Ambon
MacDONALD James Alexander - P/JX141408 - HMS Redstart - Held Hong Kong, Japan (Osaka Area, Nagoya Area)
McDONALD Thomas M - C/JX213663 - HMS Exeter - Held Celebes
McDOUALL John Crichton - HKRNVR - Lt - Ship not known - Held Hong Kong
McELROY Moses - D/SSX20995 - HMS Moth - Held Hong Kong, Japan (Osaka Area)
McELWEE Peter James - P/X2851 - HMS Tern - Held Hong Kong, Japan (Osaka Area)
McEWEN Charles - RNZN - NZD/2932 - HMS Exeter - Held Celebes
McFARLANE John Chapman - Boom Eng - HMS Tamar - Held Hong Kong, Japan (Osaka Area) - Died Japan 17.10.42 - Buried Yokohama
MacFARLANE John Wilson - D/J157360 - HMS Exeter - Held Celebes - Died Makassar 19.5.45 - Buried Ambon
McFARLING Frederick Thomas - D/J100627 - HMS Repulse - Held Sumatra (Palembang), Singapore
McGARRY William Alfred - D/JX175804 - Ship not known - Held Sumatra (Palembang)
McGEE Robert - C/JX262331 - HMS Siang Wo - Held Sumatra (Palembang)
McGLYNN Joseph Arnold - D/JX139007 - HMS Exeter - Held Celebes
McGOWAN Edward (Francis) - D/KX111367 - HMS Exeter - Held Celebes, Japan (Kyushu) - Died Japan 2.2.43 - Buried Yokohama
McGRADY Joseph Patrick - C/JX145837 - HMS Electra - Held Java, Moluccas, Java, Singapore
McGRATH William Patrick - D/J98250 - HMS Cicala - Held Hong Kong - Died Lisbon Maru 2.10.42 - Named Plymouth Memorial
McGREEN Patrick - D/MX53795 - HMS Tamar - Held Hong Kong, Japan (Osaka Area)
MacGREGOR Hugh Marshall - Sub Lt - HMS Mata Hari - Held Singapore (from Bangka Strait)
McINTYRE Duncan McAdam - D/JX152447 - HMS Jupiter - Held Java, Singapore
McINTYRE Peter - D/JX221186 - HMS Prince of Wales - Held Sumatra (Palembang), Singapore
McKAY Edward - RM - PLY/X985 - HMS Prince of Wales - Held Singapore, Thailand
MacKAY Michael Charles - SANF - SA/66812 - HMS Encounter - Held Celebes, Japan (Kyushu)
McKEEN James Graham - C/JX141526 - HMS Moth - Held Hong Kong, Japan (Osaka Area)
MacKENNY William Henry - D/MX50095 - HMS Tamar - Held Hong Kong - Died Lisbon Maru 2.10.42 - Named Plymouth Memorial
McKENZIE Royce - D/MX70451 - HMS Exeter - Held Celebes - Died Makassar 11.2.45 - Buried Ambon
McKEOWN Gerard - RM - PLY/X100142 - HMS Prince of Wales - Held Sumatra (Palembang)
McKERNEY Terrence - D/JX162961 - HMS Exeter - Held Celebes
McKINLEY James Denis - D/KX83169 - HMS Exeter - Held Celebes
McKIRLEY Kenneth Stanley - RM - PLY/X2727 - HMS Prince of Wales - Held Singapore, Thailand
MacKLEY Walter - C/KX76036 - Ship not known - Held Singapore
McLACHLAN Edgar James Roland - RNZN - NZ/3038 - HMS Sultan - Held Sumatra (Medan), Burma - Died Burma (Railway) 10.11.43 - Buried Thanbyuzayat
McLACKLAND Frank - D/X1517 - Ship not known - Held Sumatra (Palembang), Singapore, Taiwan, Japan (Tokyo Area, Sendai Area)
McLAUGHLAN Frederick - D/JX162393 - Ship not known - Held Sumatra (Medan), Burma, Thailand
McLAUGHLIN Francis Henry - RM - PLY/X1220 - HMS Exeter - Held Celebes
McLEAN Frank - D/SSX25428 - HMS Exeter - Held Celebes
McLEAN Kenneth John - D/JX169314 - HMS Stronghold - Held Celebes
McLEAN Thomas - D/JX254984 - MV Tantalus - Held Philippines, Japan (Tokyo Area)
MacLEOD Angus - C/JX240098 - MV Behar - Held Java - captured in Indian Ocean
MacLEOD Forbes - HKRNVR - Sub Lt - Ship not known - Held Hong Kong

MacLEOD James - D/SR16600 - HMS Stronghold - Held Celebes

McMAHON Robert - Gnr - SS Wellpark - Held Japan (Tokyo Area) - captured in S Atlantic

MacMILLAN John - D/JX201941 - HMS Prince of Wales - Held Sumatra (Palembang), Singapore

McMINN James Robert - D/JX194915 - HMS Prince of Wales - Held Sumatra (Palembang), Singapore

McMULLIN Daniel - MRNVR - Lt - HMS Sultan - Held Sumatra (Palembang)

McNAIR Robert Hunter - Lt - Ship not known - Held Hong Kong

McNEE Peter - D/MDX2497 - HMS Exeter - Held Celebes

McNEILL Robert - RNZN - NZ/2398 - Ship not known - Held Celebes, Japan - Died Japan 15.4.44 - Buried Yokohama

McNELLEY Francis Chas Thomas - C/JX227807 - Ship not known - Held Sumatra (Medan, Atjeh, Railway)

McPEAK Gordon - C/SSX30721 - HMS Encounter - Held Celebes - Died Makassar 12.4.45 - Buried Ambon

McQUAY Samuel - D/SSX23724 - HMS Thracian - Held Hong Kong, Japan (Osaka Area, Nagoya Area)

McQUEEN George Maclean - D/JX169654 - HMS Tamar - Held Hong Kong - Died Lisbon Maru 2.10.42 - Named Plymouth Memorial

McRAE William James Smith - FAA/FX96155 - HMS Victorious - Held Sumatra (Palembang), Singapore - Died Singapore >15.8.45 - Named Lee-on-Solent Memorial

McSHANE Francis Bertrand - D/JX184678 - HMS Exeter - Held Celebes - Died Makassar 7.4.45 - Buried Ambon

McVEY Owen - D/KX80576 - HMS Exeter - Held Celebes

McVIE James Wait Hepburn - D/SSX22667 - HMS Repulse - Held Sumatra (Palembang)

McWILLIAM John - RM - PLY/X3798 - HMS Prince of Wales - Held Singapore, Thailand

MACEY Eric Donald - D/JX131319 - Stonecutters - Held Hong Kong, Japan (Tokyo Area)

MADDAMS John Eric - D/JX200271 - HMS Exeter - Held Celebes

MAGNALL Tom - D/JX199868 - MV Empire Dawn - Held Java - captured in S Atlantic, Sumatra (Pangkalan Bali), Singapore

MAHONEY Owen Felix - NAFFI - HMS Stronghold - Held Celebes, Japan (Kyushu)

MAIDMENT Alfred George - D/KX116633 - HMS Exeter - Held Celebes

MAIR William - Skipper - HMS Robin - Held Hong Kong - Died Lisbon Maru 2.10.42 - Named - Chatham Memorial

MAJOR Richard John - D/KX120271 - HMS Sultan - Held Singapore, Taiwan, Japan (Tokyo Area)

MAKER Leslie James - D/MX55678 - HMS Exeter - Held Celebes

MAKER Norman - RM - PLY/X800 - HMS Exeter - Held Celebes - Died Makassar 14.2.42 - Buried Ambon

MAKIN James - D/JX147930 - HMS Exeter - Held Celebes

MALBON Eric Raymond - RM - PLY/X2466 - HMS Exeter - Held Celebes, Japan (Kyushu)

MALLETT William George - D/JX200308 - HMS Exeter - Held Celebes - Died Makassar 4.5.45 - Buried Ambon

MALONEY Arthur - D/KX126564 - HMS Jupiter - Held Java, Moluccas, Celebes - Died Transport 125 8.11.44 - Named Plymouth Memorial

MANDELMAN Henry - P/JX182275 - HMS Stronghold - Held Celebes

MANDER John Albert - D/J102231 - HMS Prince of Wales - Held Singapore, Thailand

MANGE Roland Maurice - MRNVR - SE/X89 - Ship not known - Held Sumatra (Palembang), Singapore

MANLEY James Edmond - D/MX67893 - HMS Sultan - Held Sumatra (Medan), Singapore, Sumatra (Railway)

MANN Charles Henry - D/JX137274 - HMS Cicala - Held Hong Kong - Died Lisbon Maru 2.10.42 - Named Plymouth Memorial

MANNING Frank Cecil - HKRNVR Lt - HMS Cornflower - Held Hong Kong

MANSFIELD Frank - Sub Lt - HMS Sultan - Held Sumatra (Medan), Singapore, Thailand

MANTLE Horace Sidney - C/KX100254 - HMS Electra - Held Java, Moluccas, Java

MARINER James Frederick - P/SSX20074 - HMS Peterel - Held Shanghai, Japan (Hokkaido)

MARKHAM Edward Arthur - RM - PLY/22169 - HMS Exeter - Held Celebes

MARLOW Frederick - D/KX105157 - HMS Tapah - Held Singapore (from Bangka)

MARR Thomas Charles Marn - Sub Lt - HMS Siang Wo - Held Java

MARRIAGE Gilbert Edward - NAAFI - HMS Exeter - Held Celebes

MARRIOTT William Henry - C/JX145860 - HMS Tamar - Held Hong Kong - Died Lisbon Maru 2.10.42 - Named Chatham Memorial

MARRIOTT William K S - D/SSX35752 - HMS Exeter - Held Celebes

MARRS William - P/JX190653 - HMS Tamar - Held Hong Kong - Died Lisbon Maru 2.10.42 - Named Plymouth Memorial

MARSH Arthur Douglas - D/J107591 - HMS Exeter - Held Celebes

MARSHALL James Henry - C/JX262328 - HMS Sultan - Held Sumatra (Palembang)

UNSUNG HEROES of the ROYAL NAVY and ROYAL MARINES

MARSHALL Stanley George - C/SSX18678 - HMS Wo Kwang - Held Java, Singapore, Japan (Osaka Area)
MARTIN Frank - W O Wardmaster - HMS Tamar - Held Hong Kong - Died Lisbon Maru 2.10.42 - Named Plymouth Memorial
MARTIN Frederick William - D/JX134559 - HMS Jupiter - Held Java, Moluccas, Celebes - Died Muna 10.4.45 Buried Ambon
MASON Charles Edward A - Surg Lt - Ship not known - Held Hong Kong
MASON Ernest Arthur - D/JX200023 - HMS Exeter - Held Celebes
MASON Leslie - P/SSX30504 - Stonecutters - Held Hong Kong, Japan (Nagoya Area)
MASSEY Edward - D/KX115612 - HMS Exeter - Held Celebes - Died Makassar 6.6.45 - Buried Ambon
MATHESON Donald - P/MX64555 - HMS Tamar - Held Hong Kong, Japan (Osaka Area) - Died Japan 17.10.42 - Buried Yokohama
MATTHEWS Francis William - Sub Lt - Ship not known - Held Sumatra (Palembang)
MATTHEWS Ronald Frederick Marcus - P/J100630 - HMS Tamar - Held Hong Kong, Japan (Osaka Area)
MATTISON William - C/JX143164 - HMS Thracian - Held Hong Kong, Japan (Osaka Area, Nagoya Area)
MAULE John - RM - PLY/X2933 - HMS Exeter - Held Celebes
MAUNDER Leslie Philip - D/JX164033 - HMS Exeter - Held Celebes - Died Makassar 13.4.45 - Buried Ambon
MAXTED Richard Leonard - C/JX140591 - HMS Tamar - Held Hong Kong, Japan (Osaka Area) - Died Japan 31.10.42 - Buried Yokohama
MAXWELL Charles - P/JX149406 - Mining Party - Held Hong Kong
MAY Ronald McKenzie - SANF - SA/68371 - HMS Stronghold - Held Celebes, Japan (Kyushu)
MAY Wilfred - C/JX219867 - HMS Tamar - Held Hong Kong - Died Lisbon Maru 2.10.42 - Named Chatham Memorial
MAYBURY Stanley Russell - D/KX118050 - HMS Exeter - Held Celebes - Died Makassar 29.2.45 - Buried Ambon
MAYNE George Stuart Otway - Act Sub Lt - HMS Cornflower - Held Hong Kong
MEACOCK Kenneth - D/KX108787 - HMS Exeter - Held Celebes - Died Makassar 22.11.44 - Buried Ambon
MEADER Fradelle - C/J102041 - HMS Electra - Held Java
MEAKER William J - D/J91552 - HMS Tamar - Held Hong Kong
MEARS Albert Edgar - D/JX141563 - HMS Cicala - Held Hong Kong, Japan (Nagoya Area) - Died Japan 30.8.45 - Buried Yokohama
MECKIN William Henry - D/JX180659 - HMS Exeter - Held Celebes
MEDLEY Albert Victor - D/JX238570 - HMS Repulse - Held Sumatra (Palembang), Singapore
MELDRUM Wallace Wright - D/KX94693 - HMS Repulse - Held Sumatra (Medan), Burma, Thailand
MELIA James - D/K56758 - HMS Exeter - Held Celebes
MELLOR Thomas Ewart - Lt - Ship not known - Held Singapore (from Bangka)
MELLOWS Stephen John - D/MX47034 - HMS Tamar - Held Hong Kong - Died Lisbon Maru 2.10.42 - Named Plymouth Memorial
MELTON John William - P/J39300 - HMS Tamar - Held Hong Kong - Died Lisbon Maru 2.10.42 - Named Plymouth Memorial
MENNELL Stanley - D/JX256038 - Ship not known - Held Sumatra (Palembang)
MERCER William Henry - C/JX213603 - HMS Exeter - Held Celebes
MERIFIELD Simon Percival - D/J108178 - HMS Encounter - Held Celebes
METCALFE Ernest - RM - PO/15951 - HMS Tamar - Held Hong Kong - Died Lisbon Maru 2.10.42 - Named Plymouth Memorial
METZ Archibald Frederick - D/K66852 - HMS Exeter - Held Celebes - Died Makassar - 12.5.45 - Buried Ambon
MICALLEF Andrew - E/LX20922 - HMS Exeter - Held Celebes
MICHAEL Samuel - D/JX170115 - Ship not known - Held Sumatra (Medan), Burma, Thailand
MIDDLETON Kenneth William - D/JX170908 - HMS Exeter - Held Celebes - Died Makassar 13.12.44 - Buried Ambon
MIDDLETON Thomas William - C/KX107161 - HMS Tern - Held Hong Kong, Japan (Tokyo Area)
MIDDLEWEEK Ronald John - D/KX111366 - HMS Exeter - Held Celebes - Died Makassar 19.4.42 - Buried Ambon
MILBANK Arthur Thomas - D/KX99137 - Ship not known - Held Singapore (from Bangka)
MILBURN Charles - C/JX190520 - HMS Exeter - Held Celebes
MILES Cyril David - RM - PLY/X4018 - HMS Exeter - Held Celebes
MILES Kenneth W - P/J94033 - Ship not known - Held Java, Singapore, Borneo
MILEY William John - D/SSX33727 - MV Tantalus - Held Philippines, Japan (Kyushu)

MILKS D - RNR - Ldg Sea - Ship not known - Held Celebes

MILL Keith Clifford - RM - PLY/X3180 - HMS Repulse - Held Singapore, Thailand - Died Thailand 26.6.43 - Buried Chungkai

MILL William Gerald - D/MX53685 - HMS Jarak - Held Sumatra (Medan), Burma, Thailand

MILLAR Edward Christopher Joseph - P/MX65302 - HMS Tamar - Held Hong Kong

MILLAR Robert - HKRNVR - Act Sub Lt - HMS Cornflower - Held Hong Kong

MILLER Charles Terence - RM - PLY/X1541 - HMS Prince of Wales - Held Singapore, Thailand, Japan (Hiroshima Area)

MILLER Henry Edward - C/J12044 - HMS Tamar - Held Hong Kong, Japan (Nagoya Area)

MILLER Horace Morgan - Lt - Ship not known - Held Hong Kong

MILLER Robert Lewis - Ldg Sea - ML 432 - Held Sumatra (Palembang)

MILLETT Herbert Claude - Com - HMS Tamar - Held Hong Kong

MILLICAN Joseph - P/MX68799 - HMS Tamar - Held Hong Kong, Japan (Osaka Area)

MILLINGTON James - D/MX60076 - HMS Exeter - Held Celebes

MILLS David Henry - RM - PLY/X100120 - HMS Prince of Wales - Held Singapore - Died Singapore 23.9.42 - Buried Kranji

MILLS John Thomas - P/JX236349 - SS Francol - Held Celebes

MILLS Lawrence - D/SSX33719 - HMS Jupiter - Held Java, Moluccas, Java

MILLS William Leonard - C/MX77256 - HMS Sultan - Held Sumatra (Medan, Railway)

MILNE James Norman - D/JX134707 - HMS Mata Hari - Held Singapore (from Bangka)

MINHINNICK Frank Burt - Capt Eng - Ship not known - Held Hong Kong, Taiwan, Manchuria

MINTO Robert - D/MX75584 - HMS Sultan - Held Singapore (from Bangka), Borneo

MIST Charles - P/J38053 - HMS Tamar - Held Hong Kong

MITCHELL Donald MacArthur - Boatswain - HMS Tamar - Held Hong KongvDied Hong Kong 9.7.42 - Buried Stanley

MITCHELL Eric Thomas Patrick - D/MX73559 - HMS Exeter - Held Celebes

MITCHELL Frederick - C/JX138032 - Ship not known - Held Hong Kong, Japan (Tokyo Area)

MITCHELL Frederick William - Lt - Boom Defence - Held Hong Kong

MITCHELL George Edward - P/JX128859 - Ship not known - Held Singapore, Thailand

MITCHELL Stanley Walter - RM - PLY/20489 - SS Francol - Held Celebes

MITCHELL William Eric - P/J110909 - RN MTB - Held Hong Kong, Japan (Tokyo Area)

MITTON John - D/SSX32939 - HMS Jupiter - Held Java, Sumatra (Railway) - Died Sumatra Railway 23.8.45 - Buried Jakarta

MOAR Gordon - D/JX177457 - HMS Exeter - Held Celebes

MOCK Charles Albert - D/JX158766 - HMS Sultan - Held Sumatra (Medan) - Died Harikiku Maru 26.6.44 - Named Plymouth Memorial

MOGRIDGE William Ronald - D/JX254855 - HMS Sultan - Held Sumatra (Palembang) - Died Palembang 25.8.45 - Buried Jakarta

MONK Donald John - D/JX169959 - HMS Grasshopper - Held Sumatra (Medan, Railway) - Died Sumatra Railway 11.11.44 - Buried Jakarta

MOODIE John - Act Lt - HMS Cornflower - Held Hong Kong

MOONEY Albert E - D/J112482 - HMS Repulse - Held Sumatra (Palembang)

MOORE Charles - Sub Lt - HMS Siang Wo - Held Sumatra (Palembang) - Died Palembang 20.6.45 - Buried Jakarta

MOORE James - RM - CH/X3397 - HMS Prince of Wales - Held Sumatra (Palembang) - Died Palembang 12.6.44 - Buried Jakarta

MOORE John Henry - D/J114975 - Stonecutters - Held Hong Kong, Japan (Osaka Area)

MOORE John William - C/MX76862 - HMS Exeter - Held Celebes - Died Makassar 25.2.45 - Buried Ambon

MOORE Thomas (12.5.02) - D/KX97330 - HMS Jupiter - Held Java, Moluccas - Died Ambon 3.10.44 - Buried Ambon

MOORE Thomas (5.8.18) - P/JX142108 - HMS Tamar - Held Hong Kong, Japan (Osaka Area)

MOORHEAD Hercules Bradshaw Forbes - Com - HMS Sultan - Held Sumatra (Palembang), Singapore

MORAHAN Bernard Joseph - HKRNVR - Lt - Ship not known - Held Hong Kong

MORGAN Charles Horace - C/MX49594 - HMS Anking - Held Celebes

MORGAN Eric Vernon StJohn - Lt Com - HMS Encounter - Held Celebes, Japan (Tokyo Area, Shikoku, Tokyo Area)

MORGAN Herbert Leslie - RM - PLY/X2384 - HMS Exeter - Held Celebes, Japan (Kyushu)

MORGAN John Stanley Austin - D/JX197972 - HMS Jupiter - Held Java, Moluccas - Died Haruku 31.5.43 - Buried Ambon

MORGAN Melville Maurice - C/KX105321 - HMS Thracian - Held Hong Kong, Japan (Osaka Area) - Died

Japan 16.10.42 - Buried Yokohama

MORLEY John - D/JX226799 - HMS Encounter - Held Celebes - Died Makassar 20.4.45 - Buried Ambon

MORRIS Ernest Richard - C/M35643 - HMS Thracian - Held Hong Kong

MORRIS George - D/JX162191 - HMS Repulse - Held Sumatra (Palembang)

MORRIS Jeffrey Michael Grave - RNZN - NZ/2923 - HMS Exeter - Held Celebes - Died Makassar 31.1.45 - Buried Ambon

MORRIS John Hinkin - D/KX141331 - HMS Exeter - Held Celebes - Died Makassar 28.3.45 - Buried Ambon

MORRIS Ronald - D/JX177481 - HMS Exeter - Held Celebes

MORRIS Walterv - D/MX48513 - HMS Dragonfly - Held Sumatra (Medan) - Died Harikiku Maru 26.6.44 - Named Plymouth Memorial

MORRIS William H - D/JX235723 - SS Willesden - Held Japan (Tokyo Area) - captured in S Atlantic

MORRISON Alexander F N - P/JX258710 - HMS Exeter - Held Celebes

MORRISON George W - Com - Ship not known - Held Hong Kong

MORROW Samuel - D/JX184694 - HMS Exeter - Held Celebes

MORSE Charles John - D/K65312 - HMS Tamar - Held Hong Kong - Died Lisbon Maru 2.10.42 - Named Plymouth Memorial

MORT Archibald Joseph - D/KX83069 - HMS Exeter - Held Celebes

MORTIMER Robert - RNZN - NZ/D2170 - HMS Encounter - Held Celebes

MORTIMORE Arthur Ernest - RM - PLY/22647 - HMS Exeter - Held Celebes - Died Makassar 2.2.45 - Buried Ambon

MORTIMORE Francis John - RM - PLY/X2759 - HMS Repulse - Held Singapore, Thailand

MORTON Frederick - D/JX184632 - HMS Exeter - Held Celebes, Japan (Kyushu)

MORTON Hugh - Lt - HMS Giang Bee - Held Java, Singapore, Japan (Hiroshima Area)

MORTON Robert Henderson - C/JX262360 - HMS Dragonfly - Held Sumatra (Medan, Atjeh, Railway)

MORTON Walter - C/J69383 - HMS Tamar - Held Hong Kong, Japan (Osaka Area)

MOSELEY Matthew - D/SSX23455 - HMS Repulse - Held Singapore (from Bangka)

MOTH Stafford George - D/JX177456 - HMS Jupiter - Held Java, Moluccas, Java

MOTLEY Ronald - P/JX290735 - SS Eugene Livano - Held Japan (Hokkaido) - captured in Indian Ocean

MOTT Joseph Edward - C/SSX32019 - HMS Encounter - Held Celebes

MOUNTSTEVENS William Henry James - D/K55610 - HMS Exeter - Held Celebes - Died Pomelaa 26.7.43 - Buried Ambon

MOXHAM Frederick - RM - PLY/X37 - HMS Tamar - Held Hong Kong, Japan (Osaka Area)

MULCAHY Michael Desmond - D/JX143657 - HMS Tamar - Held Hong Kong - Died Lisbon Maru 7.10.42 - Named Plymouth Memorial

MULLANEY Frederick Edward - D/SSX29445 - HMS Sultan - Held Sumatra (Palembang)

MULLEN Samuel George - D/MX55530 - HMS Grasshopper - Held Sumatra (Medan), Singapore, Sumatra (Railway)

MULLETT Leslie Alfred - HKRNVR - W O - Ship not known - Held Hong Kong, Japan (Osaka Area) - Died Japan 21.10.42 - Buried Yokohama

MULLOCK Alfred - D/JX144993 - HMS Exeter - Held Celebes, Japan (Kyushu)

MULOCK George Francis Arthur - Capt - RN Base Singapore - Held Sumatra (Palembang), Singapore, Taiwan, Manchuria

MULVEY Francis Patrick - D/SSX23079 - HMS Stronghold - Held Celebes

MULVIHILL Frederick - D/JX193671 - HMS Thracian - Held Hong Kong

MUNN Henry Joshua - D/SSX20893 - HMS Stronghold - Held Celebes, Japan (Kyushu)

MUNN Walter Ernest - D/JX 134960 - HMS Peterel - Held Shanghai, Japan (Tokyo Area)

MUNRO Duncan Miller - HKRNVR - Sub Lt - Ship not known - Held Hong Kong

MUNRO William John - Lt - HMS Kung Wo - Held Sumatra (Medan), Singapore, Thailand

MURCH Edward Charles - D/JX129683 - HMS Exeter - Held Celebes - Died Makassar 25.4.43 - Buried Ambon

MURFIN Francis Sydney - RM - PLY/X2233 - HMS Prince of Wales - Held Singapore, Thailand - Died Thailand 8.7.43 - Buried Kanchanaburi

MURPHY Colman Harold - D/JX164204 - HMS Exeter - Held Celebes

MURPHY John Francis - RNZN - NZ/D3033 - HMS Stronghold - Held Celebes

MURPHY Michael T - D/KX122330 - HMS Encounter - Held Celebes

MURRAY John - D/JX247784 - HMS Stronghold - Held Celebes, Japan (Kyushu)

MURRAY John Andrew - C/JX214043 - HMS Prince of Wales - Held Sumatra (Medan, Railway)

MUSSETT William Lauender - MRNVR - SE/XE2 - Ship not known - Held Sumatra (Palembang)

MUTTER Reginald Frederick - RM - PLY/X2086 - HMS Exeter - Held Celebes

MUTTON William Henry - D/K23685 - HMS Exeter - Held Celebes - Died Makassar 21.11.43 - Buried Ambon

NAGLE Arthur Michael - Pm Lt - HMS Prince of Wales - Held Sumatra (Palembang)

NAISBITT Bright - P/KX273673 - HMS Exeter - Held Celebes

NALL George - D/JX175818 - HMS Exeter - Held Celebes, Java

NASH Walter - HKRNVR - Act Sub Lt - Ship not known - Held Hong Kong

NAYLOR Leslie Francis - 2nd Eng - SS Francol - Held Celebes, Japan (Kyushu), Manchuria

NEILL Ernest Robert - D/SSX14813 - HMS Cicala - Held Hong Kong, Japan (Osaka Area) - Died Japan 16.11.42 - Buried Yokohama

NEUBRONNER Douglas Walter - MRNVR - Sub Lt - HMS Laburnum - Held Sumatra (Palembang), Singapore, Taiwan, Japan (Tokyo Area. Shikoku, Tokyo Area)

NEWALL Lewis Walter - RM - PLY/X3209 - HMS Repulse - Held Sumatra (Palembang)

NEWBY William John - D/KX106550 - HMS Sultan - Held Singapore, Thailand - Died Toyofuku Maru 21.9.44 - Named Plymouth Memorial

NEWHAM Robert Edward - C/MX47716 - HMS Encounter - Held Celebes

NEWMAN Harold Edward George - D/JX146356 - HMS Exeter - Held Celebes, Japan (Tokyo Area)

NEWMAN Joshua Frederick - P/JX126640 - HMS Sultan - Held Java - Died Java - 15.3.44 - Buried Jakarta

NEWTON Cecil - D/KX95733 - HMS Exeter - Held Celebes

NEWTON Thomas Edward Laidlaw - D/JX134895 - HMS Cicala - Held Hong Kong, Japan (Osaka Area)

NICHOLL Hugh - D/JX175811 - HMS Exeter - Held Celebes

NICHOLLS Edward Thomas - C/KX77435 - HMS Encounter - Held Celebes

NICHOLLS William Coates - D/JX167763 - HMS Ying Pin - Held Singapore (from Bangka)

NICHOLS Frank Oswald - D/JX226063 - HMS Exeter - Held Celebes - Died Makassar 28.2.45 - Buried Ambon

NICOL Jonathan Gourlay - C/J100736 - HMS Encounter - Held Celebes - Died Makassar 14.5.45 - Buried Ambon

NICOLICH Gerald Leonard - MRNVR - Sub Lt - HMS Sultan - Held Sumatra (Medan), Singapore, Thailand

NIGHTINGALE Clifford - D/MX62460 - HMS Exeter - Held Celebes, Java

NISSIM Archibald - HKRNVR - Sub Lt - HMS Cornflower - Held Hong Kong

NOBLE George - D/JX146969 - HMS Prince of Wales - Held Sumatra (Palembang)

NOBLE Herbert - HKRNVR - Senior Gnr - HMS Cornflower - Held Hong Kong

NOBLE Stanley - P/JX233305 - ML 432 - Held Sumatra (Palembang)

NORRIS Stanley Kempthorne - D/MX65280 - HMS Exeter - Held Celebes

NORTHCOTT Charles Jutland Ralph - D/JX137479 - HMS Prince of Wales - Held Sumatra (Medan, Atjeh, Railway)

NORTHOVER Ronald Clarence - RM - PLY/X1606 - HMS Tamar - Held Hong Kong, Japan (Osaka Area)

NUGUS Phillip Charles Henry - RM - PLY/X3177 - HMS Repulse - Held Singapore, Thailand - Died Thailand 29.10.43 - Buried Kanchanaburi

NUNN Henry Andrew - RM - PLY/22222 - HMS Repulse - Held Singapore

NUTTEN Leslie Harold - P/JX261165 - SS Eugene Livano - Held Japan (Hokkaido) - captured in Indian Ocean

OAKES Ernest - D/J87196 - HMS Exeter - Held Celebes - Died Makassar 18.8.44 - Buried Ambon

O'BRIEN Albert George - D/JX167418 - HMS Dragonfly - Held Sumatra (Medan, Atjeh, Railway)

O'CONNELL Henry - D/KX98095 - HMS Exeter - Held Celebes, Japan (Kyushu)

ODELL Harry Oscar - HKRNVR - Sub Lt - Ship not known - Held Hong Kong

O'FARREL William Francis - Lt - Ship not known - Held Hong Kong

O'GRADY Owen - D/KX119544 - HMS Exeter - Held Celebes, Japan (Kyushu)

O'HANLON Daniel Joseph - D/JX148638 - Stonecutters - Held Hong Kong, Japan (Osaka Area)

O'HARE Thomas Philip - P/JX247848 - HMS Exeter - Held Celebes

OLIVER John Edward - D/JX207219 - HMS Exeter - Held Celebes

OLIVER John Robert - C/SSX21162 - HMS Tamar - Held Hong Kong - Died Lisbon Maru 2.10.42 - Named Chatham Memorial

OLIVER Ronald - D/JX136673 - Ship not known - Held Hong Kong - Died Lisbon Maru 2.10.42 - Named Plymouth Memorial

O'NEILL Eugene - D/K10240 - HMS Exeter - Held Celebes

ORTON Stanley Norman - P/JX216506 - HMS Sultan - Held Sumatra (Palembang)

OSBORN Alfred James - D/J106494 HMS Sultan - Held Sumatra (Medan) - Died Harikiku Maru 26.6.44 - Named Plymouth Memorial

OSBORNE John Hepworth - Pm Lt - HMS Tamar - Held Hong Kong

OSBORNE Richard - D/JX170189 - HMS Prince of Wales - Held Sumatra (Palembang)
OSBORNE Vivian E - D/K56651 - HMS Exeter - Held Celebes
O'SHAUGHNESSY Leonard - D/JX213690 - HMS Exeter - Held Celebes
O'SHEA Patrick Finnbarr - D/JX154025 - HMS Repulse - Held Singapore (from Bangka)
OSMAN Harry James - P/J105839 - HMS Moth - Held Hong Kong - Died Lisbon Maru 2.10.42 - Named Plymouth Memorial
O'SULLIVAN Bartholomew - P/K59642 - HMS Thracian - Held Hong Kong - Died Lisbon Maru 2.10.42 - Named Plymouth Memorial
O'SULLIVAN Lawrence - D/SSX25123 - HMS Exeter - Held Celebes, Japan (Kyushu)
OSWALD Jack - D/MX74842 - HMS Sultan - Held Sumatra (Palembang)
OUSGOOD Fred - P/MX46649 - HMS Tamar - Held Hong Kong - Died Lisbon Maru 2.10.42 - Named Plymouth Memorial
OVANS John Malcolm - Lt - Ship not known - Held Hong Kong
OVENALL George Harry - C/SSX33764 - HMS Exeter - Held Celebes
OVERINGTON Norman Henry - RM - PLY/X2288 - HMS Repulse - Held Singapore, Thailand
OWEN Cyril Arton - HKRNVR - Sub Lt - HMS Cornflower - Held Hong Kong
OWEN George Thomas Richard - C/J80397 - HMS Tamar - Held Hong Kong - Died Lisbon Maru 2.10.42 - Named Chatham Memorial
OWEN Thomas William - D/MX63095 - HMS Exeter - Held Celebes, Japan (Kyushu)
PACE Jack - P/JX199505 - HMS Tamar - Held Hong Kong, Japan (Osaka Area, Nagoya Area)
PACEY William George - P/JX164925 - Boom Defence - Held Hong Kong, Japan (Osaka Area, Hiroshima Area)
PACKARD Geoffrey Percival - Lt Com - SS Harauki - Held Singapore (from Indian Ocean), Japan (Tokyo Area)
PADDEN William Arthur - D/KX121334 - ML 310 - Held Singapore (from Sinkep), Thailand
PADDON Walter - D/J30238 - HMS Exeter - Held Celebes, Japan (Kyushu)
PAGE John Allison - Surg Lt - RN Hospital - Held Hong Kong, Japan (Kyushu, Osaka Area)
PAGET Peter - P/JX214317 - HMS Tamar - Held Hong Kong, Japan (Tokyo Area, Sendai Area)
PAISH Jack - D/JX127712 - HMS Jupiter - Held Java, Sumatra (Railway)
PALMER Albert Henry - D/KX82346 - HMS Exeter - Held Celebes
PALMER Charles Henry - C/JX126168 - HMS Electra - Held Java, Moluccas, Celebes - Died Muna 28.10.44 - Buried Ambon
PALMER Edward John - D/KX91683 - HMS Repulse - Held Sumatra (Medan, Railway)
PALMER Ronald Roper - P/WRX292 - HMS Tamar - Held Hong Kong, Japan (Nagoya Area)
PARDOE Ivan - RNZN - NZ/3042 - Ship not known - Held Sumatra (Medan, Railway) - Died Sumatra Railway 29.4.45 - Named New Zealand Memorial
PARIS Carmelo - E/LX23549 - HMS Exeter - Held Celebes
PARK Louis - C/MX81951 - HMS Exeter - Held Celebes
PARK William John Annan - D/MX73020 - HMS Exeter - Held Celebes, Japan (Kyushu)
PARKER Arthur Henry - C/JX160684 - Ship not known - Held Sumatra (Medan), Burma, Thailand
PARKER Henry Thomas - W O Wr - Ship not known - Held Hong Kong, Japan (Tokyo Area)
PARKER Leonard Arthur Frederick - P/MX46039 - HMS Stronghold - Held Celebes - Died Makassar 20.2.45 - Buried Ambon
PARKER William Thomas - C/J99962 - HMS Robin - Held Hong Kong
PARKIN Robert Alan - P/MX55378 - HMS Stronghold - Held Celebes
PARKINS George Baden - C/J46941 - HMS Tamar - Held Hong Kong - Died Lisbon Maru 2.10.42 - Named Chatham Memorial
PARKINSON Maurice - D/JX238231 - HMS Exeter - Held Celebes - Died Makassar 31.3.45 - Buried Ambon
PARKINSON Robert - D/SSX33870 - Ship not known - Held Hong Kong, Japan (Osaka Area)
PARKINSON Robert Bruce - HKRNVR - Sub Lt - Ship not known - Held Hong Kong
PARKINSON William (2.8.20) - RM - PLY/X2825 - HMS Prince of Wales - Held Sumatra (Palembang)
PARKINSON William (5.4.17) - D/KX110205 - SS Nankin - Held Japan (Tokyo Area) - captured in Indian Ocean
PARKYN Leslie William - D/JX166413 - HMS Exeter - Held Celebes - Died Pomelaa 2.9.43 - Buried Ambon
PARLETTE Reginald George - C/MX86692 - HMS Tamar - Held Hong Kong - Died Lisbon Maru 2.10.42 - Named Chatham Memorial
PARMENTER John Cyril - D/J96924 - HMS Exeter - Held Celebes - Died Pomelaa 18.5.43 - Named Plymouth Memorial

PARRY Raymond - C/JX138568 - HMS Thracian - Held Hong Kong, Japan (Tokyo Area)
PARSONS Charles Archibald - MRNVR - Sub Lt - HMS Prince of Wales - Held Sumatra (Medan), Singapore, Thailand
PARSONS Charles James - D/MX67212 - HMS Repulse - Held Sumatra (Palembang)
PARSONS Henry Frederick - D/JX175278 - HMS Exeter - Held Celebes - Died Makassar 7.3.45 - Buried Ambon
PARSONS Thomas Henry - D/JX143539 - HMS Prince of Wales - Held Bangka - Escaped but see next entry
PARSONS Thomas Henry - D/JX143539 - HMS Prince of Wales - Held Java, Sumatra (Pangkalan Bali), Singapore
PARSONS William Samuel George - P/JX165583 - SS Gemstone - Held Japan (Kyushu) - captured in S Atlantic
PARTRIDGE Edward LeGreshey - MRNVR - Sub Lt - Ship not known - Held Sumatra (Palembang) - Died Palembang 5.9.45 - Buried Jakarta
PASS Cyril - D/JX213702 - HMS Exeter - Held Celebes
PATERSON Cosmos Gordon - MRNVR - Lt - HMS Sultan - Held Sumatra (Palembang)
PATEYJOHNS Robert George - D/J88068 - HMS Repulse - Held Sumatra (Medan), Singapore
PATTERSON Benjamin - C/JX144738 - HMS Moth - Held Hong Kong, Japan (Tokyo Area)
PATTERSON Carl Wight - D/MX73302 - HMS Jupiter - Held Java, Moluccas, Java
PATTERSON George Scott - RNZN - NZD/3137 - HMS Exeter - Held Celebes, Japan
PATTERSON Robert - C/J112999 - HMS Kung Wo - Held Sumatra (Medan), Burma, Thailand
PAUL Ernest Frank - D/JX148117 - HMS Thracian - Held Hong Kong, Japan (Tokyo Area)
PAYNE Albert Edward - P/SSX33262 - HMS Moth - Held Hong Kong, Japan (Osaka Area, Nagoya Area)
PAYNE Alfred George - D/JX148381 - HMS Encounter - Held Celebes
PAYNE Ernest William - C/J94361 - HMS Tern - Held Hong Kong, Japan (Osaka Area) - Died Japan 23.10.42 - Buried Yokohama
PAYNE Jack - C/SSX10766 - HMS Encounter - Held Celebes, Japan (Kyushu)
PEACEFULL James George Ernest - C/SSX17734 - HMS Electra - Held Java, Moluccas - Died Maros Maru 6.10.44 - Named Chatham Memorial
PEACH Howard - D/JX149756 - HMS Repulse - Held Sumatra (Palembang)
PEAL Eric Evelyn Fraser - MRNVR - Pm Lt - HMS Prince of Wales - Held Sumatra (Palembang), Singapore
PEARCE Anthony Frank - D/MX59050 - HMS Sultan - Held Sumatra (Medan) - Died Harikiku Maru 26.6.44 - Named Plymouth Memorial
PEARCE Denis Albert - D/KX115062 - HMS Repulse - Held Sumatra (Palembang)
PEARCE Jack - RM - PO/20483 - HMS Tamar - Held Hong Kong
PEARCE Kenneth John - D/JX140047 - HMS Exeter - Held Celebes
PEARMAN John Edward - RM - PLY/X2061 - HMS Tamar - Held Hong Kong, Japan (Osaka Area)
PEARS Arthur Luard - Com - HMS Thracian - Held Hong Kong
PEARSON Edward Ramsay - D/JX170903 - HMS Exeter - Held Celebes - Died Makassar 8.7.45 - Buried Ambon
PEARSON Ernest James - D/JX198445 - HMS Sultan - Held Singapore, Thailand - Died Thailand 29.6.43 - Buried Kanchanaburi
PEARSON Montague - D/SR8463 - HMS Thracian - Held Hong Kong - Died Hong Kong 12.10.42 - Buried Sai Wan Bay
PEARSON Thomas Wilfred - P/J54920 - HMS Moth - Held Hong Kong, Japan (Osaka Area)
PEEVOR Christopher John Gladstone - D/JX142963 - HMS Exeter - Held Celebes, Japan (Kyushu)
PELLEGRINI Emanuel - E/LX22370 - HMS Exeter - Held Celebes
PELLS James - C/SSX29989 - HMS Encounter - Held Celebes
PEMBERTON Allen Robertson - D/MX53896 - HMS Tamar - Held Hong Kong, Japan (Osaka Area)
PEMBLE Dennis M S - C/JX147713 - ML 432 - Held Sumatra (Palembang)
PENDLEBURY William - C/MX67011 - HMS Tamar - Held Hong Kong, Japan (Nagoya Area)
PENGELLY Harry - D/JX133698 - HMS Exeter - Held Celebes
PENNY Clarence - D/J208989 - HMS Exeter - Held Celebes
PERCY William Edwin - D/KX96016 - HMS Exeter - Held Celebes, Japan (Kyushu)
PERKINS Leslie George - D/MX46040 - HMS Tamar - Held Hong Kong - Died Lisbon Maru 2.10.42 - Named Plymouth Memorial
PERRY Albert Robert - C/J62778 - HMS Encounter - Held Celebes, Japan (Kyushu)
PERRYER Harold James - D/MX46556 - HMS Jupiter - Held Java, Moluccas - Died Taiwan Maru 24.8.44 - Named Plymouth Memorial
PERT William - D/JX153955 - HMS Exeter - Held Celebes, Japan (Kyushu)
PETERS Frederick Henry - D/JX188518 - HMS Exeter - Held Celebes - Died Makassar 25.3.45 - Buried

Ambon

PETERS Richard Edwin - RM - PLY/X506 - HMS Repulse - Held Singapore, Thailand

PHILLIPS Francis John James - D/JX420937 - HM Sub. Stratagem - Held Singapore (from Malacca Strait) - Died Singapore 31.12.44 - Named Plymouth Memorial

PHILLIPS Leonard - D/JX125514 - HMS Prince of Wales - Held Sumatra (Palembang)

PHILLIPS Roydon Clifford - D/JX193764 - HMS Exeter - Held Celebes, Japan (Kyushu)

PHILLIPS Sydney William Ernest - D/KX82081 - HMS Tamar - Held Hong Kong - Died Lisbon Maru 2.10.42 - Named Plymouth Memorial

PHILLIPS Walter W S - D/JX140201 - HMS Exeter - Held Celebes

PHILLIPS William Thomas - D/JX140180 - HMS Exeter - Held Celebes, Japan (Kyushu) - Died Japan 29.3.43 - Buried Yokohama

PHILP David Claude - D/KX88912 - HMS Exeter - Held Celebes - Died Makassar 23.7.42 - Buried Ambon

PHILPOTT James - C/JX173735 - HMS Encounter - Held Celebes

PHILPOTT Ronald - C/JX260594 - HMS Sultan - Held Sumatra (Palembang) - Died Palembang 10.9.45 - Buried Jakarta

PHYTHIAN Joseph - D/KX90338 - HMS Exeter - Held Celebes - Died Makassar 6.6.45 - Buried Ambon

PICKARD Harold - D/J108011 - HMS Sultan - Held Sumatra (Medan) - Died Harikiku Maru 26.6.44 - Named Plymouth Memorial

PICKERING Arnold - D/SSX17999 - HMS Exeter - Held Celebes, Japan (Kyushu)

PICKTHALL Joscelyn Richard Murrell - MRNVR - Sub Lt - HMS Mata Hari - Held Sumatra (Palembang), Singapore

PIKE Albert Stewart - D/JX177461 - HMS Jupiter - Held Java, Moluccas, Java

PIKE Horace Henry George - D/KX75591 - HMS Tamar - Held Hong Kong - Died Lisbon Maru 2.10.42 - Named Plymouth Memorial

PITT James Corrance - P/JX162022 - HMS Jupiter - Held Java, Moluccas - Died Maros Maru 1.10.44 - Named Plymouth Memorial

PLATT Frank - D/MX60255 - HMS Jupiter - Held Java, Moluccas, Java, Singapore

PLATTEN Richard Albert - D/JX169749 - HMS Dragonfly - Held Sumatra (Medan, Atjeh, Railway)

PLUMMER John Archibald Hugh - MRNVR - Lt - HMS Sultan - Held Sumatra (Palembang), Singapore

POINTING Victor Augustus - C/KX195943 - HMS Encounter - Held Celebes

POLAND Robert Edward - P/JX218158 - HMS Tamar - Held Hong Kong, Japan (Osaka Area)

POLKINGHORN Stephen - Lt - HMS Peterel - Held Shanghai, Japan (Hokkaido)

POLLARD Leonard Hugh - P/WRX622 - HMS Tamar - Held Hong Kong - Died Lisbon Maru 2.10.42 - Named Plymouth Memorial

POLLARD Walter Willliam George - C/JX129850 - Ship not known - Held Hong Kong, Japan (Osaka Area)

POLLITT Robert Henry - P/KX83981 - HMS Tern - Held Hong Kong, Japan (Osaka Area) - Died Japan 21.5.44 - Buried Yokohama

POLLOCK Joshua Thomas - Lt - Ship not known - Held Hong Kong, Japan (Osaka Area)

POOL Richard Anthony West - Lt - HMS Repulse - Held Singapore (from Jibbia), Thailand

POOLEY Charles Henry - P/SSX30155 - HMS Tamar - Held Hong Kong, Japan (Osaka Area)

POPE Alec - C/KX76805 - HMS Encounter - Held Celebes, Japan (Kyushu)

POPE Robert - C/JX239173 - SS Chilka - Held Sumatra (Medan), Singapore

POPE William Ernest - P/KX116535 - HMS Stronghold - Held Celebes - Died Makassar 19.3.45 - Buried Ambon

PORTCH William Henry Mark - D/JX168884 - HMS Scout - Held Sumatra (Medan), Singapore

PORTER Earnest K - D/JX213314 - HMS Exeter - Held Celebes

PORTER Ernest John Andrew - Lt - Ship not known - Held Hong Kong

PORTER Henry Charles - C/J97544 - Ship not known - Held Singapore (from Bangka)

PORTER John George - D/SSX19264 - HMS Exeter - Held Celebes - Died Makassar 17.3.45 - Buried Ambon

POTTER Benjamin - Lt - HMS Sultan - Held Java

POTTER John Francis - Lt - HMS Exeter - Held Celebes, Java

POTTS Jack Yuan HUTTON- see HUTTON-POTTS Jack Yuan

POTTS Richard Crossley - D/SSX28454 - HMS Jupiter - Held Java, Sumatra (Railway)

POULTER Ivor William - C/J108687 - HMS Encounter - Held Celebes

POWELL Albert Victor - D/MX46646 - HMS Tamar - Held Hong Kong - Died Lisbon Maru 2.10.42 - Named Plymouth Memorial

POWER Norman Hickey - Pm Lt - HMS Exeter - Held Celebes, Japan (Tokyo Area, Shikoku, Tokyo Area)

POWER Patrick - D/SSX22051 - HMS Stronghold - Held Celebes

POWLESLAND Alfred Sidney - D/JX177462 - HMS Exeter - Held Celebes

POWLEY John Walter - C/K63155 - HMS Tern - Held Hong Kong, Japan (Osaka Area)
PREECE Bernard John - RM - PLY/X384 - HMS Exeter - Held Celebes
PRESCOTT James - D/KX109282 - ML 432 - Held Singapore (from Bangka)
PRESS William Clifford - C/MX48233 - HMS Thanet - Held Sumatra (Medan, Railway)
PRESTON Charles - D/SSX19121 - HMS Stronghold - Held Celebes
PRESTON Frederick - P/JX259217 - HMS Exeter - Held Celebes, Japan (Kyushu)
PRESTON Kenneth James - P/MX79035 - HMS Sultan - Held Sumatra (Palembang)
PRESTON Walter Arthur Fredrich - D/KX112974 - HMS Stronghold - Held Celebes
PRICE Ernest Thomas - C/KX81053 - HMS Tern - Held Hong Kong, Japan (Tokyo Area) - Died Japan 3.2.43
- Buried Yokohama
PRICE Walter - D/JX235643 - HMS Tamar - Held Hong Kong, Japan (Osaka Area) - Died Japan 12.10.42
- Buried Yokohama
PRICE Wilfred Stephen - D/SSX25430 - HMS Prince of Wales - Held Sumatra (Palembang)
PRIEST William James - HKRNVR - W O - Ship not known - Held Hong Kong - Died Lisbon Maru 2.10.42
- Named Plymouth Memorial
PRIESTLEY Frederick - C/KX129633 - HMS Sultan - Held Sumatra (Palembang)
PRINCE Arthur Ernest - P/K67187 - HMS Peterel - Held Shanghai, Japan (Tokyo Area)
PRING Robert Henry Horatio - D/JX136601 - HMS Prince of Wales - Held Sumatra (Palembang), Singapore,
Taiwan, Japan (Tokyo Area, Sendai Area)
PRINGLE George Redmond - D/JX253839 - HMS Jupiter - Held Java, probably Moluccas, Java, Singapore
PRINGLE William - C/K58993 - HMS Tern - Held Hong Kong, Japan (Tokyo Area)
PRIOR Thomas Henry - D/JX127674 - HMS Exeter - Held Celebes - Died Pomelaa 15.6.43 - Buried Ambon
PRITCHARD Bertram Ernest - D/JX164231 - HMS Prince of Wales - Held Sumatra (Palembang)
PRITCHARD Richard - D/JX161407 - HMS Sultan - Held Sumatra (Medan) - Died Harikiku Maru 26.6.44
- Named Plymouth Memorial
PRYKE William Arthur James - P/MX68681 - HMS Tamar - Held Hong Kong - Died Lisbon Maru 2.10.42
- Named Plymouth Memorial
PUGH Edward Alexander - D/KX129123 - HMS Stronghold - Held Celebes
PULLEN Jack Arthur - D/KX123582 - HMS Exeter - Held Celebes, Japan (Kyushu)
PUNSHOW John - D/SSX26064 - Ship not known - Held Sumatra (Medan, Atjeh, Railway)
PURDY George Herbert - D/JX175810 - HMS Exeter - Held Celebes
PURNELL John Robert - D/JX140101 - HMS Exeter - Held Celebes
PURVES Alexander Graham - C/KX94791 - HMS Sultan - Held Java, Sumatra (Pangkalan Bali), Singapore
QUEEN George - D/SSX25644 - HMS Exeter - Held Celebes, Java
QUILLIAM Thomas Henry - Sub Lt - HMS Thracian - Held Hong Kong, Japan (Tokyo Area)
QUINN James - P/JX159300 - HMS Tamar - Held Hong Kong - Died Hong Kong 4.3.42 - Buried Stanley
QUINN John Joseph - RM - PLY/X3296 - HMS Tamar - Held Hong Kong, Japan (Osaka Area)
QUINN Patrick - D/SSX29386 - HMS Jupiter - Held Java, Moluccas, Celebes - Died Muna 19.10.44 - Buried
Ambon
RAE James Stewart - P/KX133843 - HMS Sultan - Held Sumatra (Medan, Railway) - Died Sumatra Railway
29.11.44 - Buried Jakarta
RAE Robert John - Midshipman - HMS Exeter - Held Celebes, Java
RAEE Wilfred James - C/KX78905 - HMS Encounter - Held Celebes, Japan (Kyushu)
RAILEY Francis David John - RM - PLY/X2102 - HMS Repulse - Held Sumatra (Palembang)
RAINBIRD Reginald - C/KX108188 - HMS Tern - Held Hong Kong, Japan (Tokyo Area, Sendai Area)
RAINEY Samuel - D/KX55652 - HMS Exeter - Held Celebes - Died Pomelaa 10.5.43 - Buried Ambon
RALPH Leslie Philip - HKRNVR - Lt - APV Shun Wo - Held Hong Kong
RAMSDEN John Richard - C/J60050 - HMS Tamar - Held Hong Kong - Died Lisbon Maru 2.10.42 - Named
Chatham Memorial
RANCE Ernest Roy - D/SSX18128 - HMS Exeter - Held Celebes - Died Makassar 27.4.45 - Buried Ambon
RASMUSSEN Kenneth Charles - RNZN - NZ/2425 - HMS Sultan - Held Sumatra (Medan), Burma - Died
Burma (Railway) 22.6.43 - Buried Thanbyuzayat
RAWLINGS Henry Thomas - C/J113653 - HMS Tern - Held Hong Kong, Japan (Osaka Area)
RAYNER Victor - C/KX101364 - HMS Tern - Held Hong Kong, Japan (Osaka Area, Nagoya Area)
READ Cecil Ernest John - P/MX65167 - HMS Stronghold - Held Celebes
READ Reginald John - HKRNVR - W O - HMS Tamar - Held Hong Kong - Died Lisbon Maru 2.10.42 -
Named Plymouth Memorial
REAMS Frederick - P/MX67983 - RN MTB - Held Hong Kong, Japan (Nagoya Area)
REDFERN Joseph Arthur - D/SSX35723 - HMS Jupiter - Held Java, Moluccas, Java
REDFERN Reginald - C/6962c - HMS Sultan - Held Java, Singapore, Borneo - Died Brunei 10.4.45 - Buried
Labuan

REDMAN Clarence William - P/JX276338 - HMS Sultan - Held Sumatra (Palembang) - Died Palembang 18.8.45 - Buried Jakarta
REDMAN James Howard - D/JX163106 - HMS Jupiter - Held Java, Sumatra (Railway)
REED Albert N S - P/J16986 - Ship not known - Held Sumatra (Palembang)
REED John Grescort - MRNVR - Surg Lt - HMS Laburnum - Held Sumatra (Palembang)
REES David Maurice - P/JX219796 - HMS Stronghold - Held Celebes
REID James Kenneth - D/MX73353 - HMS Repulse - Held Java, Sumatra (Pangkalan Bali)
REID Philip Henry Stewart - Com - Ship not known - Held Sumatra (Palembang), Singapore
RENDELL Edwin Charles - D/JX204381 - HMS Repulse - Held Sumatra (Palembang)
RENDELL John Richard - D/MX55986 - HMS Exeter - Held Celebes
REYNOLDS Alfred John - P/SS125467 - HMS Tamar - Held Hong Kong - Died Lisbon Maru 2.10.42 - Named Plymouth Memorial
REYNOLDS Harold - D/SSX22829 - HMS Exeter - Held Celebes
REYNOLDS Leonard - W O - SS Nankin - Held Japan (Tokyo Area) - captured in Indian Ocean
REYNOLDS Leonard Jack - RM - PLY/X874 - HMS Prince of Wales - Held Celebes - Died Makassar 4.4.45 - Buried Ambon
RHODES Thomas - C/SSX16072 - Ship not known - Held Hong Kong, Japan (Osaka Area)
RICE Francis Leo - D/JX134212 - HMS Exeter - Held Celebes - Died Makassar 13.4.44 - Buried Ambon
RICE Thomas - P/JX148679 - HMS Tamar - Held Hong Kong - Died Lisbon Maru 2.10.42 - Named Plymouth Memorial
RICHARDS Arthur Alfred - C/JX131039 - HMS Laburnum - Held Sumatra (Palembang)
RICHARDS Gustave Leon Charles - C/KX77360 - HMS Encounter - Held Celebes
RICHARDS Willliam Henry - D/MX54610 - HMS Exeter - Held Celebes
RICHARDSON Hector Duplessis - Com - HMS Exeter - Held Celebes, Japan (Tokyo Area, Shikoku, Tokyo Area)
RICHARDSON John Frank - D/SSX25343 - HMS Prince of Wales - Held Sumatra (Palembang)
RICHARDSON Joseph Hallsworth - RM - PO/X89 - HMS Tamar - Held Hong Kong - Died Lisbon Maru 2.10.42 - Named Plymouth Memorial
RICHARDSON Victor Ernest - W O Bwain - ˙HMS Sultan - Held Singapore (from Jibbia), Thailand
RICHENS Albert William - C/J104919 - HMS Encounter - Held Celebes
RICHMOND Alexander - D/JX184688 - HMS Exeter - Held Celebes - Died Makassar 22.1.45 - Buried Ambon
RICKETT Cedric Arthur Lacy - HKRNVR - Lt - HMS Cornflower - Held Hong Kong
RIGDEN Henry Thomas - MRNVR - Lt - HMS Sultan - Held Sumatra (Medan), Singapore, Thailand
RIGGS Reginald Henry - D/J95220 - HMS Exeter - Held Celebes, Japan (Kyushu)
RILEY Edward Patrick - RNZN - NZ/3099 - HMS Mata Hari - Held Singapore (from Bangka Strait)
RILEY William - P/K25893 - HMS Exeter - Held Celebes - Died Makassar - 8.3.45 - Buried Ambon
RILEY William George - D/JX237574 - HMS Jupiter - Held Java, Moluccas - Died Maros Maru 24.9.44 - Named Plymouth Memorial
RIPLEY Thomas - C/KX111230 - HMS Thracian - Held Hong Kong, Japan (Osaka Area, Nagoya Area)
RITCHENS Stanley Herbert - D/JX148278 - HM Sub. Stratagem - Held Singapore (from Malacca Strait) - Died Singapore 31.12.44 - Named Plymouth Memorial
RITCHIE C D - MRNVR - SE/XE5 - Ship not known - Held Sumatra (Palembang) - Died Palembang 16.10.43 - Buried Jakarta
RIX John Arthur - RNZN - NZD/7426 - HMS Barlight - Held Hong Kong, Japan (Osaka Area)
ROACH Walter Herbert - C/J105329 - HMS Encounter - Held Celebes
ROBB David Scott - HKRNVR - Pm Sub Lt - Ship not known - Held Hong Kong
ROBBINS John Sydney - D/KX92150 - HMS Exeter - Held Celebes
ROBERTS Arthur - C/JX206218 - ML 432 - Held Sumatra (Palembang)
ROBERTS Charles John - D/MX49997 - HMS Exeter - Held Celebes, Japan (Kyushu)
ROBERTS Christmas - C/JX176872 - HMS Sultan - Held Singapore
ROBERTS David Elio - P/MX68557 - HMS Sultan - Held Sumatra (Palembang)
ROBERTS Fred - D/KX114267 - HMS Exeter - Held Celebes - Died Makassar 22.3.45 - Buried Ambon
ROBERTS George - D/JX222004 - HMS Encounter - Held Celebes
ROBERTS Raymond William - P/JX132133 - HMS Sultan - Held Sumatra (Medan) - Died Harikiku Maru 26.6.44 - Named Plymouth Memorial
ROBERTSON William - HKRNVR - W O - Ship not known - Held Hong Kong
ROBINS Arthur - D/JX143549 - Ship not known - Held Singapore, Taiwan, Japan (Tokyo Area)
ROBINS Joseph Clifford - D/MX57736 - HMS Exeter - Held Celebes, Japan (Kyushu)
ROBINS Peter Eric - D/MX70269 - HMS Repulse - Held Sumatra (Palembang)
ROBINSON Charles R (29.4.15) - C/MX48323 - HMS Tamar - Held Hong Kong - Died Lisbon Maru 2.10.42

- Named Chatham Memorial

ROBINSON Charles Rupert (29.12.04) - HKRNVR - Act Sub Lt - Ship not known - Held Hong Kong

ROBINSON F N - MRNVR - SE/XE/1 - HMS Sultan - Held Sumatra (Palembang)

ROBINSON Henry Charles - P/MX69813 - HMS Tamar - Held Hong Kong - Died Lisbon Maru 2.10.42 - Named Plymouth Memorial

ROBINSON Henry William - D/JX248187 - HM Sub. Stratagem - Held Singapore (from Malacca Strait), Japan (Tokyo Area)

ROBINSON James (<12.9.16) - RM - PLY/X3175 - HMS Repulse - Held Singapore (from Jibbia), Thailand - Died Rakuyo Maru 12.9.44 - Named Plymouth Memorial

ROBINSON James (28.7.21) - P/MX72523 - HMS Laburnum - Held Sumatra (Palembang)

ROBINSON Leslie - P/JX276280 - HMS Sultan - Held Sumatra (Palembang)

ROBSON James - D/KX115303 - HMS Repulse - Held Java, Sumatra (Railway)

ROBSON John - Lt - HMS Fuh Wo - Held Sumatra (Palembang), Singapore, Taiwan, Japan (Tokyo Area. Shikoku, Kyushu)

ROCKETT Ronald William - D/JX234235 - HMS Jupiter - Held Java, Moluccas - Died Maros Maru 3.10.44 - Named Plymouth Memorial

RODGERS Ernest Rex - HKRNVR - W O - Ship not known - Held Hong Kong, Japan (Osaka Area)

RODGERS Stephen Patterson - D/MX54162 - HMS Tamar - Held Hong Kong - Died Lisbon Maru 2.10.42 - Named Plymouth Memorial

RODRIGUES Edward L - HKRNVR - Sgm - Ship not known - Held Hong Kong

RODRIGUES Leandro M - HKRNVR - Sgm - Ship not known - Held Hong Kong

ROE John Andrew - D/JX145900 - HMS Exeter - Held Celebes

ROEBUCK Donald Vivian - Sub Lt (A) - HMS Victorious - Held Sumatra (Palembang), Singapore - Died Singapore >15.8.45 - Named Lee-on-Solent Memorial

ROGAN William G - D/X181788 - HMS Exeter - Held Celebes, Japan (Kyushu)

ROGERS Albert - RM - PLY/X2257 - HMS Repulse - Held Sumatra (Medan, Railway)

ROGERS Charles - FAA/FX82905 - HMS Illustrious - Held Andaman Is., Japan (Tokyo Area)

ROGERS Charles Halma - D/JX125387 - HMS Repulse - Held Sumatra (Palembang)

ROGERS Frederick - P/KX87726 - HMS Grasshopper - Held Sumatra (Medan), Burma - Died Burma (Railway) - 18.12.43 - Buried Thanbyuzayat

ROGERS George Henry - RM - PO/13198 - HMS Tamar - Held Hong Kong, Taiwan, Manchuria

ROGERS Henry Albert - RM - PLY/20713 - HMS Tamar - Held Hong Kong

ROGERS James - HKRNVR - W O - HMS Cornflower - Held Hong Kong, Japan (Osaka Area) - Died Japan - 15.1.45 - Buried Yokohama

ROGERS Joseph Thomas - P/MX50729 - HMS Redstart - Held Hong Kong, Japan (Osaka Area) - Died Japan 19.10.42 - Buried Yokohama

ROGERS Joseph William - RM - PLY/X100028 - HMS Exeter - Held Celebes - Died Makassar 24.3.45 - Buried Ambon

ROGERS Thomas - C/KX107168 - HMS Thracian - Held Hong Kong, Japan (Osaka Area)

ROGERS William Ambrose - D/MX64723 - HMS Sultan - Held Sumatra (Palembang)

ROGERSON George - RM - PLY/X1748 - HMS Tamar - Held Hong Kong, Japan (Osaka Area)

ROGERSON Jack - FAA/JX604478 - HMS Indefatigable - Held Japan (Tokyo Area)

ROGERSON Thomas John - Lt - HMS Tamar - Held Hong Kong - Died Hong Kong 11.3.42 - Buried Stanley

ROLFE William Redvers - C/J57713 - HMS Cicala - Held Hong Kong - Died Hong Kong 16.12.42 - Buried Stanley

ROOK Cyril - D/JX241054 - HMS Exeter - Held Celebes

ROOME David Gordon - Sub Lt - HMS Exeter - Held Celebes, Java

ROONEY William - D/SSX23161 - HMS Mata Hari - Held Singapore (from Bangka)

ROOS Victor Edward - C/JX141248 - HMS Tamar - Held Hong Kong - Died Lisbon Maru 2.10.42 - Named Chatham Memorial

ROPER James - D/MX48153 - HMS Sultan - Held Sumatra (Medan) - Died Harikiku Maru 26.6.44 - Named Plymouth Memorial

ROSE John Stephenson - HKRNVR - Sub Lt - Ship not known - Held Hong Kong

ROSE Stanley Frederick - C/JX126536 - HMS Encounter - Held Celebes

ROSS David Pryde - HKRNVR - Act Sub Lt - HMS Cornflower - Held Hong Kong

ROSS Stephen Campbell - D/JX184660 - HMS Exeter - Held Celebes, Japan (Kyushu)

ROSS William Simpson - HKRNVR - Sub Lt - HMS Cornflower - Held Hong Kong

ROSSITER Frederick Charles - RM - PLY/X100135 - HMS Prince of Wales - Held Singapore, Thailand - Died Thailand 18.7.43 - Named Plymouth Memorial

ROUE James Nicholas - D/JX169187 - HMS Grasshopper - Held Sumatra (Medan, Atjeh, Railway)

UNSUNG HEROES of the ROYAL NAVY and ROYAL MARINES

ROUGHLEY Robert Henry - D/JX146250 - HMS Tamar - Held Hong Kong, Japan (Osaka Area)
ROWE Frank - D/J32869 - HMS Prince of Wales - Held Java, Singapore, Borneo
ROWLAND Kenneth Cleadon - P/JX239541 - HMS Exeter - Held Celebes
ROWSE Joseph Arthur Cecil - D/MX84341 - HMS Exeter - Held Celebes
RUDDICK Charles - D/SSX16227 - HMS Exeter - Held Celebes
RUFFLES Harry - D/SSX29590 - HMS Jupiter - Held Java, Moluccas - Died Maros Maru 14.11.44 - Named Plymouth Memorial
RULE Charles Arnold - P/MX67982 - RN MTB - Held Hong Kong, Japan (Osaka Area)
RUSE Roy Samuel Charles - D/M22034 - HMS Exeter - Held Celebes
RUSHMAN Mervyn Francis - RM - PLY/X488 - HMS Tamar - Held Hong Kong - Died Lisbon Maru 2.10.42 - Named Plymouth Memorial
RUSSELL Edmund - P/M38592 - HMS Encounter - Held Celebes - Died Makassar 13.2.45 - Buried Ambon
RUSSELL James Frederick - D/MX66241 - HMS Exeter - Held Celebes - Died Makassar 22.3.45 - Buried Ambon
RUSSELL Reginald Charles - C/LDX2725 - HMS Encounter - Held Celebes
RUTHERFORD Robert - HKRNVR - Lt - HMS Cornflower - Held Hong Kong
RYALLS David Noel - Lt Com Surg - HMS Exeter - Held Celebes, Java, Singapore - Died Tamahoko Maru 24.6.44 - Named Plymouth Memorial
RYAN Raymond Frank William - C/MX76018 - HMS Encounter - Held Celebes - Died Makassar 19.4.45 - Buried Ambon
RYAN Thomas Henry - D/JX172380 - HMS Sultan - Held Sumatra (Medan), Burma, Thailand, Indo China Died Saigon - 26.8.44 - Buried Kranji
SAMPSON Ronald - RM - PLY/X2755 - HMS Repulse - Held Sumatra (Palembang)
SANDERSON Ronald - RM - PLY/X714 - HMS Tamar - Held Hong Kong, Japan (Osaka Area)
SARGEANT Ronald Kenneth - C/JX81447 - HMS Sultan - Held Sumatra (Palembang)
SARNEY John Horace - RNZN - NZ/1631 - HMS Kuala - Held Sumatra (Medan), Burma, Thailand
SAUNDERS Albert Edward - D/J109279 - HMS Exeter - Held Celebes - Died Pomelaa 2.9.43 - Buried Ambon
SAVAGE James Ogle - D/JX188536 - HMS Exeter - Held Celebes
SAVAGE Robert - D/JX180546 - HMS Exeter - Held Celebes
SAWYER William Arthur - C/J101193 - HMS Tamar - Held Hong Kong - Died Lisbon Maru 2.10.42 - Named Chatham Memorial
SAYERS Mark - D/KX77821 - HMS Repulse - Held Singapore
SCALLY Dennis Frederick Joseph - P/MX80371 - HMS Tamar - Held Hong Kong, Japan (Osaka Area) - Died Japan 11.5.43 - Buried Yokohama
SCANTLEBURY Edward Ernest - RM - PLY/X1056 - HMS Prince of Wales - Held Singapore, Thailand Died Rakuyo Maru 12.9.44 - Named Plymouth Memorial
SCHOFIELD Norman Neville - D/JX145469 - HMS Exeter - Held Celebes, Japan (Tokyo Area)
SCHOFIELD Ralph - D/SSX19755 - HMS Thracian - Held Hong Kong, Japan (Osaka Area) - Died Japan 27.10.42 - Buried Yokohama
SCOTT Bernard - MRNVR - Com - HMS Laburnum - Held Sumatra (Palembang), Singapore
SCOTT Frederick - D/KX102776 - HMS Sultan - Held Sumatra (Medan), Burma - Died Burma (Railway) 9.2.44 - Buried Thanbyuzayat
SCOTT-LINDSLEY Mervyn Ewart - Lt - Ship not known - Held Hong Kong
SCRIPPS Terence Austin - D/J166590 - HMS Exeter - Held Celebes - Died Makassar 29.3.45 - Buried Ambon
SCUDAMORE Cecil Charles - D/MX69893 - HMS Exeter - Held Celebes
SCUTTS Jack M - D/KX111624 - HMS Prince of Wales - Held Singapore (from Bangka)
SEABY John - HKRNVR - W O - HMS Cornflower - Held Hong Kong, Japan (Osaka Area)
SEARLE Leslie Bertram - P/KX99269 - HMS Dragonfly - Held Sumatra (Medan, Railway)
SEAWARD Lloyd - D/JX191531 - HMS Exeter - Held Celebes
SEDDON Robert Henry - RM - PLY/X1717 - HMS Repulse - Held Sumatra (Palembang)
SEDGEBEER Ashley - D/KX105957 - Ship not known - Held Sumatra (Medan), Burma, Thailand
SELBY Henry Charles Sylveter Collinwood - Lt Com - HMS Redstart - Held Hong Kong
SENIOR Cyril Alderman - RM - PLY/X3769 - HMS Repulse - Held Singapore, Thailand
SERCOMBE William Morley - D/MX49610 - HMS Tamar - Held Hong Kong - Died Lisbon Maru 2.10.42 - Named Plymouth Memorial
SHARP Henry Thomas - C/M38907 - HMS Tamar - Held Hong Kong - Died Lisbon Maru 2.10.42 - Named Chatham Memorial
SHARPE Adrian Leslie - MRNVR - Pm Lt - HMS Sultan - Held Sumatra (Palembang)
SHARPLES John - MRNVR - Sub Lt - HMS Siang Wo - Held Java

SHARPLEY Thomas - D/JX184682 - HMS Exeter - Held Celebes

SHAW Arthur Bernard - D/JX180615 - HMS Exeter - Held Celebes

SHAW Herbert - D/JX148031 - HMS Exeter - Held Celebes - Died Makassar 5.4.45 - Buried Ambon

SHAW John - RM - PLY/X100068 - HMS Exeter - Held Celebes

SHAW Reginald James Anthony - Sub Lt (A) - HMS Illustrious - Held Sumatra (Palembang), Singapore - Died Singapore >15.8.45 - Named Lee-on-Solent Memorial

SHAW Stanley Walter - D/JX167441 HMS Sultan - Held Sumatra (Palembang) - Died Palembang 6.8.45 - Buried Jakarta

SHAWCROSS Wilfred - D/MX72876 - HMS Exeter - Held Celebes, Japan (Kyushu)

SHEARGOLD Kenneth - C/KX127552 - HMS Sultan - Held Singapore, Taiwan, Japan (Tokyo Area, Sendai Area) - Died Japan 12.7.45 - Buried Sydney

SHELLARD Patrick Philip - Lt - HMS Sultan - Held Singapore (from Indian Ocean), Thailand

SHELLEY George Gilbert - W O Gnr - HMS Exeter - Held Celebes

SHEPHERD Basil Lawrence Howard - MRNVR - Sub Lt - HMS Laburnum - Held Sumatra (Palembang), Singapore

SHEPHERD William Grant - P/MX78147 - HMS Cicala - Held Hong Kong, Japan (Osaka Area)

SHERIDAN Gerald Thomas Brinsley - RM - Lt - HMS Prince of Wales - Held Singapore, Thailand

SHERMAN Solomon - D/JX192821 - HMS Tamar - Held Hong Kong - Died Lisbon Maru 2.10.42 - Named Plymouth Memorial

SHERRATT Clifford William - D/JX194998 - HMS Exeter - Held Celebes - Died Makassar 29.8.43 - Buried Ambon

SHEWRING William James - D/JX166616 - HMS Repulse - Held Sumatra (Palembang)

SHIELDS Douglas Walter - D/SSX29267 - HMS Jupiter - Held Java, Moluccas, Celebes - Died Muna 26.10.44 - Buried Ambon

SHIELDS Thomas Perkins - P/ED195 - HMS Tamar - Held Hong Kong - Died Lisbon Maru 2.10.42 - Named Plymouth Memorial

SHILTON Robert Percival Henry - D/J69414 - HMS Exeter - Held Celebes, Japan (Tokyo Area) - Died Japan 19.4.45 - Named Plymouth Memorial

SHINNER Raymond Claud - D/KX98106 - HMS Jupiter - Held Java, Moluccas - Died Ambon 3.10.44 - Buried Ambon

SHIPMAN Ian Frances George - RNZN - NZ/2171 - HMS Exeter - Held Celebes, Japan

SHIPSIDES Kenneth - D/MX50718 - HMS Tamar - Held Hong Kong, Japan (Nagoya Area)

SHIRKEY John Dollar - P/SSX14017 - HMS Tern - Held Hong Kong - Died Lisbon Maru 2.10.42 - Named Plymouth Memorial

SHIRLEY Allan - D/JX134375 - HMS Exeter - Held Celebes

SHORT Gerald Bartlett - D/JX184619 - HMS Exeter - Held Celebes - Died Makassar 3.5.45 - Buried Ambon

SHORT Henry Edward - C/J40659 - Mining Party - Held Hong Kong, Japan (Osaka Area)

SHRIGLEY William - D/JX134156 - Ship not known - Held Hong Kong, Japan (Osaka Area, Hiroshima Area)

SHUTE Ernest George - P/KX90520 - HMS Tapah - Held Singapore (from Bangka)

SIDDANS John - D/J115494 - HMS Tamar - Held Hong Kong - Died Lisbon Maru 2.10.42 - Named Plymouth Memorial

SIDLEY William Frank - P/SSX25548 - HMS Sultan - Held Java, Sumatra (Railway)

SIEWCZYNSKI Frederick William - D/JX149134 - HMS Sultan - Held Sumatra (Palembang) - Died Palembang 6.8.45 - Buried Jakarta

SILVERTHORNE Thomas Charles Moss - C/JX135001 - Ship not known - Held Hong Kong, Japan (Osaka Area)

SIM Alexander Woodrow Stuart - MRNVR - Sub Lt - Ship not known - Held Sumatra (Medan), Singapore, Sumatra (Railway)

SIMCOCK Henry Hugh - P/MX65693 - HMS Sultan - Held Sumatra (Medan), Burma - Died Burma (Railway) 1.10.43 - Buried Thanbyuzayat

SIMMONDS Cecil Stanley - C/JX152643 - HMS Pelandok - Held Sumatra (Palembang)

SIMMONDS George William - RM - PLY/X3814 - HMS Prince of Wales - Held Singapore, Thailand

SIMMONDS Harold Augustine Pearce P - P/J32688 - HMS Tamar - Held Hong Kong - Died Lisbon Maru 2.10.42 - Named Plymouth Memorial

SIMONDS Frank Hartley - D/JX136537 - HMS Thracian - Held Hong Kong

SIMONS Albert Edward Ronald - D/KX112322 - HMS Encounter - Held Celebes

SIMPSON Charles - C/JX175976 - HMS Ying Pin - Held Singapore (from Bangka)

SIMPSON William - C/KX104981 - Ship not known - Held Java, Singapore, Borneo - Died Labuan 20.1.45 - Named Chatham Memorial

SINCLAIR Charles - C/JX151440 - HMS Moth - Held Hong Kong - Died Hong Kong 28.9.42 - Buried

Stanley
SISSON Ralph Edward - Pm Lt - Ship not known - Held Hong Kong
SKEDGELL Albert - D/JX135065 - HMS Repulse - Held Sumatra (Palembang)
SKELLEY Albert William - Lt - HMS Barlight - Held Hong Kong
SKELTON Rupert John - D/MX54820 - HMS Exeter - Held Celebes, Japan (Kyushu)
SKERITT Everett Albert - C/JX190950 - HMS Electra - Held Java, probably Moluccas, Java, Singapore
SKINNER Sidney Albert - C/JX132691 - HMS Tern - Held Hong Kong, Japan (Osaka Area) - Died Japan 3.3.43 - Buried Yokohama
SLADE Norman Alan - P/JX125897 - HMS Sultan - Held Java, Moluccas, Java, Singapore, Sumatra (Railway)
SLATER Arthur - D/JX94870 - HMS Repulse - Held Sumatra (Palembang)
SLATER Roland - P/JX162454 - HMS Grasshopper - Held Sumatra (Medan) - Died Harikiku Maru 26.6.44 - Named Plymouth Memorial
SMALE Albert Edward - C/J27525 - HMS Tamar - Held Hong Kong - Died Lisbon Maru 2.10.42 - Named Chatham Memorial
SMALE William Thomas Gordon - D/KX105373 - Ship not known - Held Sumatra (Medan), Burma, Thailand
SMALL Eric William - D/KX80043 - HMS Thracian - Held Hong Kong, Japan (Nagoya Area)
SMALL Frederick C - D/J114826 - HMS Exeter - Held Celebes
SMALL Matthew - D/KX94477 - Ship not known - Held Sumatra (Medan), Singapore, Sumatra (Railway)
SMALLEY Walter Norman Adams - HKRNVR - Sub Lt - Ship not known - Held Hong Kong
SMART Sidney James - D/JX204426 - HMS Exeter - Held Celebes
SMART Stanley George - D/KX81418 - HMS Tamar - Held Hong Kong, Japan (Osaka Area) - Died Japan 1.2.43 - Buried Yokohama
SMITH Alexander - P/KX83885 - HMS Peterel - Held Shanghai, Japan (Tokyo Area)
SMITH Alfred Albert Charles - C/JX260616 - HMS Sultan - Held Sumatra (Palembang)
SMITH Basil George - D/J79589 - HMS Pelandok - Held Sumatra (Palembang)
SMITH Cecil Kennedy Stewart - HKRNVR - Act Sub Lt - Ship not known - Held Hong Kong
SMITH Clarence Frederick Frank - P/JX143405 - HMS Grasshopper - Held Sumatra (Medan, Railway)
SMITH Cyril - D/JX239595 - HMS Exeter - Held Celebes
SMITH Edward James - C/JX165169 - HMS Dragon - Held Java, Singapore, Japan (Osaka Area)
SMITH Edwin Leslie George - P/J28740 - HMS Tamar - Held Hong Kong, Japan (Osaka Area) - Died Japan 12.11.42 - Buried Yokohama
SMITH Eugene Patrick - D/JX125408 - HMS Exeter - Held Celebes
SMITH Frank Claud - D/SSX19337 - HMS Repulse - Held Java, Sumatra (Pangkalan Bali), Singapore
SMITH Frank William - C/JX175717 - HMS Thracian - Held Hong Kong, Japan (Tokyo Area, Sendai Area)
SMITH Frederick - D/JX23382 - HMS Prince of Wales - Held Sumatra (Palembang)
SMITH Frederick Charles Henry - MRNVR - Pm Lt - HMS Sultan - Held Sumatra (Palembang), Singapore
SMITH George Henry - P/JX169274 - Ship not known - Held Sumatra (Medan), Burma, Thailand
SMITH James Eric - RM - PLY/X3831 - HMS Repulse - Held Sumatra (Palembang)
SMITH John Basil Gustave - HKRNVR - Sub Lt - Ship not known - Held Hong Kong
SMITH John D - P/JX273681 - HMS Exeter - Held Celebes
SMITH John Kynan - D/KX82612 - HMS Exeter - Held Celebes
SMITH John William Gilbert - D/JX158070 - HMS Jupiter - Held Java, Moluccas, Celebes, Java
SMITH Kenneth Roy - D/JX184557 - HMS Exeter - Held Celebes
SMITH Leonard George - P/J19217 - Mining Party - Held Hong Kong
SMITH Leslie Alexander - D/JX22129 - HMS Sultan - Held Java, Singapore - Died Tamahoko Maru 24.6.44 - Named Plymouth Memorial
SMITH Leslie Spurrell - D/MX23140 - HMS Exeter - Held Celebes - Died Makassar 28.2.45 - Buried Ambon
SMITH Maurice Arthur - W O Elect - HMS Exeter - Held Celebes
SMITH Ralph Richard Thomas - HKRNVR - Act Lt - HMS Cornflower - Held Hong Kong
SMITH Robert Alexander MacMillan - D/JX188577 - HMS Exeter - Held Celebes
SMITH Sidney - D/KX75526 - HMS Tamar - Held Hong Kong, Japan (Tokyo Area) - Died Japan 27.11.42 - Buried Yokohama
SMITH Stanley George - RM - PLY/X3803 - HMS Prince of Wales - Held Sumatra (Palembang)
SMITH Stanley Robert - D/KX112348 - HMS Encounter - Held Celebes - Died Makassar 24.3.45 - Buried Ambon
SMITH Thomas - C/KX128239 - HMS Exeter - Held Celebes, Japan (Kyushu)
SMITH Walter T - P/KX112350 - HMS Grasshopper - Held Sumatra (Medan), Burma, Thailand
SMITH William Edward - P/KX87116 - HMS Grasshopper - Held Sumatra (Medan, Railway) - Died Sumatra

Railway 25.7.45 - Buried Jakarta
SMITH William McRory - D/KX87075 - HMS Exeter - Held Celebes, Japan (Kyushu)
SMITH William Reginald Thomas - RM - PLY/X1916 - HMS Repulse - Held Singapore (from Sinkep), Borneo
SMYTH William - D/JX143426 - Ship not known - Held Sumatra (Medan), Burma, Thailand
SNEDDON James - RM - PLY/X1375 - Ship not known - Held Singapore (from Sinkep), Thailand
SOLE Arthur Lawrence - P/JX236167 - HMS Exeter - Held Celebes
SOLOMAN James - C/SSX14431 - HMS Encounter - Held Celebes, Japan (Kyushu)
SOLWAY Edward George - Lt Com - Ship not known - Held Hong Kong
SOMMERFELT Allister - HKRNVR - Pm Lt - Ship not known - Held Hong Kong
SOPER George Sydney Norman - D/MX51596 - HMS Exeter - Held Celebes, Japan (Kyushu) - Died Japan 7.3.43 - Buried Yokohama
SOPER Leonard Charles - C/JX177500 - HMS Tamar - Held Hong Kong, Japan (Tokyo Area)
SOUTER Farquhar - D/SSX35795 - HMS Exeter - Held Celebes
SOUTH James - D/K65629 - Ship not known - Held Hong Kong, Japan (Tokyo Area)
SOUTHGATE Dennis Thomas Harry - RM - PLY/X3806 - HMS Prince of Wales - Held Singapore, Thailand, Japan (Kyushu)
SOUTHWORTH Eric - Lt - HMS Exeter - Held Celebes, Java
SPALDING Robert - C/J91849 - HMS Encounter - Held Celebes
SPALLE Roy Ernest - D/MX48891 - HMS Exeter - Held Celebes
SPARKS William John - D/JX125134 - HMS Prince of Wales - Held Sumatra (Medan, Atjeh, Railway)
SPASHETT Peter Arthur - D/JX184945 - HMS Encounter - Held Celebes, Java
SPAULL G R - MRNVR - Lt Com - HMS Sultan - Held Sumatra (Palembang), Singapore
SPEAR Philip - Sub Lt - HMS Exeter - Held Celebes, Java
SPENCER Victor - D/SSX23078 - HMS Sultan - Held Sumatra (Palembang) - Died Palembang 24.7.45 - Buried Jakarta
SPENCER Victor Henry - -/FX96677 - HMS Indefatigable - Held Japan (Tokyo Area)
SPENDLOVE Albert - C/JX131500 - HMS Li Wo - Held Sumatra (Palembang)
SPENDLOVE Aubrey John - RM - PLY/X1278 - HMS Exeter - Held Celebes
SPICER Richard Kingsley - D/JX144685 - HMS Exeter - Held Celebes
SPILLER William Ronald - C/JX178739 - HMS Dragonfly - Held Sumatra (Medan, Railway) - Died Sumatra Railway 5.6.45 - Buried Jakarta
SPILMAN Frank - Lt Com - HMS Siang Wo - Held Sumatra (Palembang), Singapore
SPINKS John William - C/SSX14312 - HMS Encounter - Held Celebes
SPIRIT Robert - D/JX131484 - RN MTB - Held Hong Kong, Japan (Osaka Area)
SPRAGUE James Samuel - D/JX169031 - HMS Anking - Held Java, Sumatra (Railway)
SPREADBURY William James - P/JX144106 - Stonecutters - Held Hong Kong, Japan (Osaka Area)
SPREAT Arthur Charles - D/JX130162 - HMS Jupiter - Held Java, Moluccas, Celebes - Died Muna 1.3.45 - Buried Ambon
SQUIRE Albert Victor - D/JX137856 - HMS Repulse - Held Singapore (from Bangka Strait)
SQUIRE Arthur Alfred - D/JX208413 - HMS Exeter - Held Celebes
STACEY Edward - P/J22877 - Mining Party - Held Hong Kong, Japan (Osaka Area, Nagoya Area)
STAFFORD Herbert William - C/JX197602 - HMS Electra - Held Java, Moluccas, Java
STAGG Ernest Albert - C/JX265607 - SS Willesden - Held Japan (Tokyo Area) - captured in S Atlantic
STAINER Victor Vulcan - P/JX2583 - Mining Party - Held Hong Kong, Japan (Osaka Area)
STALEY Thomas William - P/JX131007 - HMS Moth - Held Hong Kong, Japan (Osaka Area)
STALLARD Joseph Joyner - P/JX159202 - HMS Jupiter - Held Java, Moluccas, Java
STANTON Ronald George Gladstone - Sub Lt - HMS Li Wo - Held Sumatra (Palembang), Singapore
STANWORTH Joseph - D/MX64942 - HMS Exeter - Held Celebes, Japan (Kyushu)
STAPLES John William - P/SSX28017 - HMS Kedah - Held Singapore, Thailand
STARE George Christopher - P/SSX31692 - HMS Tamar - Held Hong Kong, Japan (Osaka Area) - Died Japan 7.3.43 - Buried Yokohama
STAUNTON Harold - D/JX184685 - HMS Exeter - Held Celebes
STEARNS Harry Roger - C/K62955 - HMS Encounter - Held Celebes
STEDMAN John Frederick - P/J112040 - HMS Tamar - Held Hong Kong, Japan (Osaka Area)
STEED Thomas Henry - C/SR59 - HMS Tamar - Held Hong Kong - Died Lisbon Maru 2.10.42 - Named Chatham Memorial
STEEL Robert Alexander - C/JX169711 - HMS Encounter - Held Celebes, Japan (Kyushu)
STEELE William John - D/MX52695 - HMS Exeter - Held Celebes
STEIN George Keir - MRNVR - Lt - ML 1062 - Held Sumatra (Palembang), Singapore
STEPHENSON William - RM - PLY/X1622 - HMS Exeter - Held Celebes, Japan (Kyushu)

STEPHENSON William Ralph Ewing - HKRNVR - Lt - Ship not known - Held Hong Kong
STEVENS Alfred Watson - P/J22598 - HMS Tamar - Held Hong Kong - Died Hong Kong 9.12.42 - Buried Stanley
STEVENS Leonard - P/JX239344 - HMS Exeter - Held Celebes - Died Makassar 28.4.44 - Buried Ambon
STEVENSON Leslie James - HKRNVR - Lt Com - APV Frosty - Held Hong Kong
STEWART Donald Campbell - D/JX146752 - HMS Tamar - Held Hong Kong, Japan (Osaka Area) - Died Japan 7.5.44 - Buried Yokohama
STEWART James - P/WRX497 - Stonecutters - Held Hong Kong, Japan (Osaka Area)
STEWART James H - D/JX188567 - HMS Exeter - Held Celebes
STEWART Murdo - RNZN - NZ/7421 - Ship not known - Held Hong Kong - Died Lisbon Maru 2.10.42 - Named New Zealand Memorial
STICKLAND Francis Alfred - P/KX110216 - HMS Thracian - Held Hong Kong, Japan (Tokyo Area)
STIMSON Douglas Charles - C/KX100699 - HMS Thracian - Held Hong Kong, Japan (Osaka Area)
STOCK Robert - HKRNVR - Lt - Ship not known - Held Hong Kong
STOKER Ralph William - P/ED190 - HMS Tamar - Held Hong Kong - Died Lisbon Maru 2.10.42 - Named Plymouth Memorial
STOKES David - P/J34983 - HMS Tamar - Held Hong Kong, Japan (Osaka Area) - Died Japan 24.1.43 - Buried Yokohama
STOKES John Leslie - RM - PLY/22226 - HMS Repulse - Held Singapore, Thailand
STONE Bernard Oliver Benjamin - D/JX213055 - HMS Exeter - Held Celebes, Japan (Kyushu)
STONE Harold - D/JX204446 - HMS Exeter - Held Celebes, Java
STONE Joseph Mathias Hippsley - RM - PLY/X100136 - HMS Prince of Wales - Held Sumatra (Palembang)
STONE Thomas John - D/KX94034 - HMS Tamar - Held Hong Kong - Died Lisbon Maru 2.10.42 - Named Plymouth Memorial
STONES Joseph Herbert - D/JX155907 - HMS Repulse - Held Sumatra (Palembang)
STOTT Geoffrey Holt - D/JX170952 - HMS Exeter - Held Celebes, Japan (Kyushu)
STOVOLD Arthur Bryant - C/J39344 - HMS Thracian - Held Hong Kong
STOW Albert Ernest - P/JX261738 - MV Empire Dawn - Held Java - captured in S Atlantic, Sumatra (Pangkalan Bali), Singapore
STRATFORD Ronald A - D/MX53331 - Ship not known - Held Hong Kong
STRINGFELLOW William - D/JX198358 - HMS Exeter - Held Celebes
STRONG Charles - Chaplain Lt - Ship not known - Held Hong Kong
STRONG Frederick - RM - PLY/X100148 - HMS Tapah - Held Sumatra (Palembang)
STRONG Raymond Percival - D/SSX82869 - HMS Jupiter - Held Java, Moluccas, Java, Singapore
STROTHER Robert - RM - PLY/X996 - HMS Prince of Wales - Held Singapore, Thailand, Japan (Kyushu)
STROUD Alfred Ernest - C/JX127848 - HMS Encounter - Held Celebes
STUBBS Norman - P/MX54062 - HMS Grasshopper - Held Sumatra (Medan) - Died Harikiku Maru 26.6.44 - Named Plymouth Memorial
STUBBS Peter George - D/JX184644 - HMS Exeter - Held Celebes - Died Makassar 16.7.45 - Buried Ambon
STUBBS Raymond Stanley - C/JX205607 - HMS Sultan - Held Sumatra (Palembang)
STUDLEY Ernest Wallace George - D/KX88244 - HMS Exeter - Held Celebes, Japan (Kyushu)
SUMMERS Albert Henry Whiteron - RM - PLY/X100191 - HMS Prince of Wales - Held Singapore, Borneo Died Labuan 1.12.44 - Named Plymouth Memorial
SUNSBURG Harry - D/JX144314 - HMS Jupiter - Held Java, Singapore, Japan (Osaka Area)
SUTCH Donald Jack - C/FX30393 - SS Nankin - Held Japan (Tokyo Area) - captured in Indian Ocean
SUTHERLAND Francis - RM - PLY/X2021 - HMS Tamar - Held Hong Kong, Japan (Osaka Area)
SUTHERLAND George Harry - MRNVR - Lt - Ship not known - Held Sumatra (Palembang), Singapore
SUTTON George - D/JX161117 - HMS Exeter - Held Celebes
SUTTON George Oliver - RM - PLY/X3755 - HMS Exeter - Held Celebes - Died Makassar 18.3.45 - Buried Ambon
SUTTON John - C/KX104645 - HMS Encounter - Held Celebes, Japan (Kyushu)
SUTTON Lawrence - D/J110989 - HMS Prince of Wales - Held Sumatra (Palembang)
SWAIN Ronald - RM - PLY/X2111 - HMS Prince of Wales - Held Singapore, Thailand, Japan (Kyushu)
SWANSON Cyril Noble - C/TDX2194 - HMS Encounter - Held Celebes
SWEENEY Daniel Christopher - P/M37259 - HMS Tamar - Held Hong Kong - Died Lisbon Maru 2.10.42 - Named Plymouth Memorial
SWETLAND Stanley Joseph - HKRNVR - Lt Com - Ship not known - Held Hong Kong
SWIFT George - P/MX69930 - HMS Sultan - Held Sumatra (Palembang)
SWIFT Henry John - D/JX134186 - ML 311 - Held Java, Singapore, Japan (Hiroshima Area)
SWINFIELD Albert Edward - D/JX181941 - HMS Exeter - Held Celebes

SYMONS Harold Edward - D/M35857 - HMS Exeter - Held Celebes
SYMONS Robert Charles - D/JX147813 - HMS Tamar - Held Hong Kong - Died Shanghai after sinking of Lisbon Maru 12.10.42 - Buried Yokohama
SYMS Malcolm Henry - RM - Lt - HMS Exeter - Held Celebes, Java
SYRED Deryck Ralph - Surg Lt - HMS Encounter - Held Celebes, Japan (Kyushu)
TABB Clive William Jarvis - RM - PLY/X3791 - HMS Exeter - Held Celebes
TAFFS Frederick - P/MX71668 - Ship not known - Held Sumatra (Palembang), Singapore, Taiwan, Japan (Hokkaido)
TAIT John George - SANF - SA/68579 - HMS Encounter - Held Celebes
TAIT Robert - D/JX188492 - HMS Exeter - Held Celebes
TALLON Leslie Brian - P/JX299512 - HMS Exeter - Held Celebes, Japan (Kyushu)
TATTERSFIELD Cyril - D/JX256659 - HMS Jupiter - Held Java, Moluccas, Java
TAYLOR Arthur William Francis - W O - HMS Tamar - Held Hong Kong, Japan (Tokyo Area) - Died Japan 25.7.45 - Buried Yokohama
TAYLOR Clifford - D/M22029 - HMS Sultan - Held Singapore - Died Singapore 15.11.42 - Buried Kranji
TAYLOR Edward William James - P/J109562 - Mining Party - Held Hong Kong, Japan (Osaka Area)
TAYLOR Frank William - C/JX151634 - RNLMS Java - Held Celebes, Japan (Kyushu)
TAYLOR George Herbert - C/J53184 - HMS Encounter - Held Celebes
TAYLOR Stanley - D/MX70683 - HMS Sultan - Held Sumatra (Palembang), Singapore, Taiwan, Japan (Tokyo Area) - Died Japan 13.3.43 - Buried Yokohama
TAYLOR Sydney John - D/SSX33879 - HMS Tamar - Held Hong Kong - Died Lisbon Maru 2.10.42 - Named Plymouth Memorial
TAYLOR Thomas - D/JX232536 - Ship not known - Held Hong Kong, Japan (Osaka Area)
TAYLOR Thomas Tennant - D/MX62121 - HMS Exeter - Held Celebes, Japan (Kyushu)
TAYLOR William Benjamin - D/SSX18852 - HMS Stronghold - Held Celebes - Died Makassar 22.5.45 - Buried Ambon
THEW Norman Vivian Joseph Thomas - Lt Com - HMS Jupiter - Held Java
THISTLETHWAITE Richard - D/JX157114 - HMS Sultan - Held Sumatra (Medan) - Died Harikiku Maru 26.6.44 - Named Plymouth Memorial
THOM Allan Duncan - D/JX184602 - HMS Exeter - Held Celebes - Died Makassar 31.5.45 - Buried Ambon
THOMAS Cyril Edward - D/MX46963 - HMS Rahman - Held Java, Sumatra (Railway)
THOMAS David Gough - D/JX184177 - Ship not known - Held Sumatra (Medan), Burma, Thailand
THOMAS David Lewis - D/MX81581 - HMS Exeter - Held Celebes - Died Makassar 24.3.45 - Buried Ambon
THOMAS Elder B - 2nd Lt - HMS Indefatigable - Held Japan (Tokyo Area)
THOMAS Frederick Hubert - RM - PLY/X516 - HMS Exeter - Held Celebes
THOMAS Gwynfor - P/MX64986 - HMS Tamar - Held Hong Kong - Died Shanghai after sinking of Lisbon Maru 15.10.42 - Buried Yokohama
THOMAS Idris - P/JX219786 - HMS Sultan - Held Java, Singapore, Japan (Hiroshima Area) - Died Japan 28.11.43 - Buried Yokohama
THOMAS Ivor Edward - P/SSX28641 - HMS Redstart - Held Hong Kong, Japan (Osaka Area) - Died Japan 18.10.42 - Buried Yokohama
THOMAS Jack - C/JX299516 - Ship not known - Held Sumatra (Palembang)
THOMAS Leonard - D/JX166621 - HMS Exeter - Held Celebes
THOMAS Leslie - D/JX212822 - HMS Sultan - Held Sumatra (Medan, Railway) - Died Sumatra Railway 2.3.45 - Buried Jakarta
THOMAS Owen Meredith - D/JX171484 - HMS Exeter - Held Celebes
THOMAS Stanley - RM - RMB/X1580 - HMS Exeter - Held Celebes, Japan (Kyushu)
THOMAS Walter Reginald Alfred - RM - PLY/X579 - HMS Prince of Wales - Held Singapore, Thailand
THOMAS William - P/JX193356 - HMS Fuh Wo - Held Sumatra (Palembang)
THOMAS William Llewellyn - D/JX143337 - HMS Stronghold - Held Celebes, Java
THOMASON George Henry - D/JX133144 - HMS Exeter - Held Celebes
THOMPSON Arthur William - D/JX129898 - HMS Li Wo - Held Sumatra (Palembang)
THOMPSON David George - D/KX96172 - HMS Exeter - Held Celebes, Java
THOMPSON Frederick Whittaker - P/JX938 - HMS Encounter - Held Celebes, Japan (Kyushu)
THOMPSON John Henry - D/SSX16022 - HMS Exeter - Held Celebes - Died Makassar 19.2.45 - Buried Ambon
THOMPSON John Howard - C/MX72850 - HMS Sultan - Held Sumatra (Medan), Burma, Thailand
THOMPSON Lionel Charles - RM - PLY/X1521 - HMS Prince of Wales - Held Singapore, Thailand - Died Thailand 7.12.43 - Buried Kanchanaburi

THOMPSON Richard - D/JX160235 - HMS Stronghold - Held Celebes
THOMPSON Robert Harold - C/JX173932 - HMS Encounter - Held Celebes, Japan (Kyushu)
THOMPSON Thomas - D/KX106492 - HMS Jupiter - Held Java, probably Moluccas, Java, Singapore
THOMPSON Walter William Henry - D/J107406 - HMS Dragonfly - Held Sumatra (Medan), Singapore
THOMS William Robert - P/JX219787 - HMS Danae - Held Java, Singapore - Died Tamahoko Maru 24.6.44 - Named Plymouth Memorial
THOMSON Basil William - Lt - Ship not known - Held Hong Kong
THOMSON Christopher Grimson - D/JX211905 - HMS Exeter - Held Celebes, Japan (Kyushu)
THORNE Reginald Albert - P/K46936 - HMS Redstart - Held Hong Kong, Japan (Osaka Area)
THORNHILL John McCorn Herbert - Act Sub Lt - HMS Cornflower - Held Hong Kong
THORNTON John Tasker - C/JX260635 - HMS Siang Wo - Held Sumatra (Palembang)
THRIFT John Howard - D/JX150445 - HMS Repulse - Held Singapore (from Bangka)
THUNDER Allan Henry - C/JX137686 - HMS Sultan - Held Sumatra (Medan, Railway) - Died Sumatra Railway 6.4.45 - Named Chatham Memorial
THUNDER Jack E - D/KX107031 - Ship not known - Held Singapore, Thailand
THYER William Frederick - D/JX154315 - HMS Exeter - Held Celebes, Japan (Kyushu)
THYNNE William - D/J105854 - HMS Tamar - Held Hong Kong, Japan (Osaka Area)
TIDY George Horace - RCNVR - Lt - HMS Exeter - Held Celebes, Java
TILL Ernest H J - D/JX181977 - HMS Exeter - Held Celebes
TILTON James Povey - D/SSX19929 - HMS Exeter - Held Celebes, Java
TIMPSON Alexander - D/JX188517 - HMS Exeter - Held Celebes
TINCKER Robert Wise Holden - Surg Com - Ship not known - Held Hong Kong, Japan (Tokyo Area, Sendai Area)
TINCKNELL Francis Herbert Jack - RM - PLY/X100103 - HMS Prince of Wales - Held Singapore, Thailand - Died Thailand 17.12.43 - Buried Chungkai
TINDALL Arthur Horace William - P/JX290242 - HMS Exeter - Held Celebes
TINK William - D/K21308 - HMS Exeter - Held Celebes - Died Makassar 10.1.44 - Buried Ambon
TIPPING William Gamble - P/SSX20329 - HMS Peterel - Held Shanghai, Japan (Tokyo Area)
TIVEY Joseph - D/JX161959 - HMS Prince of Wales - Held Sumatra (Medan, Railway) - Died Sumatra Railway 26.3.45 - Buried Jakarta
TOBIN James - D/JX177497 - HMS Prince of Wales - Held Singapore (from Bangka)
TODD Frederick Charles - C/J32991 - HMS Sultan - Held Sumatra (Palembang) - Died Palembang 12.3.42 - Buried Jakarta
TODD James Somerville - D/JX149160 - HMS Tamar - Held Hong Kong - Died Shanghai after sinking of Lisbon Maru 14.10.42 - Buried Yokohama
TOLLEMACHE Lawrence Lyonel A - Com - Ship not known - Held Hong Kong
TOMBS Frederick Francis William - P/FX25856 - HMS Exeter - Held Celebes
TOMLINSON Frank John - C/MX76640 - HMS Sultan - Held Sumatra (Palembang)
TOOLE Joseph - D/KX87455 - HMS Exeter - Held Celebes
TOOMBS John Douglas William - D/JX181982 - HMS Exeter - Held Celebes
TOPPING Charles Arthur - P/JX294873 - HMS Anking - Held Java, Singapore, Thailand, Singapore
TOTTERDELL Ronald Thomas Frank - D/KX116542 - HMS Exeter - Held Celebes
TOUT Clarence - D/BDX1508 - HMS Prince of Wales - Held Sumatra (Palembang)
TOWNSEND Leslie Thomas - RM - PLY/22090 - HMS Repulse - Held Singapore, Thailand
TOWNSEND-GREEN Kenneth A - Sub Lt - HMS Exeter - Held Celebes, Java
TOZER Rupert Peter - D/MX53346 - HMS Exeter - Held Celebes
TOZER Stanley Herbert - Com Shipwr - HMS Tamar - Held Hong Kong - Died Lisbon Maru 2.10.42 - Named Plymouth Memorial
TRACEY Percy - D/KX128680 - HMS Repulse - Held Sumatra (Medan), Burma, Thailand
TRAHAIR Thomas - D/KX90586 - HMS Exeter - Held Celebes - Died Makassar 12.4.45 - Buried Ambon
TREACHER Archie Frank - C/KX128989 - HMS Anking - Held Java
TREGIDGO Alfred Francis George - D/K60133 - HMS Thracian - Held Hong Kong, Japan (Osaka Area)
TRENNERRY Edmund John - D/KX84648 - HMS Exeter - Held Celebes - Died Makassar 25.2.45 - Buried Ambon
TRERISE Richard John - D/MX54111 - HMS Sultan - Held Sumatra (Palembang) - Died Palembang 4.11.44 - Buried Jakarta
TRIM Albert Cyril - RM - PLY/22198 - HMS Tamar - Held Hong Kong, Japan (Osaka Area)
TRIPP Cyril - D/JX162761 - HMS Exeter - Held Celebes, Japan (Kyushu)
TROUGHTON Frederick Walter - P/MX48086 - HMS Sultan - Held Sumatra (Palembang)
TROWELL Harold William - C/K64339 - HMS Encounter - Held Celebes
TRUSCOTT Reginald Charles - D/JX140590 - HMS Exeter - Held Celebes - Died Makassar 3.5.45 - Buried

Ambon

TUCKER Hubert Norman - C/KX128988 - ML 310 - Held Singapore (from Jibbia), Borneo

TUCKER Reginald John - D/SSX13849 - HMS Sultan - Held Sumatra (Palembang) - Died Palembang 12.8.45 - Buried Jakarta

TUCKER William Henry - D/J107882 - HMS Jarak - Held Sumatra (Medan), Burma, Thailand

TUCKETT Douglas Henry Hamblyn - D/MX57970 - HMS Exeter - Held Celebes

TUFFS Edward - C/J69264 - Ship not known - Held Hong Kong, Shanghai, Japan (Hokkaido)

TUNNICLIFFE Robert Richardson - D/KX78175 - HMS Jupiter - Held Java, Moluccas - Died Maros Maru 26.9.44 - Named Plymouth Memorial

TUPLIN James Edward - D/KX120221 - Ship not known - Held Singapore, Thailand

TURNBULL John William - Lt - HMS Sultan - Held Sumatra (Medan), Singapore, Thailand

TURNER Abraham - P/K43828 - HMS Sultan - Held Singapore, Japan (Hokkaido) - Died Japan 28.12.43 - Buried Yokohama

TURNER Donald Deacon - P/JX173983 - Boom Defence - Held Hong Kong, Japan (Osaka Area)

TURNER George - RM - PLY/X3340 - HMS Repulse - Held Sumatra (Palembang)

TURNER Jack - D/JX140369 - HMS Exeter - Held Celebes

TURNER James Crowley - RM - PLY/X2216 - HMS Prince of Wales - Held Singapore, Thailand

TURNER Lewis Arthur - D/J106618 - HMS Exeter - Held Celebes - Died Pomelaa 5.9.43 - Buried Ambon

TURNER Robert James - D/JX162865 - HMS Exeter - Held Celebes, Japan (Kyushu)

TURNER William Arthur - P/KX109310 - HMS Tamar - Held Hong Kong - Died Lisbon Maru 2.10.42 - Named Plymouth Memorial

TWEEDALE Allan - P/JX252040 - HMS Sultan - Held Singapore (from Jibbia), Thailand - Died Thailand 25.7.43 - Buried Kanchanaburi

TWISS Frank Roddam - Lt Com - HMS Exeter - Held Celebes, Japan (Tokyo Area, Shikoku, Tokyo Area)

TYACK William James - D/JX129803 - HMS Exeter - Held Celebes, Japan (Kyushu)

TYLER Graham Oliver - SANF - SA68556 - HMS Encounter - Held Celebes, Japan

TYRRELL Edward - Lt - HMS Encounter - Held Celebes, Japan (Tokyo Area, Shikoku, Tokyo Area)

ULRICK Desmond - D/KX105132 - HMS Prince of Wales - Held Sumatra (Medan), Burma, Thailand

UNIACKE Michael - D/K23867 - HMS Exeter - Held Celebes - Died Makassar 12.2.45 - Buried Ambon

UNWIN John Arthur - D/JX172214 - HMS Thracian - Held Hong Kong

UPTON George W - D/KX82169 - HMS Exeter - Held Celebes

UPTON Herbert Cooper - MRNVR - Lt - HMS Rahman - Held Java, Sumatra (Railway)

USBORNE Frank Eric - C/MX45570 - HMS Encounter - Held Celebes - Died Makassar 10.4.45 - Buried Ambon

USHER Hubert - P/KX86806 - HMS Peterel - Held Shanghai, Japan (Hokkaido)

USHER Norman - P/JX161231 - Ship not known - Held Sumatra (Palembang)

VALENTINE George Frederick William - P/J20240 - HMS Tamar - Held Hong Kong - Died Lisbon Maru 2.10.42 - Named Plymouth Memorial

VALENTINE Kenneth Courtney - C/MX77292 - ML 432 - Held Sumatra (Palembang)

VARNEY Harry - P/J18390 - HMS Tamar - Held Hong Kong, Japan (Osaka Area) - Died Japan 1.10.43 - Buried Yokohama

VARTY Richard - RM - PLY/X2518 - HMS Prince of Wales - Held Singapore, Thailand - Died Thailand 8.8.43 - Buried Kanchanaburi

VENNER Peter - D/JX166623 - HMS Exeter - Held Celebes

VENTERS John MacKie - MRNVR - Lt - HMS Laburnum - Held Sumatra (Palembang)

VERDON Charles Jack - RM - Lt - HMS Prince of Wales - Held Singapore, Thailand

VERNALL Richard John - HKRNVR - Lt Com - Ship not known - Held Hong Kong

VERRION Walter John - P/J109631 - HMS Stronghold - Held Celebes

VERRY Maurice William - RNZN - NZ/3115 - Ship not known - Held Sumatra (Palembang) - Died Palembang 13.7.45 - Buried Jakarta

VESEY Francis Michael - D/KX64799 - HMS Exeter - Held Celebes - Died Makassar 8.8.44 - Buried Ambon

VIDLER Victor Harold - RM - RMB/X178 - HMS Exeter - Held Celebes - Died Makassar 24.4.45 - Buried Ambon

WADE Richard Beswick - RM - PLY/X100138 - HMS Prince of Wales - Held Singapore, Thailand

WADE Vernon Nicholas - MRNVR - Lt - HMS Siang Wo - Held Java, Singapore, Borneo

WAGER Sidney James - C/JX223144 - HMS Scorpion - Held Sumatra (Palembang)

WAGNER Richard James - RNZN - NZ/D2409 - HMS Exeter - Held Celebes

WAINSCOTT Kenneth Alfred - P/J104088 - HMS Peterel - Held Shanghai, Japan (Tokyo Area)

WAINWRIGHT James Anthony - D/JX152280 - ML 432 - Held Sumatra (Palembang)

WAKEHAM William John - D/KX113186 - HMS Jupiter - Held Java, Moluccas, Java

WALKER Charles F - D/JX180588 - Ship not known - Held Singapore, Thailand, Japan (Kyushu)
WALKER Edward Thomas - D/J94545 - HMS Jupiter - Held Java, Moluccas - Died Maros Maru 25.9.44 - Named Plymouth Memorial
WALKER Harry - C/M34377 - HMS Encounter - Held Celebes - Died Makassar 17.5.45 - Buried Ambon
WALKER Henry Desmond - D/JX221670 - HMS Exeter - Held Celebes, Japan (Kyushu)
WALKER John - D/MX65132 - HMS Laburnum - Held Sumatra (Palembang)
WALKER Patrick J - D/LX24564 - Ship not known - Held Sumatra (Medan), Burma, Thailand
WALKER Peter Caudle - P/KX116556 - HMS Cicala - Held Hong Kong, Japan (Osaka Area, Nagoya Area)
WALKER Robert William - P/JX183396 - HMS Thracian - Held Hong Kong
WALKER Stanley George - D/J25010 - HMS Exeter - Held Celebes
WALL Thomas Mervyn - RM - PLY/22054 - HMS Tamar - Held Hong Kong, Japan (Osaka Area) - Died Japan 13.10.42 - Buried Yokohama
WALLACE Charles Eric - D/KX79789 - HMS Repulse - Held Sumatra (Palembang)
WALLACE George William - RM - PLY/100351 - HMS Exeter - Held Celebes, Japan (Kyushu)
WALSH Vincent Francis - Surg Com HMS Exeter - Held Celebes, Java
WALTERS Joseph Richard - RM - PLY/X100053 - HMS Exeter - Held Celebes, Japan (Kyushu)
WALTON John Edward - RM - PLY/X100019 - HMS Prince of Wales - Held Sumatra (Palembang)
WANN Alan - P/JX274009 - HMS Encounter - Held Celebes, Java
WANNOP Norman Shaw - C/JX250148 - Ship not known - Held Sumatra (Palembang)
WANSTALL David Y - D/K56387 - HMS Tamar - Held Hong Kong
WARBURTON Charles - D/JX176793 - HMS Repulse - Held Java, Sumatra (Pangkalan Bali), Singapore
WARD Frederick - P/JX192551 - HMS Stronghold - Held Celebes
WARD Henry Dodington - D/SR16347 - HMS Thracian - Held Hong Kong
WARD Sidney - C/KX126834 - HMS Sultan - Held Singapore, Thailand
WARDROPE T - RM - PLY/X774 - Ship not known - Held Sumatra (Palembang)
WARE Edwin Arthur - P/JX192523 - HMS Kuala - Held Sumatra (Medan), Singapore
WAREHAM William John Alex - D/JX214858 - MV Empire Dawn - Held Java - captured in S Atlantic, Sumatra (Pangkalan Bali), Singapore
WARING Henry - W O - HMS Tamar - Held Hong Kong, Japan (Tokyo Area, Sendai Area)
WARLOW Benjamin Herbert - D/KX77226 - HMS Encounter - Held Celebes - Died Makassar 20.4.45 - Buried Ambon
WARN Reginald Theodore - RM - PLY/X524 - HMS Prince of Wales - Held Singapore
WARNER Alfred Henry - RM - PLY/X2245 - HMS Exeter - Held Celebes, Japan (Kyushu)
WARNER Percy - Com - Ship not known - Held Hong Kong
WARNER Reginald Frederick - C/SSX26349 - HMS Encounter - Held Celebes
WARNER William Robert - D/JX152064 - HMS Sultan - Held Sumatra (Medan), Burma - Died Tavoy 14.9.42 - Buried Thanbyuzayat
WARREN Alan George - RM - Lt Col - Ship not known - Held Sumatra (Medan), Singapore, Thailand
WATERS Ronald George Mascott - D/J114822 - HMS Sultan - Held Sumatra (Palembang) - Died Palembang 19.10.44 - Buried Jakarta
WATKINS Ernest Hector - C/J50389 - HMS Electra - Held Java, Sumatra (Railway)
WATMORE Francis George - D/KX100904 - HMS Thracian - Held Hong Kong, Japan (Nagoya Area)
WATSON Arthur - HKRNVR - AB - Ship not known - Held Hong Kong - Died Lisbon Maru 2.10.42 - Named Plymouth Memorial
WATSON Harry - D/KX90348 - HMS Exeter - Held Celebes
WATSON Kenneth Albert - HKRNVR - Lt - APV Minnie - Held Hong Kong
WATSON Percy - C/J41288 - HMS Sultan - Held Sumatra (Medan), Burma, Thailand - Died Thailand (Mergui Road) 4.6.45 - Buried Kanchanaburi
WATSON Rennie - D/JX272102 - HMS Repulse - Held Sumatra (Palembang)
WATT Peter - C/K64991 - HMS Encounter - Held Celebes
WATTS Albert Leonard - D/SSX32352 - Ship not known - Held Sumatra (Medan), Burma, Thailand
WATTS John - C/J36255 - HMS Sultan - Held Sumatra (Palembang)
WATTS Thomas William - P/J14612 - HMS Tamar - Held Hong Kong, Japan (Osaka Area) - Died Japan 25.10.42 - Buried Yokohama
WEAVER Jack - P/JX162188 - HMS Sultan - Held Sumatra (Medan), Burma - Died Mergui 12.7.42 - Buried Thanbyuzayat
WEAVER Randle - D/JX198627 - HMS Sultan - Held Sumatra (Palembang) - Died Palembang 31.8.45 - Buried Jakarta
WEBB Albert George - C/SSX30940 - HMS Encounter - Held Celebes, Java
WEBB Donald - D/MX57578 - HMS Tamar - Held Hong Kong - Died Lisbon Maru 2.10.42 - Named Plym-

outh Memorial
WEBB George William - D/L12084 - HMS Exeter - Held Celebes
WEBB Peter Jack - P/JX382419 - HM Sub. Stratagem - Held Singapore (from Malacca Strait) - Died Singapore 31.12.44 - Named Plymouth Memorial
WEBB Sidney - C/J110817 - HMS Tamar - Held Hong Kong - Died Lisbon Maru 2.10.42 - Named Chatham Memorial
WEBBER Bertram - P/MX69233 - Ship not known - Held Hong Kong, Japan (Tokyo Area)
WEBBER Thomas Albert - RM - PLY/X2652 - HMS Prince of Wales - Held Singapore, Thailand
WELCH James Dennis - P/JX212444 - HMS Vyner Brooke - Held Sumatra (Palembang)
WELDON Denis - P/JX289272 - Ship not known - Held Sumatra (Palembang)
WELLS Arthur William Clement - C/JX299677 - SS Nankin - Held Japan (Tokyo Area) - captured in Indian Ocean - Died Japan 31.5.45 - Buried Yokohama
WELLS Edgar Arthur Benjamin - P/JX236321 - HMS Exeter - Held Celebes, Japan (Kyushu)
WELLS Gordon - D/JX22456 - HMS Prince of Wales - Held Sumatra (Palembang)
WELSH John Patrick - D/JX238087 - HMS Exeter - Held Celebes
WELSH Patrick - D/KX121518 - HMS Encounter - Held Celebes - Died Makassar 14.3.45 - Buried Ambon
WENT Charles Edward - C/JX150008 - HMS Encounter - Held Celebes
WEST Albert Edward - D/MX37662 - HMS Exeter - Held Celebes, Japan (Kyushu) - Died Japan 2.2.43 - Buried Yokohama
WEST Frederick William C - C/KX130208 - HMS Sin-Aik-Lee - Held Java, Singapore, Borneo
WEST Kenneth Harvey Victor - D/JX177236 - HMS Exeter - Held Celebes
WESTCOTT Sydney Kenneth - D/JX161068 - HMS Exeter - Held Celebes
WESTGATE Noel Frank Ferrow - RM - PLY/X3758 - HMS Prince of Wales - Held Singapore, Thailand
WESTGATE Robert Henry - P/J13916 - Mining Party - Held Hong Kong, Japan (Nagoya Area)
WESTHUIZEN John William - SANF - SA68825 - HMS Exeter - Held Celebes, Japan (Kyushu)
WESTWOOD Arthur Leonard - P/JX220335 - HM Sub. Stratagem - Held Singapore (from Malacca Strait) - Died Singapore 31.12.44 - Named Plymouth Memorial
WESTWOOD Ernest William - HKRNVR - Sub Lt - Ship not known - Held Hong Kong
WESTWOOD Reginald Robert - D/BDX1575 - HMS Exeter - Held Celebes, Java
WEXHAM Robert Martin - W O Supply - HMS Tamar - Held Hong Kong - Died Lisbon Maru 2.10.42 - Named Chatham Memorial
WHEELDON Robert Joseph - D/KX121392 - HMS Exeter - Held Celebes
WHELAN Kevin Shaun - D/JX188569 - HMS Exeter - Held Celebes
WHERRY Robert - Lt - Ship not known - Held Hong Kong
WHILEY Kenneth - P/JX162054 - HMS Sultan - Held Sumatra (Medan) - Died Harikiku Maru 26.6.44 - Named Plymouth Memorial
WHITAKER Frederick - RM - PLY/X100130 - HMS Prince of Wales - Held Sumatra (Palembang)
WHITE Albert Edward - D/JX190199 - Ship not known - Held Sumatra (Medan), Burma, Thailand
WHITE Albert John - D/J107206 - HMS Tamar - Held Hong Kong, Japan (Tokyo Area)
WHITE Charles James Stanley - P/J46351 - Mining Party - Held Hong Kong, Japan (Tokyo Area)
WHITE Edward Charles Peter - C/JX259190 - SS Ben Nevis - Held Shanghai, Japan (Osaka Area) - Died Japan 9.3.44 - Buried Yokohama
WHITE Eric - D/MX66188 - HMS Tamar - Held Hong Kong
WHITE James Cusak Stacey - MRNVR - Lt Com - HMS Sultan - Held Sumatra (Palembang), Singapore
WHITE John - W O Gnr - HMS Exeter - Held Celebes
WHITE John McGrath - D/JX168863 - HMS Mata Hari - Held Sumatra (Palembang), Singapore, Taiwan, Japan (Tokyo Area, Sendai Area)
WHITE Ralph James - P/JX146392 - HMS Tamar - Held Hong Kong - Died Lisbon Maru 2.10.42 - Named Plymouth Memorial
WHITE Raymond Bert - P/SSX28990 - HMS Sultan - Held Sumatra (Palembang)
WHITE Ronald Leslie - RM - PLY/X1299 - HMS Exeter - Held Celebes, Japan (Kyushu)
WHITE Stanley William - C/KX130200 - Ship not known - Held Sumatra (Palembang)
WHITE Thomas Henry - P/J24692 - HMS Sultan - Held Singapore, Thailand
WHITE William Percy - D/KX116552 - HMS Exeter - Held Celebes
WHITEHALL Alfred - D/MX73019 - HMS Exeter - Held Celebes, Japan (Kyushu)
WHITEHEAD Harry - D/JX212907 - HMS Exeter - Held Celebes - Died Makassar 1.3.45 - Buried Ambon
WHITELEY Norman - D/SSX25325 - HMS Repulse - Held Sumatra (Palembang)
WHITFIELD Richard Sarel - Surg Lt - HMS Tamar - Held Hong Kong, Japan (Tokyo Area)
WHITING Kenneth George - D/BDX1559 - HMS Exeter - Held Celebes
WHITMAN George Frederick - RM - PLY/2159 - HMS Prince of Wales - Held Sumatra (Palembang)
WHITMAN Richard Arthur - D/SSX32080 - HMS Jupiter - Held Java, Singapore, Japan (Osaka Area)

WHITTAKER William - D/SSX27259 - HMS Exeter - Held Celebes, Java
WHITTINGHAM Harold - C/MX69410 - HMS Tern - Held Hong Kong, Japan (Osaka Area)
WHORTON Laurence - RM - PLY/X993 - HMS Repulse - Held Singapore, Thailand
WHORWOOD Cyril - D/MX68285 - HMS Exeter - Held Celebes
WIGNALL Francis - P/JX189108 - HMS Tien Kwang - Held Sumatra (Medan), Burma - Died Burma (Railway) 9.12.43 - Buried Thanbyuzayat
WIGNALL John - RM - PLY/X100430 - HMS Prince of Wales - Held Sumatra (Palembang)
WILCOX Leonard - P/MX62124 - HMS Tamar - Held Hong Kong, Japan (Osaka Area)
WILDE Alfred James - D/LX24297 - HMS Exeter - Held Celebes - Died Makassar 15.4.45 - Buried Ambon
WILDERS Frederick William - C/KX128011 - HMS Encounter - Held Celebes
WILDING William Dick - C/SSX18460 - HMS Laburnum - Held Sumatra (Palembang)
WILKIN Douglas Havard - RM - RMB/X1152 - HMS Exeter - Held Celebes - Died Pomelaa 6.9.43 - Buried Ambon
WILKINSON John - D/KX103847 - HMS Exeter - Held Celebes
WILKINSON Patrick Ormond Howard - MRNVR - Lt - HMS Ying Pin - Held Sumatra (Palembang), Singapore
WILKINSON Roy Ian - D/LX23606 - HMS Exeter - Held Celebes, Japan (Kyushu)
WILKINSON William Ernest Basil - D/JX137073 - HMS Cicala - Held Hong Kong - Died Hong Kong 2.9.42 - Buried Sai Wan Bay
WILLCOCK Thomas R - D/JX198245 - HMS Repulse - Held Sumatra (Medan, Railway)
WILLCOCK William Francis - D/J109977 - HMS Exeter - Held Celebes
WILLCOCKS Charles Henry - D/KX83588 - HMS Exeter - Held Celebes
WILLETTS Henry - C/SSX28192 - HMS Exeter - Held Celebes - Died Makassar 1.6.45 - Buried Ambon
WILLIAMS Caradoc Morgan - P/SSX14600 - HMS Peterel - Held Shanghai, Japan (Tokyo Area)
WILLIAMS Charles Stanley - C/J15845 - HMS Sultan - Held Singapore (from Bangka)
WILLIAMS David John - D/J108186 - HMS Repulse - Held Java, Singapore, Borneo
WILLIAMS George Albert - D/M37680 - HMS Tamar - Held Hong Kong - Died Shanghai after sinking of Lisbon Maru 7.10.42 - Buried Yokohama
WILLIAMS Hannibal - D/JX226936 - HMS Moth - Held Hong Kong, Japan (Osaka Area)
WILLIAMS Harry Edward Iles - D/JX208165 - HMS Tamar - Held Hong Kong - Died Lisbon Maru 2.10.42 - Named Plymouth Memorial
WILLIAMS Henry Llewellyn - RM - PLY/X1057 - HMS Tamar - Held Hong Kong, Japan (Osaka Area)
WILLIAMS Ivor - RM - PLY/22374 - HMS Prince of Wales - Held Sumatra (Palembang)
WILLIAMS James Alun - D/KX97554 - HMS Exeter - Held Celebes
WILLIAMS John - RM - PLY/X2803 - HMS Prince of Wales - Held Sumatra (Palembang)
WILLIAMS John Alfred - C/J90467 - HMS Encounter - Held Celebes - Died Makassar 13.5.45 - Buried Ambon
WILLIAMS John Etna - Sub Lt - HMS Fuh Wo - Held Sumatra (Palembang), Singapore
WILLIAMS John Phillip Moss - D/M52566 - HMS Prince of Wales - Held Singapore - Died Singapore 18.7.42 - Buried Kranji
WILLIAMS Joseph George - D/KX108221 - HMS Redstart - Held Hong Kong, Japan (Tokyo Area, Sendai Area)
WILLIAMS Leonard Walter - C P O - HMS Dragonfly - Held Sumatra (Medan), Singapore, Sumatra (Railway)
WILLIAMS Ronald - D/JX170990 - Ship not known - Held Sumatra (Medan, Railway) - Died Sumatra Railway 7.4.45 - Buried Jakarta
WILLIAMS Roy William - Lt - Ship not known - Held Sumatra (Palembang), Singapore
WILLIAMS Victor George - P/JX236353 - HMS Exeter - Held Celebes, Japan (Kyushu) - Died Japan 30.6.43 - Buried Yokohama
WILLIAMS William Robert - Lt - HMS Sultan - Held Sumatra (Medan) - Died Harikiku Maru 26.6.44 - Named Plymouth Memorial
WILLIAMSON Arthur Sidney - RM - PLY/X2322 - HMS Prince of Wales - Held Java, Singapore, Borneo
WILLIAMSON Herbert - P/FX75168 - SS Nankin - Held Japan (Tokyo Area) - captured in Indian Ocean
WILLIAMSON John - P/JX190366 - HMS Dragonfly - Held Sumatra (Medan, Railway) - Died Sumatra Railway 16.9.45 - Buried Jakarta
WILLIMOT Stanley Gordon - Lt - HMS Sultan - Held Java, Singapore, Japan (Hiroshima Area, Shikoku, Kyushu)
WILLIS Bertram Drew - D/K63420 - HMS Thracian - Held Hong Kong, Japan (Osaka Area, Nagoya Area)
WILLISON Walter - D/SSX22117 - HMS Thracian - Held Hong Kong, Japan (Tokyo Area, Sendai Area)
WILLOUGHBY Algernon Frank - P/J34873 - HMS Stronghold - Held Celebes
WILMOT John Charles - D/MX50500 - HMS Sultan - Held Sumatra (Medan, Railway) - Died Sumatra Rail-

way 18.7.45 - Buried Jakarta

WILSMORE Frank - D/M35484 - HMS Exeter - Held Celebes, Japan (Kyushu)

WILSON Alan James Richmond - Lt - HMS Sultan - Held Sumatra (Medan), Singapore, Thailand

WILSON Cecil - P/SSX18268 - HMS Sultan - Held Sumatra (Palembang)

WILSON Charles - D/JX238251 - HMS Exeter - Held Celebes

WILSON David - D/JX127781 - HMS Repulse - Held Sumatra (Palembang)

WILSON Ernest - D/KX132275 - HMS Siang Wo - Held Singapore (from Bangka)

WILSON Frederick Cyril - D/MX51882 - HMS Exeter - Held Celebes, Japan (Kyushu)

WILSON George Jacob - D/MDX2079 - HMS Exeter - Held Celebes

WILSON Henry - P/SSX21285 - HMS Stronghold - Held Celebes, Japan (Kyushu)

WILSON James Cairns - RM - PLY/X3801 - HMS Prince of Wales - Held Singapore (from Bangka Strait)

WILSON John Campbell - P/WRX489 - HMS Thracian - Held Hong Kong - Died Lisbon Maru 2.10.42 - Named Plymouth Memorial

WILSON John Stephen - C/JX163163 - HMS Grasshopper - Held Sumatra (Medan) - Died Harikiku Maru 26.6.44 - Named Chatham Memorial

WILSON Robert Archibald - D/MX73304 - HMS Exeter - Held Celebes, Japan (Kyushu)

WILSON Robert Griffen - D/KX94035 - HMS Thracian - Held Hong Kong

WILSON William Edward - P/MX52828 - Ship not known - Held Hong Kong, Japan (Osaka Area, Hiroshima Area)

WINSTANLEY Frederick - RM - PLY/X752 - HMS Prince of Wales - Held Sumatra (Palembang), Singapore

WINTER Charles William - MRNVR - Lt - Ship not known - Held Sumatra (Palembang) - Died Palembang 14.5.45 - Buried Jakarta

WINTER Dennis Ambrose - HKRNVR - Act Sub Lt - Ship not known - Held Hong Kong

WITHERLEY Howard William - C/SSX18347 - Ship not known - Held Sumatra (Medan), Burma, Thailand

WITTER Squire Francis - P/MX79323 - HMS Sin-Aik-Lee - Held Java, Singapore, Borneo

WITTS George Henry - D/M40092 - HMS Prince of Wales - Held Sumatra (Palembang)

WOOD Charles - D/SSX35798 - HMS Exeter - Held Celebes, Japan (Kyushu)

WOOD Charles Henry - C/KX104156 - HMS Encounter - Held Celebes

WOOD Henry Robert - C/K52154 - HMS Encounter - Held Celebes, Japan (Kyushu) - Died Japan 4.1.44 - Buried Yokohama

WOOD Reginald Bertram - HKRNVR - Lt - HMS Cornflower - Held Hong Kong

WOOD Richard Kerslake - W O Schoolmaster - HMS Exeter - Held Celebes

WOOD Samuel Robert Roy - D/MX52124 - HMS Electra - Held Java, Moluccas, Celebes - Died Muna 28.5.45 - Buried Ambon

WOODALL Ernest Edward David - D/KX82509 - HMS Exeter - Held Celebes

WOODHAMS Frederick H - C/JX249777 - SS Wellpark - Held Japan (Tokyo Area) - captured in S Atlantic

WOODIER Eric Raymond - D/SSX35721 - HMS Repulse - Held Sumatra (Palembang) - Died Palembang 18.3.42 - Buried Jakarta

WOODING George Charles Harris - D/JX180520 - HMS Exeter - Held Celebes - Died Makassar 28.2.45 - Buried Ambon

WOODINGS Percy - RM - PLY/X1586 - HMS Tamar - Held Hong Kong, Japan (Osaka Area)

WOODLEY Archie - Lt - HMS Siang Wo - Held Sumatra (Palembang), Singapore

WOODS Donald Albert - P/J114343 - HMS Dragonfly - Held Sumatra (Medan), Singapore, Sumatra (Railway)

WOODS James - D/J96507 - HMS Exeter - Held Celebes, Java

WOODS John Tinline Henderson - D/KX103015 - HMS Jupiter - Held Java, probably Moluccas, Java, Singapore

WOOLEY John Blaxland - Com - Shanghai Consulate - Held Shanghai - Escaped 6.10.44

WOOLFENDEN George - RM - PLY/X100174 - HMS Exeter - Held Celebes - Died Pomelaa 28.8.43 - Buried Ambon

WOOTTON Frederick Joseph - RM - PLY/X3064 - HMS Prince of Wales - Held Sumatra (Medan), Burma, Thailand

WOPLIN George Christopher - P/JX164895 - HMS Barlight - Held Hong Kong - Died Hong Kong 10.9.42 - Buried Stanley

WORDEN Harry - D/SSX32966 - HMS Exeter - Held Celebes - Died Makassar 11.5.45 - Buried Ambon

WORRALL Dennis - D/JX200453 - HMS Exeter - Held Celebes, Java

WORRALL Geoffrey Clare - HKRNVR - W O - Ship not known - Held Hong Kong, Japan (Osaka Area) - Died Japan 13.12.44 - Buried Yokohama

WORRALL George - D/MX69904 - HMS Exeter - Held Celebes

WORRALL Thomas - D/KX88704 - HMS Exeter - Held Celebes, Japan (Kyushu)

WORT Stanley David - P/JX189266 - Ship not known - Held Hong Kong, Japan (Nagoya Area)
WORTHINGTON Herbert Edward - D/MX72871 - HMS Exeter - Held Celebes
WREN James - RM - PLY/X3712 - HMS Repulse - Held Sumatra (Palembang)
WREYFORD John - D/J102921 - Ship not known - Held Hong Kong, Japan (Osaka Area, Hiroshima Area)
WRIGHT Bertram Charles - D/KX46991 - HMS Exeter - Held Celebes
WRIGHT Edgar - D/SSX13434 - HMS Exeter - Held Celebes, Japan (Kyushu)
WRIGHT Harold - D/KX104672 - HMS Prince of Wales - Held Singapore (from Bangka)
WRIGHT Harold Charles - C/JX143483 - HMS Encounter - Held Celebes
WRIGHT James - P/JX273690 - HMS Exeter - Held Celebes, Java
WRIGHT Robert - D/J94639 - HMS Exeter - Held Celebes - Died Makassar 31.3.45 - Buried Ambon
WRIGHT Thomas O'Rourke - D/JX169857 - HMS Stronghold - Held Celebes, Japan (Kyushu)
WRIGLEY Winston - D/SMX802030 - HMS Exeter - Held Celebes, Japan (Kyushu)
WYATT John Cameron - Surg Lt - HMS Exeter - Held Celebes, Java, Sumatra (Railway)
WYATT William George - D/JX130789 - HMS Exeter - Held Celebes
WYNN Arthur - RM - PLY/100418 - HMS Prince of Wales - Held Java, Singapore, Sumatra (Railway)
WYNN John William - RM - PLY/X721 - HMS Prince of Wales - Held probably Singapore, Taiwan, Japan (Tokyo Area)
WYNN Leonard Thomas - RM - PLY/X439 - HMS Prince of Wales - Held Sumatra (Palembang)
YARWOOD Colin - P/WRX617 - HMS Cicala - Held Hong Kong, Japan (Osaka Area) - Died Japan 18.2.43 - Buried Yokohama
YATES Thomas Ostend - D/KX82669 - HMS Cicala - Held Hong Kong, Japan (Tokyo Area)
YEATES Jonas John Henry - P/J98702 - RN MTB - Held Hong Kong, Japan (Osaka Area, Hiroshima Area)
YELLAND Russell Edwin Richard - D/MX54851 - HMS Encounter - Held Celebes, Japan (Kyushu)
YEO Thomas Gordon - RM - PLY/X3477 - HMS Exeter - Held Celebes - Died Makassar 18.7.45 - Buried Ambon
YOUDAN Geoffrey John - D/JX136295 - HMS Exeter - Held Celebes - Died Makassar 23.2.45 - Buried Ambon
YOUENS George Alfred - C/JX279856 - HMS Anking - Held Java, Singapore, Thailand, Singapore
YOUNG Albert Edward - P/JX136543 - HMS Thanet - Held Sumatra (Palembang)
YOUNG Alexander M - D/JX170209 - HMS Exeter - Held Celebes
YOUNG James Robert - RM - CH/X1939 - Ship not known - Held Sumatra (Palembang)
YOUNG John William Rose - HKRNVR - Sub Lt - HMS Cornflower - Held Hong Kong
YOUNG Leonard - Lt - Ship not known - Held Hong Kong
YOUNG Patrick Elliott - HKRNVR - Sub Lt - HMS Cornflower - Held Hong Kong
YOUNG Reginald Seymour - HKRNVR - Lt Com - Ship not known - Held Hong Kong
YOUNGMAN Jack Leslie - HKRNVR - Sub Lt - Ship not known - Held Hong Kong
YOUNGS George Roland - D/SSX16954 - HMS Exeter - Held Celebes, Java
ZAMMITT John - E/L12431 - HMS Exeter - Held Celebes

EPILOGUE

—■—

Talk to any FEPOW about his having survived his captivity, the chances are that he will say "I was lucky".

Those who remained in the country of capture will say "I was lucky not to have been transported". Those from Hong Kong not transported on the *Lisbon Maru* will invariably say "I was lucky not to have been on the *Lisbon Maru*". Those transported back to Java from the Molucca Islands, even those transported on the *Maros Maru (Haruyoshi Maru)*, will usually say "I was lucky not to have been on the *Suez Maru*. Usually other instances of "luck" are then given. Invariably these will tell of help received from other FEPOWs when at a low ebb.

Russell Braddon, author of "The Naked Island", once said in a television interview that the families of those who did not survive their captivity could rest assured that no-one who died as a prisoner of war of the Japanese died unloved. That spiritual love has continued ever since, as epitomised in the words of the FEPOW Prayer:

> And we that are left grow old with the years
> Remembering the heartache, the pain and the tears,
> Hoping and praying that never again
> Man may sink to such sorrow and shame
> The price that was paid we will always remember
> Every day, every month, not just in November.

TABLE 1
Into Singapore

———————————————————— ■ ————————————————————

FROM	ARRIVED	POW TOTAL	UK	AUS	US	DUTCH
Sumatra (Padang)	March 1942	26	26	-	-	-
Sumatra (Palembang)	July 1942	127	90	4	33	-
Java	18.9.42	725	700	25	-	-
Java	26.9.42	1300	1299	1	-	-
Java	8.10.42	400	-	88	191	121
Java	12.10.42	1499	-	1499	-	-
Java	17.10.42	1500	418	378	554	150
Java	20.10.42	63	-	-	1	62
		Others remained on board for Burma				
Java	21.10.42	2002	-	-	1	2001
Java	23.10.42	2001	500	-	-	1501
Java	26.10.42	32	32	-	-	-
		Others remained on board for Japan				
Java	27.10.42	1000	-	-	-	1000
Java	29.10.42	400	-	-	-	400
Java	28.10.42	500	(Nationalities not known)			
		Transhipped to Dai Nichi Maru for Japan				
Java	31.10.42	1000	-	-	-	1000
Java	2.11.42	1000	-	-	94	906
Java	2.1.43	74	16	1	1	56
Java	7.1.43	1970	-	1484	-	486
Java	7.1.43	992	-	-	-	992
Java	17.1.43	1699	-	-	-	1699
Java	19.1.43	3188	-	-	-	3188
Java	29.1.43	2000	-	-	-	2000
Java	2.2.43	500	-	-	-	500
Java	9.2.43	1705	3	-	-	1702
Java	13.2.43	1000	704	-	-	296
Java	13.2.43	650	-	-	-	605
Java	2.3.43	7	3	-	-	4
Java	14.9.43	519	360	-	-	159
Java	1.10.43	2600	429	2	-	2169
Java	1.10.43	35	10	8	4	13
Java	22.1.44	30	2	-	-	28
Java	21.5.44	800	194	258	42	306
Sumatra (Medan)	26.6.44	720 (Dutch, UK and Aus) aboard Van Waerwijck (Harikiku Maru) sunk 26.6.44				

off Medan (543 survivors)

Java	1.7.44	1260	286	123	8	843
Java	17.9.44	1080	47	2	-	1028
Java	11.1.45	958	275	4	-	679
Java	18.1.45	639	117	106	8	408
Sumatra (Palembang)	25 5.45 and 30.5.45	1500	434	-	-	1066

TABLE 2
Into Saigon, Burma and Thailand

■

FROM	LEFT	POW DETAILS	ARRIVED
Singapore	4.4.42	1125 UK	Saigon
Singapore	14.5.42	3000 Aus	Mergu, Burma
Sumatra (Medan)	15.5.42	2000 (1500 Dutch, 500 UK)	Mergui, Burma aboard England Maru
Singapore	18,20,22,24,26 June 42	5 parties of 600 totalling 3000 (UK)	Bam Pong, Thailand
Singapore	9,10,11,12,15 Oct 42	5 parties of 650 totalling 3250 (UK)	Bam Pong, Thailand
Kuala Lumpur	14 Oct 42	401 (UK)	Bam Pong, Thailand
Singapore	14 Oct 42	390 (UK)	Bam Pong, Thailand
Singapore	17,18,20,22 23,24 Oct 42	6 parties of 650 totalling 3900 (UK)	Bam Pong, Thailand
Singapore	16.10.42	1800 from Java (1499 Aus, 190 USA, and 111 Dutch)	Moulmein, Burma
Java	20.10.42	1600 Dutch	Moulmein. Burma aboard Tacoma Maru
Singapore	25,26,27,28,29 30,31 Oct 42	7 parties of 650 totalling 4550 (UK)	Bam Pong, Thailand
Singapore	1,2,3,4,5,6 Nov 42	6 parties of 650 totalling 3900 (UK)	Bam Pong, Thailand
Singapore	7,9 Nov 42	2 parties of 630 totalling 1260 (UK)	Bam Pong, Thailand
Singapore	20.12.42	1000 (Dutch from Java)	Moulmein
Singapore	27.12.42	401 (Dutch from Java)	Moulmein
Singapore	7 Jan 43	1002 from Java	Bam Pong, Thailand (159 Dutch, 456 USA, 383 Aus, 4 UK)

Singapore	10.1.43	1000	Nichimei Maru sunk
	15.1.43	(Dutch from Java)	Andaman Sea
			(961 survivors)
Singapore	14,15,16,17,20,	16 parties of 625	Bam Pong, Thailand
	21,22,23,27,28	totalling 10,000	
	29,30 Jan 43	from Java	
	2,3,4,5 Feb 43	(8750 Dutch, 1250 Aus)	
Singapore	14 Mar 43	7 from Java	Bam Pong, Thailand
		(4 Dutch, 3 UK)	
Singapore	14,16,17,18,	9 parties (approx 555)	Bam Pong, Thailand
	19,20,21,22,23	totalling 5000	
	March 1943	(2780 UK, 2220 Aus)	
Singapore	13,14,15,16	5 parties of 600	Bam Pong, Thailand
	17 April 43	totalling 3000	
		from Java	
		(2831 Dutch, 155 Aus,	
		11 USA, 3UK)	
Singapore	18,19,20,21,22	13 parties (approx 538)	Bam Pong, Thailand
(F Force)	23,24,25,26,27	totalling 7000	
	28,29,30 Apr 43	(3334 UK, 3666 Aus)	
Singapore	5,6,8,9,13	6 parties of 545	Bam Pong, Thailand
(H Force)	17 May 43	totalling 3270 from Java	
		(1949 UK, 705 Aus,	
		26 USA, 590 Dutch)	
Singapore	25 Jun 43	230 (164 UK,	Bam Pong, Thailand
		55 Aus, 11 Dutch)	
Singapore	24 Aug 43	115 (42 UK, 73 Aus)	Bam Pong, Thailand
Singapore	8 Feb 44	30 from Java	Bam Pong, Thailand
		(28 Dutch, 2 UK)	

TABLE 3
Into Japan, Korea and Taiwan

■

FROM	LEFT	POW DETAILS	ARRIVED
Celebes	3.4.42	????	Tokyo
Singapore	16.8.42	1000	Korea
		(885 UK and 115 Aus)	
Singapore	16.8.42	400	Takao, Taiwan
		(378 UK and 22 Aus)	
		(inc POWs from Sumatra)	
Hong Kong	-. 8.42	????	Tokyo

Hong Kong	17.9.42	1816	Lisbon Maru sunk East China Sea 2.10.42 (977 survivors)
Celebes	14.10.42	1000 (213 UK)	Nagasaki aboard Asama Maru
Singapore	25.10.42	1100 (UK)	Takao, Taiwan aboard England Maru
Singapore	27.10.42	1205 from Java (719 Non-Dutch, 486 Dutch)	Moji aboard Tofuku Maru
Singapore	28.10.42	500 from Java (Nationalities not known)	Moji aboard Dai Nichi Maru
Singapore	28.10.42	900 (UK)	Takao, Taiwan aboard Dai Nichi Maru
Singapore	30.10.42	1100 from Java (Nationalities not known)	Moji aboard Singapore/ Shonan Maru
Singapore	28.11.42	1152 from Java (324 Non-Dutch, 828 Dutch)	Nagasaki aboard Kamakura Maru
Singapore	28.11.42	557 (555 Aus and 2 UK)	Moji aboard Kamakura Maru
Singapore	10.1.43	74 from Java (56 Dutch, 16 UK, 1 Aus, 1 USA)	Takao Taiwan aboard Aki Maru
Hong Kong	19.1.43	1200	Nagasaki aboard Tatsuta Maru
Singapore	2.4.43	1003 From Java (3 Non-Dutch, 1000 Dutch)	Moji aboard Hawaii Maru
Singapore	25.4.43	1500 from Java (500 Non-Dutch, 1000 Dutch)	Moji aboard Kyoko Maru
Singapore	15.5.43	900 (600 UK and 300 Aus)	Moji aboard Wales Maru
Hong Kong	15.8.43	501	Osaka aboard Banryo Maru
Singapore	20.9.43	507 from Java (353 Non-Dutch, 154 Dutch)	Moji aboard Uslii Maru
Singapore	21.10.43	1155 from Java (419 Non-Dutch, 736 Dutch)	Moji aboard Matsue Maru
Singapore	6.11.43	1229 from Java (11 Non-Dutch, 1218 Dutch)	Moji aboard Hawaii Maru
Hong Kong	-.12.43	500	Unknown ship to Taiwan then Moji aboard Toyama Maru
Singapore	5.6.44	800 from Java (494 Non-Dutch, 306 Dutch)	Bijou Maru to Taiwan then Tamahoko Maru sunk 24.6.44 Nagasaki Bay (212 survivors)

Singapore	5.6.44	approx 2200 from Thailand (UK, Aus and Dutch)	Moji probably aboard Kokusei Maru, Hioki Maru and Teiwa Maru
Singapore	4.7.44	1287 UK from Thailand (Aus and Dutch)	Toyofuku Maru Sunk 21.9.44 off Manilla Philippines remaining 2 months (383 survivors)
Thailand	? 7.44	1065 from Thailand (Nationalities not known)	Rashin Maru
Thailand	? 7.44	609 from Thailand (Nationalities not known)	Hakushika Maru
Thailand	? 7.44	709 from Thailand UK and Aus	Asaka Maru Sunk 13.8.44 off Taiwan (690 survivors)
Singapore	4.9.44	1318 from Thailand UK and Aus	Rakuyo Maru Sunk 12.9.44 South China Sea (136 rescued by the Japanese. Others rescued by US submarines)
Singapore	4.9.44	950 from Thailand UK and Aus	Kachidoki Maru Sunk 12.9.44 South China Sea (520 rescued by the Japanese. Others rescued by US submarines)
Hong Kong	29.9.44	220	Osaka aboard Naura Maru
Singapore	23.12.44	525 from Thailand (Aus, USA and Dutch)	Moji aboard Awa Maru

TABLE 4
Into Borneo

∎

FROM	LEFT	POW DETAILS	ARRIVED
Singapore	8.7.42	1500 (Aus)	Sandakan
Singapore	9.10.42	1886 from Java (1886 UK)	1048 at Kuching 838 at Jesselton (Kota Kinabalu)
Singapore	3.2.43	104 from Java (104 UK)	Kuching
Singapore	28.3.43	1000 (500 UK and 500 Aus)	Kuching Aus later to Sandakan

TABLE 5
Into New Britain, The Moluccas and Floress

FROM	LEFT	POW DETAILS	ARRIVED
Singapore	18.10.42	600 UK	New Britain
Java	22.4.43	1025 predominantly Dutch	Ceram (Seram) Moluccas aboard Kunitama Maru
Java	22.4.43	2061 (1716 UK, 345 Dutch)	Haruku, Moluccas Aboard Amagi Maru and Matsukawa Maru
Java	24.4.43	1024 predominantly UK	Ambon, Moluccas aboard Mayahashi Maru and Nishii Maru
Java	25.4.43	1975 predominantly Dutch	Flores aboard Tenzio Maru, Tazima Maru and Koam Maru

TABLE 6
Into Java and Celebes

FROM	LEFT	POW DETAILS	ARRIVED
Celebes (Makassar)	October 1943	43	Probably Surabaya
Moluccas	26.11.43	548 (411 UK, 137 Dutch)	Suez Maru sunk 29.11.43 North of Bali (0 survivors)
Moluccas	14.12.43	437	Surabaya aboard Nichinan Maru
Flores	27.1.44	725	Surabaya
Moluccas	1.5.44	200	Surabaya aboard Tencho Maru
Flores	12.5.44	170	Surabaya
Flores	22.6.44	479	Surabaya
Moluccas	7.8.44	599	Surabaya aboard Taiwan Maru
Flores	29.8.44	430	Surabaya
Moluccas	31.8.44	300	Surabaya aboard Kenzen Maru
Moluccas	31.8.44	200	Surabaya aboard Sugi Maru

Moluccas	9.9.44	150	Unknown ship to Muna Island then Kaishun Maru sunk 20.9.44 off Muna (138 survivors)
Moluccas	17.9.44	500	Surabaya aboard Maros/Haruyoshi Maru)
Flores	12.9.44	20	Surabaya
Moluccas	8.& 9.10.44		
		435	Muna Island
Celebes (Muna)	8.11.44	100	Japanese Transport 125 sunk 8.11.44 off Muna Island (73 survivors)
Celebes (Muna)	13.4.45	80	Surabaya
Celebes (Muna)	28.7.45	60	Surabaya
Celebes (Makassar)	August 1945	45	Probably Surabaya
Celebes (Muna)	16.8.45	80	Celebes (Makassar)

TABLE 7
Into Sumatra

■

FROM	LEFT	POW DETAILS	ARRIVED
Java	10.11.43	2100 (419 UK, 1680 Dutch,1 Aus)	Pangkalan Bali
Java	14.5.44	1925 (310 UK, 1615 Dutch)	Padang
Singapore	-.7.44	approx 530	Pakanbaru
Singapore	1.7.44	1260 from Java (286 UK, 123 Aus, 8 USA, 843 Dutch)	Pekanbaru
Java	15.9.44	2200 Dutch and UK	Junyo Maru sunk 18.9.44 off Padang (738 survivors)

APPENDIX 1
RN and RM Personnel who survived the sinking of the Lisbon Maru

◼

ADAMS Leonard George
ALEXANDER John
ALLISON John
ALLISTONE Albert Percy
ANDERSON Thomas Albert
ANDREWS William Henry Austin
ASHTON Cyril Richard
BAGGS Kenneth George
BAILEY Stanford Arthur
BAINBOROUGH George Harry
BAKER Edwin Douglas
BALL Denis Ronald
BANKS Gerald
BARTON George William
BATER Harold Charles
BAYRAM Allan George
BELL Norman McLeod
BEVIS Harry
BIGNALL Gordon Howard
BOW Stanley Henry
BREESE George Edwin
BROWN Frank
BROWN George Frederick
BULL Francis Charles
BURFORD Frederick James
BURROWS Kenneth George
BUTCHER Eric Robert
BUTLER Harry
BUTTERWORTH John
CARTER Charles Walter
CARTER John Douglas Haig
CASEY Jeremiah

CASSIDY John McFerran
CASTLETON Reginald Gaze
CHAMBERS James
CHILDS George Montague
CHISWELL Reginald Clarence G
CLARKE Alfred Horatio James
COLE Frank
COLLARD Charles Walter
CONNOR Herbert Howard
COOK Clifford Montague
CORDON John Henry
COWLING John Hedley
CRABBE William Gordon
CROFT Sidney
DAVIES Hedley Walter
DAVIS Edward T A
DAWSON John
DEERING William
DOW Robert
DOWLING Maurice
DOWSETT Samuel
DUFFY James Edwin
DUFFY John
DYKE Leslie Edward
EADES Thomas
ECCLESTON Thomas James
EDGE Ellis Taylor
ELDRIDGE Harry Norman
ELSWORTH William James
ENDRES Francis Walter
ENNIFER Arthur Vincent B
EVANS Arthur Jack William

EVERARD Henry Joseph
FACER William James
FALLACE James Wilfred
FLYNN Patrick Joseph
FRENCH Stanley James
FURZER Donald Frank
GARDINER Leslie John
GARTON Frank Kekewich
GAY Harry
GEORGE Frederick Charles G
GIBSON Robert Alderson
GODDARD Alfred Gruncell
GORE Dudley Eric
GOULD William John Arthur
GREEN Jack
GRIFFITH Robert Alex Skilling
GRIFFITH Robert Thomas
GRIFFITHS Kenneth Cecil
GROCOCK Charles
HAGGER Kenneth Leslie
HAINES Stanley John
HASTINGS Wallace George M
HAVELOCK William
HAWKINS Arthur
HENLEY James
HERMAN Albert Frank
HEWETT Edward Tucker
HINDMARSH Leslie
HODGSON Thomas
HORDER Douglas George
HUGHES Kenneth Wynford
HUGHIESON Jack H
HUNT Alfred Dennis
IRELAND Michael Norman
IRVINE George Robert
JACKSON Charles Antony
JEFFERY Garfield Harry
JEFFS Sydney Hill
JOHNSTONE William Charles
JONES Thomas Theodore
JUPP John Edmund
KELLEHER James

KIM George Victor
KING Reginald Arthur
LALOE Michael Francis
LAMPARD Victor George
LAVER Ronald
LAWRENCE Frank
LEARY Harry
LEVI Charles Henry
LILLEY Bernard Charles
LIVESEY Ellis Norman
LLOYD John
LONG George Lloyd
LYNNEBERG Ross
McAFEE David
McCREADY Thomas
McELROY Moses
McELWEE Peter James
McFARLANE John Chapman
McGREEN Patrick
McKEEN James Graham
MATHESON Donald
MATTHEWS Ronald Frederick M
MAXTED Richard Leonard
MILLIGAN Joseph
MOORE John Henry
MOORE Thomas
MORGAN Melville Maurice
MULLETT Leslie Alfred
NEILL Ernest Robert
NEWTON Thomas Edward L
NORTHOVER Ronald Clarence
O'HANLON Daniel Joseph
PARKINSON Robert
PAYNE Ernest William
PEARMAN John Edward
PEARSON Thomas Wilfred
PEMBERTON Allen Robertson
POLAND Robert Edward
POLLARD Walter Willliam George
POLLOCK Joshua Thomas
POOLEY Charles Henry
POWLEY John Walter

PRICE Walter
QUINN John Joseph
RAWLINGS Henry Thomas
RHODES Thomas
RIX John Arthur
RODGERS Ernest Rex
ROGERS Joseph Thomas
ROGERS Thomas
ROUGHLEY Robert Henry
RULE Charles Arnold
SCALLY Dennis Frederick Joseph
SCHOFIELD Ralph
SEABY John
SHEPHERD William Grant
SHORT Henry Edward
SILVERTHORNE Thomas Charles
SKINNER Sidney Albert
SMART Stanley George
SMITH Edwin Leslie George
SPIRIT Robert
SPREADBURY William James
STAINER Victor Vulcan
STALEY Thomas William
STEDMAN John Frederick

STEWART Donald Campbell
STEWART James
STIMSON Douglas Charles
STOKES David
SYMONS Robert Charles
TAYLOR Edward William James
THOMAS Gwynfor
THOMAS Ivor Edward
THORNE Reginald Albert
THYNNE William
TODD James Somerville
TREGIDGO Alfred Francis George
TRIM Albert Cyril
TUFFS Edward
TURNER Donald Deacon
VARNEY Harry
WALL Thomas Mervyn
WATTS Thomas William
WHITTINGHAM Harold
WILCOX Leonard
WILLIAMS George Albert
WILLIAMS Henry Llewellyn
WOODINGS Percy
YARWOOD Colin

APPENDIX 2
FEPOWs Identified as Working on the Mergui Road

———■———

BARRATT Herbert
BREAKSPEAR Edward James
BROWN Robert William Charles
BROWNING Robert
COOKMAN James
CORNFORD Donald Edward
DAVIES Richard John
DAWSON-GROVE Antony W
EDWARDS Maurice Francis George
EDWARDS Richard John Gilbert
EVANS Ronald John
GAMMON James Henry
HERMAN Harold George
HOUSLEY Clifford
JONES John Glyn
LOCKLIN Thomas
McKIRLEY Kenneth Stanley

MANDER John Albert
PADDEN William Arthur
SENIOR Cyril Al/derman
SHELLARD Patrick Philip
SHERIDAN Gerald Thomas B
SIMMONDS George William
SNEDDON James
STAPLES John William
STOKES John Leslie
THUNDER Jack E
TUPLIN James Edward
TURNER James Crowley
WADE Richard Beswick
WATSON Percy
WEBBER Thomas Albert
WESTGATE Noel Frank Ferrow
WHORTON Laurence

APPENDIX 3
Vessels Sunk/Captured/Scuttled
North of Sumatra in February 1942

■

Alert (captured)
Aquarious (sunk)
Blumut (captured)
Changeh (sunk)
Dymas (captured)
Dragonfly (sunk)
Elizabeth (sunk)
Eureka (beached and sunk)
Excise (captured)
Fan Lin (sunk)
Florence Nightingale (beached)
Fuh Wo (beached)
Giang Bee (beached)
Grasshopper (beached)
Hua Tonk (sunk)
Hung Jao (sunk)
Hung Tatt (captured)
Jackal (captured)
Jarak (sunk)
Jeruntut (sunk)
Kalama (captured)
Katong (bombed)
Kingfisher (scuttled)
Klias (scuttled)
Kuala (sunk)
Kung Wo (sunk)
Li Wo (sunk)
Majang (captured)
Malacca (sunk)

Mary Rose (captured)
Mata Hari (captured)
ML 36 (captured)
ML 311 (sunk)
ML 432 (captured)
ML 433 (sunk)
ML 1062 (sunk)
Pahlawan (captured)
Pelandok (probably sunk)
Pengawal (sunk)
Poelau Soegi (sunk)
Rantau (captured)
Redang (sunk)
Relau (captured)
Rompin (captured)
Rosemary (captured)
St Breock (sunk)
Scorpion (sunk)
Shu Kwang (bombed)
Shunan (captured)
Siang Wo (beached)
Tanjong Pinang (sunk)
Tapah (captured)
Tenggaroh (scuttled)
Tien Kwang (scuttled)
Trang (sunk)
Vyner Brooke (sunk)
Ying Pin (sunk)

APPENDIX 4
FEPOWs in the Party from
Makassar to Pomelaa

■

ADAMS Thomas John George
AINDOW Frederick
ALLEN Graeme Phillip
ANSON Peter
ARBUCKLE Robert
BACON Richard Stanley
BALL John William George
BALL Richard Gregson
BATCHELOR William Arthur
BEAUGIE Raymond George
BETTENSON Sidney Henry G
BIRD James Campbell
BLACK James Robert
BLATHERWICK William James
BOND Ernest Alexander
BOWDEN John William
BOWLER Arthur William Spicer
BRADLEY Joseph Douglas
BRADSHAW Reginald James
BRAKEWELL George
BRITTON Douglas
BROMLEY Ythil C L
BROOK Herbert Eric
BROUGHTON William Edward D
BUCKLE John Terence
BUTCHER David
BUTTERFIELD Dennis
CALLEJA Hugo
CAMPBELL John Alexander
CARSON William Henry
CARTER John Hall
CASTRO George William
CHAFFE Leonard
CHAMBERS Charles Ernest
CHRISTOPHER Ronald Francis
CLAMP Joseph William

CLAY Norman Leslie
COLLIER Nelson Leslie Bailey
CORK Samuel Henry
CORY William Edward
COWDALL Leslie
COWELL Stanley Phillip
CRANEFIELD Philip C
CROCKER George Isaac
CROCKER William Harry
CRUMP Ronald Charles
CURRUTHER Leonard Gordon
CUTHBERT John
DAVIES Evan Hywel
DESVERGEZ Francis Pierre Louis
DIGGLE Herbert
DITCHBURN John
DIXON Frederick
DODDS Andrew Kenneth
DYOS Walter John
EVANS William Edwin
EYNON William John
FALLE Samuel
FAULKNER William Frederick Bt
FENNELL Eric Rodney
FORBES Ian Dudley Stewart
FOWLER George William
GLOVER Albert Tudor
GRAHAM Robert
GREGORY Herbert Frederick
GRIMA Paul
HALL Roy
HAMMOND Percy John
HANMAN John Patrick
HANNAFORD Frederick John
HANNAFORD Victor Frederick
HARKNESS James Percy K

HARRIS Sidney John
HAWKEY Albert
HAWORTH Norman
HAZELL Francis Charles
HAZELTON David Carson
HEGNEY James Henry
HENNESSEY Ronald James
HENSON Arthur Peter
HICKLEY John Allen Victor
HICKS John Arthur
HIGMAN Mark Edward
HILL Francis
HILTON-FINN Thomas
HORSFALL Leo Herbert
HUDSON Frank
HUGGON David Edmund
HUTCHESON Hugh Anthony
JACKSON Richard Thomas
JEFFERIES Frank Edward
JEFFERY Frederick Alfred
JEFFERY Ralph
JENKINS Frederick
JEREMIAH David
JOHNS William Edward
JONES Douglas Harold
JORDAN Reginald Henry
KAVANAGH Henry
KERMODE William R
KERR Mark William Brownrigg
KIRKHAM Louis
LANGRIDGE Basil Frederick Jack
LAST Frederick James
LEIR Richard Hugh
LETHEBY William Arthur
LEWIS Alfred Leslie
LEWIS Kenneth Thomas
LITTLE Frederick C
McCAHON John Hamilton
McCARTHY Francis Henry
McCLURE George Richmond
McDONALD Thomas M
McKENZIE Royce
McKERNEY Terrence
McNEE Peter
McSHANE Francis Bertrand
MARKHAM Edward Arthur
MARRIOTT William K S

MAULE John
METZ Archibald Frederick
MICALEFF Andrew
MILLINGTON James
MITCHELL Eric Thomas Patrick
MOAR Gordon
MOUNTSTEVENS William Henry
MURPHY Colman Harold
MUTTON William Henry
NEWHAM Robert Edward
NEWTON Cecil
NICHOLS Frank Oswald
O'NEILL Eugene
OSBORNE Vivian E
PARIS Charley/Carnelo
PARKINSON Maurice
PARKYN Leslie William
PARMENTER John Cyril
PASS Cyril
PEARCE Kenneth John
PELEGRINE Emanuel
PHILLIPS Walter W S
PRIOR Thomas Henry
RAE Robert John
RAINEY Samuel
RICHARDS William Henry
RILEY William
ROACH Walter Herbert
ROBBINS John Sydney
ROE John Andrew
ROGERS Joseph William
ROOME David Gordon
ROWLAND Kenneth Cleadon
RUSE Roy Samuel Charles
RYALLS David Noel
SAUNDERS Albert Edward
SCRIPPS Terence Austin
SCUDAMORE Cecil Charles
SHARPLEY Thomas
SHAW Arthur Bernard
SHAW John
SHIRLEY Allan
SHORT Gerald Bartlett
SMITH Cyril
SMITH John Kynan
SMITH Kenneth Roy
SMITH Leslie Spurrell

SMITH Maurice Arthur
SOUTHWORTH Eric
SPALLE Roy Ernest
SPEAR Philip
SWINFIELD Albert Edward
SYMS Malcolm Henry
TABB Clive William Jarvis
THOM Allan Duncan
THOMAS Owen Meredith
THOMASON George Henry
TIDY George Horace
TILL Ernest H J
TINDALL Arthur Horace William
TOOLE Joseph
TOOMBS John Douglas William
TOTTERDELL Ronald Thomas F
TOWNSEND-GREEN Kenneth A

TOZER Rupert Peter
TURNER Lewis Arthur
UNIACKE Michael
VIDLER Victor Harold
WALKER Harry
WALSH Vincent Francis
WARLOW Benjamin Herbert
WATSON Harry
WELSH John Patrick
WHITE John
WHITING Kenneth George
WHITTINGHAM Harold
WILCOCKS Charles Henry
WILKIN Douglas Havard
WILKINSON John
WOOLFENDEN George
WORRALL George
YOUDAN Geoffrey John

APPENDIX 5
Makassar FEPOWs Transported to Java in October 1943

ALLEN Graeme Phillip
ANSON Peter
BEADLE Denis Mark
BROMLEY Yrhil Charles Lewis
COOPER George Tyndale
CRANEFIELD Philip C
DITCHBURN John
FALLE Samuel
FAULKNER William Frederick
FORBES Ian Dudley Stewart
HARKNESS James Percy K
HAZELTON David Carson
HICKLEY John Allen Victor
HILTON-FINN Thomas

HUTCHESON Hugh Anthony
KERR Alexander William
LEIR Richard Hugh
McCAHON John Hamilton
POTTER John Francis
ROOME David Gordon
RYALLS David Noel
SOUTHWORTH Eric
SPEAR Philip
SYMS Malcolm Henry
TIDY George Horace
TOWNSEND-GREEN Kenneth A
WALSH Vincent Francis
WYATT John Cameron

APPENDIX 6
Ships Carrying UK FEPOWs Sunk by Allied Action

———————————————————————■———————————————————————

ASAKA MARU - 709 UK and Australian POWs on board being transported from Thailand to Japan. Sunk 13.8.44 by typhoon off Taiwan. Survivors 690. Died 19 (0 RN/RM). (ref Sumio Adachi).

HARIKIKU MARU/VAN WAERWIJCK - 720 UK and Dutch POWs on board being transported from Medan to Pekanbaru, Sumatra. Sunk 26.6.44 by HMS Truculent near Belawan, Sumatra. Survivors 543. Died 177 (25 RN/RM). (ref Nat Arch CO/980/224).

JUNYO MARU - 2200 Dutch and UK POWs on board being transported from Java to Padang, Sumatra. Sunk 18.9.44 by HMS Tradewind near Moeko Moeko, Sumatra. Survivors 723 Died or Missing 1477 (1 RN). (ref Nat Arch CO/980/224) .

KAISHUN MARU - 150 UK and Dutch POWs on board being transported from the Molucca Islands, to Java. Sunk 20.9.44 by aircraft off Muna Island, south of Celebes (now Sulawesi). Died 12 (0 RN/RM) Survivors 138 picked up by Maros Maru (otherwise known as the Haruyoshi Maru) also transporting POWs from Ambon to Java. (ref Nat Arch AIR2/6955/5299).

KACHIDOKI MARU(See also RAKUYO MARU) - 950 UK and Australian POWs on board being transported from Thailand via Singapore to Japan. Sunk 12.9.44 by US Submarine Pampanito.
Survivors from both ships - Picked up by Japanese "whale factory" vessel Kibibi Maru 656. Picked up by US Submarines Pampanito 73 (1 died), Sealion 54 (4 died), Queenfish 18 (2 died) and Barb 14. Deaths from both ship 1460 (4 RN) including those after rescue by US submarines. (ref John and Clay Blair "Return from the River Kwai").

LISBON MARU - 1816 UK and Canadian POWs on board being transported from Hong Kong to Japan. Sunk 2.10.42. by US Submarine Growler. Survivors 977. Died 839 (159 RN/RM). (ref Nat Arch CO/980/224).

RAKUYO MARU (see also KACHIDOKI MARU) 1318 UK and Australian POWs on board being transported from Thailand via Singapore to Japan. Sunk 12.9.44 by US Submarine Sealion.

Survivors from both ships - Picked up by Japanese "whale factory" vessel Kibibi Maru 656. Picked up by US Submarines Pampanito 73 (1 died), Sealion 54 (4 died), Queenfish 18 (2 died) and Barb 14. Deaths from both ship 1460 (4 RN) including those after rescue by US submarines. (ref John and Clay Blair "Return from the River Kwai").

SUEZ MARU - 548 UK and Dutch POWs on board being transported from the Molucca Islands to Java. Sunk 29.11.43 by US Submarine Bonefish near island of Kangean, north of Bali. Died 548 (1 RN). (ref Nat Arch CO/980/224).

TAMAHOKO MARU - 772 Australian, Dutch, UK and USA POWs on board being transported from Java to Japan. Sunk 24.6.44 by US Submarine Tang in Nagasaki Bay. Survivors 212. Died 560 (5 RN). (ref Nat Arch CO/980/224).

TOYOFUKU MARU - 1287 UK, Australian and Dutch POWs on board being transported from Thailand via Singapore to Japan. After breaking down and remaining in Manila, Philippines, for two months sunk on 21.9.44 by aircraft 5 miles off Manila. Survivors 383. Died 904. (3 RN). (ref Sumio Adachi).

TRANSPORT 125 - 104 UK and Dutch POWs from the Molucca Islands on board being transported from Muna Island, south of Celebes (now Sulawesi), to Java. Sunk on 8.11.44 by aircraft 6 miles off Muna. Survivors 77. Died 27 (1 RN). (ref Nat Arch AIR2/6955/5299).

VAN WAERWIJCK/HARIKIKU MARU - 720 UK and Dutch POWs on board being transported from Medan to Pekanbaru, Sumatra. Sunk 26.6.44 by HMS Truculent near Belawan, Sumatra. Survivors 543. Died 177 (25 RN/RM). (ref Nat Arch CO/980/224).

APPENDIX 7
War Cemeteries and Memorials Relating to RN and RM FEPOWs

■

AMBON, INDONESIA - Within the cemetery lie those who died in Ambon, Ceram (now Seram), Flores, Timor, Haruku, Makassar (now Ujung Padang) and Muna. In 1961 at the request of the Indonesian Government the cemetery at Makassar (now Ujung Padang), which also held those who died on Muna Island, was closed and those buried there re-interred in Ambon.

CHATHAM MEMORIAL - Named on the memorial are the RN and RM men with no known grave whose home port was Chatham.

CHUNGKAI, THAILAND - Within the cemetery lie those who died at the Hospital Camp for No 4 Group at Chungkai.

JAKARTA, INDONESIA - Within the cemetery with those who died in Java lie those who died in Sumatra as some time after the war the two Commonwealth War Cemeteries in Sumatra at Palembang and Medan were closed and those who were buried there re-interred in Jakarta. At the entrance to the Cemetery is a Memorial honouring 130 Commonwealth men buried about twelve miles from Jakarta at Antjol, 58 of whom are named.

KANCHANABURI, THAILAND - Those who died on the Burma/Thailand Railway to the East of Nikki lie within Kanchanaburi War Cemetery.

KRANJI, SINGAPORE - Within Kranji Cemetery as well as FEPOWs lie many who were not prisoners of war, for instance Rear Admiral Spooner who left Singapore before it fell and died on 15.4.42

LABUAN, MALAYSIA - In Labuan Cemetery lie those who died in Borneo at Jesselton (now Kota Kinabalu), Sandakan, Kuching and Labuan.

LEE on SOLENT MEMORIAL - Names on the Memorial are those from the Fleet Air Arm with no known grave.

LIVERPOOL MEMORIAL - Named on the Memorial are those from the Merchant Navy who volunteered to serve on Royal Naval armed merchant cruisers with no known grave, Liverpool being their manning port establishment.

NEW ZEALAND MEMORIAL (AUKLAND) - Named on the Memorial are those New Zealand Naval personnel with no known grave.

PLYMOUTH MEMORIAL - Named on the memorial are the RN and RM men with no known grave whose home port was Plymouth

PORTSMOUTH MEMORIAL - Named on the memorial are the RN and RM men with no known grave whose home port was Portsmouth

SAI WAN BAY, HONG KONG - In the cemetery lie those who died in Taiwan and some of those who died in Hong Kong.

STANLEY, HONG KONG - Most of those who died in Hong Kong lie in the Stanley Cemetery.

SYDNEY, AUSTRALIA - Buried in the cemetery are those who died in Concord Military Hospital and also Far East Prisoners of War whose ashes were taken to Australia.

THANBYUZAYAT, BURMA - Those who died on the Burma/Thailand Railway in Burma or in Thailand to the West of Nikki, lie within Thanbyuzayat Cemetery.

YOKOHAMA, JAPAN - It is believed that those who died in Japan were all cremated. Most have graves but the ashes of 335 could not be individually identified and lie in an urn housed within a shrine in the Cemetery. Their names, save for the 51 who were not identified, are inscribed on the walls of the shrine.

Bibliography

Adachi, Sumio "Unprepared Regrettable Events" unpublished report

Anderson,Ted and Rowe, Robin "Nippon's Guest - a Sailor Prisoner of War in Japan" published 1995 by Devonshire House, Christow (ISBN 0-952413-2-8

Apthorp A A "The British Sumatra Battalion" published 1988 by The Book Guild, Lewes, Sussex (ISBN 0 86332 285 3)

Audus, Leslie "Spice Island Slaves - A History of Japanese Prisoner of war Camps in Eastern Indonesia May 1943-August 1945" published 1996 by Alma Publishers, Richmond, Surrey (ISBN 0 9517497 2 2)

Banham, Tony "The Lisbon Maru" published 2006 by the Hong Kong University Press (ISBN 962 209 7715).

Brooke, Geoffrey "Singapore's Dunkirk" published 1989 by Leo Cooper, London (ISBN 0 85052 051 7)

Few, Don "A Helping Hand" unpublished narrative

Cooper, George T "Never Forget Nor Forgive" published 1995 by Navigator Books (ISBN 0 902830 53 8). First published as "Ordeal in the Sun" in 1963 by Robert Hale Ltd.

Gough, Richard "The Escape from Singapore" first published 1987 by William Kimber & Co Ltd (ISBN 07183-0655-4)

Haining, Peter "The Banzai Hunters - the forgotten Armada of little ships that defeated the Japanese 1944-1945" published 2006 by Robson Books (ISBN 1 86105 941 8)

Hough, Richard "The Hunting of Z Force", first published in 1963 by William Collins.

Jones, Allan, "The Suez Maru Atrocity" published
(ISBN 0 9542 725 0 1)

Lock, Harold "The Forgotten Men" unpublished narrative.

Nelson, David "The Story of Changi, Singapore" published 1974 by Changi Publication Co, Australia (ISBN 0 9503243 1 0)

Neumann H & Van Witsen E "The Sumatra Railway" published 1989 by Studio Pieter Mulier, Holland (ISBN 90 70393 09 3)

Poidevin, Leslie "Samurais and Circumcisions" published 1985 by the author (ISBN 0 9590087 21)

Roberts, David Elio "No Bamboo for Coffins" published 1996 by Gee and Sons, Denbigh (ISBN 0 7074 0280 8)

Lord Russell of Liverpool "The Knights of Bushido" first published 1959 by Cassell & Co Ltd)

Sibley, David "The Behar Massacre" published 1998 by A Lane Publishers (ISBN 1 897 666 13 5)

Silver, Lynette Ramsay "Sandakan - a Conspiracy of Silence" published 1998 by Sally Milner Publishing, Australia (ISBN 1 86351 223 3)

Stubbs, Ray "Prisoner of Nippon" published 1995 by Square One Publications, Worcs (ISBN 1 872017 88 6)

Veenstra J H W et al "Als Krijgsgevangene naar de Molukken en Flores" published 1982 by Unigeverij Martinus Nijhoff's-Gravenhage, Holland.

Wall, Don "Kill the Prisoners" published 1996 by D Wall, New South Wales (ISBN 0646 278 347)

Wettern, Desmond "The Lonely Battle" published 1960 by W H Allen &Co, London.